COBOL LOGIC AND PROGRAMMING

COBOL

LOGIC AND PROGRAMMING

Fritz A. McCameron, Ph.D., CPA
Professor, Accounting Department
Louisiana State University

1966

RICHARD D. IRWIN, INC.
Homewood, Illinois

First Printing, August, 1966
Second Printing, May, 1967
Third Printing, January, 1968
Fourth Printing, April, 1968
Fifth Printing, September, 1968
Sixth Printing, January, 1969
Seventh Printing, July, 1969

Library of Congress Catalog Card No. 66-27461

PRINTED IN THE UNITED STATES OF AMERICA

PREFACE

COBOL is the newest widely-accepted programming language; the product of a refining process which in a few years has led from machine language—to symbolic programming—to compilers. After what seemed to be a slow beginning (partly because equipment lacked the ability to cope with the language adequately), COBOL is fast gaining popularity, and promises to be used even more widely than it is today.

Unfortunately, literature dealing with the language has for the most part followed a reference-manual format at the expense of instructional clarity. Most manuals have set forth the basic characteristics of the language concisely, but have included a minimum of descriptive information. While this is quite proper in a manual designed to be used by persons versed in programming, it is very difficult for the novice to understand.

On the other hand, this is a COBOL manual for beginning programmers. It is assumed that the reader knows nothing about computers or their control. The objective of this manual is to present the basic nature of COBOL, after introducing the electronic computer, in such a way that the reader may gain an understanding of the language's use as well as its composition.

In attaining this objective, the manual departs in several major respects from conventional programming material. In the first place, it is written in regular textbook style, rather than in the somewhat abbreviated form of a reference manual. As a part of the language is introduced, its nature is explained and the relationship between commands is illustrated. Observations on the characteristics of language components are designed to give insight into the construction of a program. Numerous exercises are furnished, challenging the reader to find new ways of achieving results by combining language components.

A second unique feature of this manual is to be found in its separation of logical and coding functions. The major part of the manual is devoted to instruction in COBOL logic through the device of diagramming. Thus, without becoming mired in technique, the novice may learn something of the general nature of this language. Coding techniques are introduced only after logic has been explored thoroughly; in this way the beginner can tell the difference between the conceptual and the procedural.

The manual differs from most, finally, in that no attempt is made to introduce all facets of COBOL. The skilled programmer or systems analyst has access to several sources of accurate, detailed information on the language as it is used with his particular computer, and this manual makes no attempt to intrude in this area. On the other hand, only those commands which several years' instruction have shown to be an integral part of the basic COBOL structure are presented here. These serve to introduce the notion of electronic computers and COBOL without overwhelming the student with a number of optional commands.

The order of the manual's material reflects its viewpoint. The first chapter is devoted to a brief introduction to electronic computers and a general explanation of COBOL processing. Chapter 2 is concerned with the concept of data as found in electronic data processing, and investigates the order of data in the COBOL language.

Chapters 3 and 4 contain an exploration of basic COBOL logic. Chapter 3 introduces the basic data-manipulation commands, such as READ, MØVE, WRITE, and the arithmetic instructions. Chapter 4 describes most of the computer-control verbs, emphasizing the nature and use of conditionals.

Chapters 5 and 6 contain information on program coding. The requirements of the Identification, Environment, and Data Divisions are set out in Chapter 5. Chapter 6 describes the coding requirements of the Procedure Division. In each chapter numerous related examples are designed to bring reason and meaning to the somewhat tedious coding rules.

All parts of the COBOL language required to prepare computer programs are thus covered in the first six chapters of the text. However, not all instructions have been covered at this point. The most sophisticated control command in the language—the PERFØRM—is covered in Chapter 7, where data arrays are also treated. In this chapter, considerable attention is paid to the use of these as well as to their structure.

Matters of logic and coding are related by problems. These require that logical design be prepared in certain chapters, and are followed with coding requirements in later material. Thus, the student actually prepares programs for these problems. It is strongly recommended that the students be permitted to run these on a computer, using test data, so they may gain experience in program compilation, debugging, and execution.

This manual is designed to be used by persons beginning a study of electronic computers and COBOL. It should be useful to college freshmen or upper-level students, although certain problems may require some explanation to students with limited business administration backgrounds. The manual may serve as the only text in a short course dealing with computer introduction and programming, or as a supplementary text in a regular course on electronic data processing.

Fritz A. McCameron

August, 1966

ACKNOWLEDGEMENT

Any organization interested in reproducing the COBOL report and specifications (of the Conference on Data Systems Language) in whole or in part, using ideas taken from this report as the basis for an instructional manual or for any other purpose is free to do so. However, all such organizations are requested to reproduce this section as part of the introduction to the document. Those using a short passage, as in a book review, are requested to mention "COBOL" in acknowledgement of the source, but need not quote this entire section.

COBOL is an industry language and is not the property of any company or group of companies, or of any organization or group of organizations.

No warranty, expressed or implied, is made by any contributor or by the COBOL committee as to the accuracy and functioning of the programming system and language. Moreover, no responsibility is assumed by any contributor, or by the committee, in connection therewith.

Procedures have been established for the maintenance of COBOL. Inquiries concerning the procedures for proposing changes should be directed to the Executive Committee of the Conference on Data Systems Languages.

The authors and copyright holders of the copyright material used herein

> FLOW-MATIC (Trademark of Sperry Rand Corporation), Programming for the UNIVAC (R) I and II, Data Automation Systems copyright 1958, 1959, by Sperry Rand Corporation; IBM Commercial Translator Form No. F28-8013, copyrighted 1959 by IBM; FACT, DSI27A5260-2760, copyrighted 1960 by Minneapolis-Honeywell

have specifically authorized the use of their material in whole or in part, in the COBOL specifications. Such authorization extends to the reproduction and use of COBOL specifications in programming manuals or similar publications.

TABLE OF CONTENTS

CHAPTER 1

THE ELECTRONIC COMPUTER

Before one may hope to master the control and use of an electronic computer, he must have some notion of the tool he plans to use. Thus a brief description of the typical electronic computer is in order before giving consideration to its programming.

BASIC NATURE

The electronic computer is in the general family of computing devices, along with such common machines as adding machines and desk calculators. Certain of its characteristics are so different from other calculating instruments that the analogy cannot be carried too far, however.

One basic characteristic of the electronic computer is its lack of moving parts. Whereas desk calculators ordinarily do their work of computing through the rotation of dials or disks, the electronic computer achieves its results through the movement of electronic impulses. This makes the computer much faster than an ordinary calculator; it can almost operate at the speed of light. The absence of moving parts has also permitted the miniaturization of parts and the construction of an instrument much more capable than its mechanical counterpart. The electronic computer can accept data at high speeds, store vast amounts of information in its "memory," perform arithmetic in nanoseconds (billionths of a second), and emit information very rapidly. Thus, although many of its capabilities are to some extent duplicated by the desk calculator, the magnitude of work capability is entirely different.

The electronic computer consists of several major parts, each of which may be housed in a different unit—indeed, some parts may be located many feet or miles from the central processor. Types of components are standard, however. These are data input devices, data storage, the arithmetic unit, the control unit, and data output units. A computer may have more than one of each of these. The typical computer has several data input-output units, perhaps two kinds of storage (high-speed and slow), one or more arithmetic units, and a single control unit.

The very high speed of the electronic computer would be wasted if it were controlled step by step by a human operator, as is the desk calculator. Instead, the electronic computer is guided by instructions prepared in advance and read into its memory. Then, when the computer is to perform operations, its control is turned over to the set of instructions, or program, and the device analyzes this program at electronic speeds and acts accordingly.

The Computer Program

The set of instructions used to control an electronic computer is called a program. Since a computer is too fast to allow human control on a step-by-step basis, a complete set of instructions covering all imaginable conditions is given the machine prior to its execution of any kind of operation. This is quite similar to the way in which a clerk is employed, when he is first told exactly what to do and then allowed to work at the assigned project.

In illustration of the concept of the program, assume that a particular firm quotes sales prices on a per unit basis and that most sales are for more than one unit. Thus, to determine the total sales price, unit prices must be multiplied by the number of units sold. This is commonly referred to as a process of extending the sales ticket.

If one employed a clerk to perform this task, he would probably be told something like the following: "Please extend these prices by multiplying the unit price on each ticket by the corresponding number of units sold." The clerk would understand that he was expected to extend all tickets, and would then begin his task and continue until finished.

A computer program for the same task might read, in a non-English language sensible to the computer, somewhat as follows: "Take a sales ticket, and look in certain places for two values. Compute a third value by multiplying the first by the second. Write all three values on a new piece of paper. Take up another sales ticket and repeat the process. Continue until there are no more sales tickets." This program would be prepared in a machine-sensible form and read into the computer. The computer's data input unit would then be loaded with sales tickets, and it would begin to execute the program.

There is, then, much similarity in the manner of using a computer and a clerk. In each instance, instructions are given before execution of the actual job is begun. These instructions comprise the program. Different programs are created for different tasks. They may be long and involved, or they may be quite short, like the one in the example above. In any event, no computer is able to operate until properly programmed, just as no clerk can perform his tasks until properly instructed. When they are acquired, computers typically have no programs of direct utility to the user. They must be "trained" through the creation of programs, just as a new employee must be trained in his job.

Although a computer's memory is quite large, it is ordinarily too small to contain all the programs executed by the computer in its use. Therefore, many programs are kept in the form of punched cards or on magnetic tape, and are read into the computer just before the particular job is to be performed.

Computer-Sensible Data

In communicating, man almost always uses symbols as abstractions of the actual subject. For example, the word "apple" is a symbol used to represent a particular fruit, and "12 apples" is used to represent 12 units of the fruit. Man has used such symbolism for so long that the process is taken for granted. Tangibles and intangibles are symbolized by sounds, shapes, or written symbols.

Computer communication is carried out in the same general way, but unusual symbols are employed. Computers have a very delicate "touch"; therefore a major way of entering data is by punching holes in paper strips or cards. The presence or absence of a hole symbolizes data, and communication is thus effected. Computers are also able to make distinction between the presence and absence of electronic impulses, and this ability is used in communication.

Recently, computer input units have been developed with the ability to distinguish shapes, permitting the use of written characters in data input. Sounds may also be recognized, but this form of data recognition is not very well developed at the present time. It is probable that some day the computer will recognize oral commands, permitting the programmer to operate his machine by giving oral instructions.

At present, the most widely used means of computer data input are the punched card and magnetic tape. The former is a card containing several columns, each having space for one or more punches to represent data—for example, the standard IBM card has 80 columns, and each column has 12 punching positions. Certain combinations of punches represent different characters—numbers, letters, or special symbols. Any column may contain any character, making the card roughly the equivalent of an 80-character line. The computer "reads" by determining the location of holes in the card, rather by recognizing character shapes.

Magnetic tapes are used in both computer input and computer output in a similar fashion. Rather than having punched holes, however, tiny magnetic impulses are deposited on the surface of plastic tape. This gives a communication medium much more compact than punched cards, and one which can be used much more rapidly. Where a punched card measures slightly more than 7" x 3" and contains 80 characters, magnetic tape one-half inch wide may contain over 1,000 characters in a single inch. And while few card readers can accept more than 64,000 characters per minute, magnetic tape may be read at a rate of 100,000 characters per second.

Basic Computer Components

As mentioned previously, all computers consist of certain basic sections. While the exact form of these may change, the roles they play in the computer's use is standard. The basic configuration of a computer is outlined in Figure 1-1 (page 6); comments below should be associated with this diagram.

Input. The computer input units are used to enter programs and data for manipulation. Input units frequently used are punched-card and tape readers for paper cards and tape, and magnetic tape units. Optical scanners, capable of reading information written in certain type fonts, are becoming a common means of input. Readers capable of scanning characters written in a magnetic ink are popular input units in banking and a few other industries.

Input units have been greatly improved in the last few years. Small data input terminals have been developed which may be located far from the computer proper at any point where recordable events take place. Data may thus be entered at their origin and transmitted over telephone or telegraph lines to the central processor.

Memory. Electronic computers have data storage units for the retention of programs, data in the course of being processed, and results being stored prior to writing. A common memory form consists of tiny metal washers, called cores, strung on a series of wires. These cores are capable of being magnetized or demagnetized and, when used in sets, may represent letters or numbers.

The memory of a computer is divided into sections. The exact nature of these sections differs from one machine to another. If the section is capable of representing more than one character, it is known as a "word" of storage. If the section can represent only one character, it is called a "character" of storage. No matter which means of constructing memory is used, the total storage capacity of most computers amounts to thousands or even millions of characters.

Each section of computer memory has a known address. Thus the computer's memory is divided into many small compartments, each of them having an address, or name. The memory may then be thought of as a set of mailboxes, where each box is capable of containing a small amount of mail and each box has a name corresponding to that of its renter. It is important to note at this point that the name of the compartment and its contents are very definitely two different things.

The computer's memory is designed to store the program being executed as well as data. Each instruction in the program is stored at a different memory address and is called for by the machine as needed. Each different kind of data is also stored at a different memory address and may be called for by the program. As will be seen later, COBOL commands frequently refer to the addresses of data rather than to the data themselves. For example, the command "ADD A TØ B" really assumes that A and B are data addresses and says: "Add the contents of memory address A to the contents of memory address B, and store the sum at address B." This assumes, of course, that data are stored at A and B, and that their summation is a logical undertaking. How data may be gotten to A and B is another matter and is discussed at length in a later section.

Modern electronic data processors frequently have two basic types of memory as an integral part of the machine, or "on line." One memory unit is relatively small, with a storage capacity of 4,000 to 800,000 characters. This is used to contain the program in process of execution and data currently being manipulated. Data may be entered or withdrawn very quickly. Many modern computers have an "access time" to this memory which is measured in nanoseconds.

The second memory unit is used for storage of great masses of data, such as entire ledgers of accounting data or files of personnel information. These units may contain hundreds of millions of characters. Access time is slow when compared with fast storage, being measured in milliseconds (thousandths of a second), but incomparably faster than that of any other information retrieval system presently available.

The memory of modern computers is nonvolatile; that is, information stored therein will not automatically be erased by reading it out. Data stored in memory are erased only by storing new information in the same location.

Control. The computer has a control unit capable of causing the execution of commands in the program. When the computer's control is turned over to its program, each instruction in the program is brought into the control unit in sequence. It is analyzed, and the machine is activated. After an instruction is executed, its successor is brought into the control unit and executed, and so forth, until the program has been completed. Then, operations may be terminated or repeated, according to the commands in the program.

Arithmetic. A fourth common computer unit is the arithmetic sector, where all arithmetic is performed. An electronic computer has the ability to add, subtract, multiply, and divide, but these are its only arithmetic capabilities.

Output. Once a program has been executed, the results of the computer's operations must be communicated to its user. Several output devices are available for this. The simplest may be an electric typewriter connected to the computer, on which it may type its output. A faster means of data output is the card punch, which punches cards that must be taken to a printer for listing. Another data output unit frequently found is the high-speed printer, many models of which are capable of printing over 600 lines per minute. Magnetic tapes are also used for data output and provide the fastest output means commonly in use, although the results are not in a man-sensible form. Television units are sometimes used to display information in remote units.

The Computer's Use Illustrated

Figure 1-1 illustrates the way in which an electronic computer is used in a typical application. Steps in the process are as follows:

1. The program to be executed is loaded into the computer's memory through an input unit. This may be a card reader or a magnetic tape drive, or some other unit.

2. After the program has been loaded, control of the computer is turned over to the program. The first instruction is brought into the control unit and analyzed, and the computer is directed accordingly.

3. Assuming that the program is to involve the manipulation of data, a READ command will be encountered. Data may come into the computer's memory from the same input unit used to read the program, from some other input device, or from large secondary storage.

4. If arithmetic is to be done, data read in will be brought into the arithmetic unit, processed, and returned to another memory position.

5. Answers will be written out through some output device—a high-speed printer, a card punch, or some other unit, or returned to secondary storage.

Once the computer is turned over to the control of the program, it is directed by that program until some other condition prevails. The program may call for a single reading of data, processing, and output, and then return control of the computer to the operator. It may require that control be returned to the operator if circumstances make operation impossible, such as attempting to read improper input information or the occurrence of an event which should never take place. On the other hand, the computer program may require that the machine operate in a repetitive cycle, completing its process only to return, read in new data, and go through the program again. These are matters wholly under the control of the programmer when he makes up the set of computer instructions.

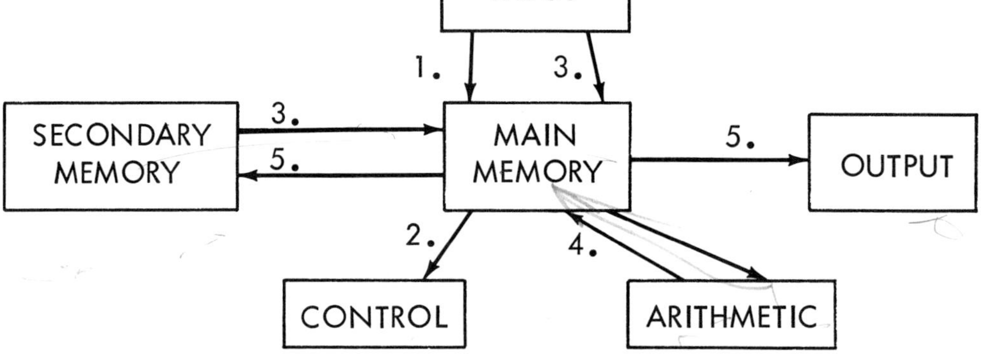

FIG. 1-1. Schematic of Computer Operation

THE NATURE OF COBOL

A computer has the ability to perform several different possible activities. It may read, test data, perform arithmetic, and do a number of other things. Each different activity of which the computer is capable is referred to by a code symbol, usually a number or letter combination.

Programming a computer in its own "language," that is, with the set of symbols representative of different possible actions, is a very tedious process. It requires that the programmer remember these codes for operational steps, as well as the memory location used for all data and program storage.

The COBOL Language

A recent advance in programming technology permits the programmer to write instructions in an English-like language and then use the computer itself to translate this set of commands into its machine language equivalent. One of the most advanced versions of this modern programming method is called COBOL.

COBOL is a word coined from the phrase "common business-oriented language," taking the letters underlined to form the name. As the phrase implies, it is a language primarily designed for use in the processing of business data. It makes use of all parts of the computer, however, and can be used in scientific as well as business data-processing applications.

COBOL is designed to make use of the regular business data-processing vocabulary to the greatest extent possible. Its logic is similar to that used in noncomputer data-processing situations. By creating a language as similar as possible to that in current business use, programming is made understandable to persons familiar with business situations much more quickly than if machine language programming were required.

One objective of the creators of COBOL is to develop a programming language which will be usable on the equipment of any manufacturer. Thus a program written in COBOL might be executed on computers manufactured by IBM, Remington Rand, RCA, or some other firm. This permits the computer user to be much more independent of his equipment than has formerly been the case, and means that a change from one model of equipment to another is an easier task, even when a new kind of equipment is employed.

Using the Computer with COBOL

The COBOL program is of a nature easily readable by man and is referred to as being "man-sensible." Before the computer can execute the program, however, it must be translated into the machine's own programming language. This translation process is called compilation and is done by the computer itself.

A survey of the steps involved when a COBOL program is compiled and executed follows. The computer is assumed to have a card reader, and program and data are to be read in through this device.

1. Create the Program. The first step in the computer's utilization is, of course, the creation of the program. This requires a careful analysis of the situation to be programmed and its reduction to solution through the use of COBOL logic. Thus, while a certain end might be attained by one process when the computer is not used, introduction of the computer and COBOL to the situation requires that the logic of solution be carefully restricted to that of the language.

After mapping the proper logic for resolving the situation in question, this logic is transformed into COBOL by coding. This results in the creation of what is called the source program. It is a set of COBOL instructions setting out the actions to be performed by the computer. This is similar to instructions which might be prepared for an employee designated to perform the task in question.

2. Translate into Machine Language. After the COBOL program is written, it is transcribed into a form readable by the machine, by punching into standard cards. These cards are read into the computer. By means of referring to another program prepared by the computer manufacturer, this COBOL program is translated into a machine language program. Thus the set of man-sensible instructions is transformed by the computer itself into a set of machine-sensible commands. This latter is known as the object program.

During the translation phase the computer checks the source program for errors. It makes a list of any errors detected and writes these out for the benefit of the programmer. Translation may or may not continue, depending on the magnitude of the errors found. Of course, the computer cannot check on the accuracy of the programmer's logic, because it has no way of knowing just what is intended. Therefore, while the computer may be able to detect errors of a clerical nature, it is not able to detect mistakes in logic or strategy.

After the source program is translated into machine language, it may be executed immediately, or it may be written out for later use.

3. Executing the Program. Once the translation phase is completed, the computer is available for any task. Assuming that the newly created object program is to be executed, it is read back into the computer's memory (the process of translation causes it to be stored on a magnetic tape or disk). As soon as the process of reading in the object program is completed, computer control is surrendered to this program, and execution commences. The object program may be saved and rerun later without retranslating, if desired.

The COBOL Character Set

A set of characters has been selected by all equipment manufacturers preparing COBOL compilers for their machines. This is known as the

COBOL character set, and only those symbols included in the set are recognized by the language. The character set encompasses three basic types of characters: numeric, such as the arabic numerals 0-9; alphabetic, including the letters A-Ƶ and the space; and alphameric, a category including both letters and numbers, and certain special characters. These special characters are shown in Table 1-1.

Table 1-1

Name	Character
Space	
Plus sign	+
Minus sign / Hyphen	-
Multiplication sign	*
Division sign	/
Left parenthesis	(
Right parenthesis	)
Comma	,
Period / Decimal point	.
Dollar sign	$
Equal sign	=
Quotation mark	'

This is not a complete list of allowable special COBOL characters, but it represents those in most frequent use which are implemented in almost all versions of the language.

Writing Certain Characters. Because programming requires extreme accuracy, certain writing conventions have evolved to insure clarity of meaning. First, programs are always printed, rather than being written in longhand. Second, capital alphabetic characters are always used, never small letters. Third, certain characters are made in unique ways to distinguish them from some other similar symbols.

The letter Ø is always written with a slash through it, as shown, to distinguish it from the number zero (0). The letter Ƶ is also slashed to differentiate it from the number two (2); the two are very similar when written in small characters. The letter I should always have a head and foot, as shown, and the number one (1) should be made as displayed here to avoid confusion.

CHAPTER 2

COBOL STRUCTURE AND DATA ORGANIZATION

An electronic computer, as it is used in business administration, is essentially a data-processing device. Problems are solved by reading variable data or accepting fixed data, manipulating the data in an appropriate fashion, and emitting results.

The COBOL language is designed expressly to facilitate this kind of data processing. Its structure reflects emphasis on problems of massive data input and output, where relatively simple processing steps are involved. This, in turn, makes the matter of data organization more important than when other computer languages are used.

EXAMPLE OF A COBOL PROGRAM

These matters may be pointed out to some extent, even though the nature of COBOL has not yet been explored, by examining a simple data-processing situation and its associated COBOL program.

The Problem

In being told how to extend sales tickets and prepare a total of all sales amounts processed, an accounting clerk might be given the following instructions: "Take this file of sales tickets, each containing a single sales item. Calculate the total sales amount by multiplying unit prices by the number of units sold. Then, calculate sales tax as 3 percent of the sales amount, and add this to the sales amount, giving the total billed price. Accumulate the billed prices for all tickets so extended."

This statement is reasonably concise, assuming the clerk to be versed in the nomenclature of accounting. He should be able to take the tickets and, with perhaps a question or two, complete his assigned task.

A computer program must be a great deal more explicit, however. It must "explain" to the computer the exact appearance of the sales ticket. What bits of data are included? Where are they shown on the input document? How large are they? Exactly what is to be included in the output record, which must be different from the input document? Answers to these and other questions must be provided before the computer is able to cope with the data processing problem.

Data Input

First, the sales ticket must be in a form understandable to the computer. Assuming that it is converted to punched cards, the machine-sensible sales ticket might appear as in Figure 2-1.[1] Here, spaces are devoted to the recording of the account number (Acct. No.), the number of units sold (Qty.), and the sales price per unit (Amt.) in card areas called "fields." The exact size of the field and its location on the card are frozen when the card is originally planned; according to the format of this card, the account number must appear in card columns 1-5, the quantity sold in columns 6-10, and the sales price per unit in columns 11-14. Although the accounting clerk might be able to find these bits of data even if they were slightly misplaced, the computer has no such ability. It will programmed to look for these items in these areas only, and it will follow its instructions explicitly.

Data Output

More exact information must be furnished the computer on the nature of required output also. It cannot write answers back on the input document, as a clerk might do. Therefore, it must be programmed to transfer certain data to output, as well as to compute other information to be written. The computer must be "told" the order in which output items are to appear and their field size.

Assuming that output records are to be written on magnetic tape, a

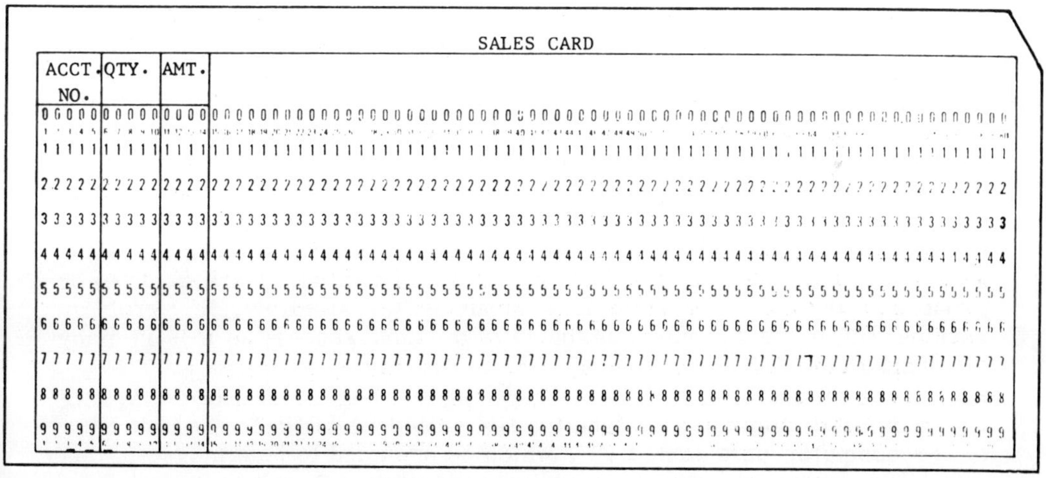

FIG. 2-1 The Sales Card

[1] In practice, the input documents would doubtless contain much more information than is shown here. However, this example is purposely kept simple for ease of explanation.

FIG. 2-2 The Output Record

record might appear as in Figure 2-2. Since magnetic tape reels are quite lengthy, records are separated from one another by an invisible symbol called a record mark (‡).

Simplified COBOL Program

Once the nature of data input and output is understood, the program required to link the two may be constructed. A simplified program is shown in Figure 2-3. In this, several parts essential to proper execution, but not required for understanding the general nature of the language, have been omitted.

It may be seen that the overall program is divided into the identification, environment, data, and procedure divisions, captions for which may be seen on lines 01, 03, 06, and 19 of Figure 2-3. The identification division is the shortest, serving only to give the program a name.

The other three divisions are closely related. The environment division tells the computer which of its several input-output units are to be used, and the file of data to be associated with each. The data division sets out space in the computer's memory as required by the data records and items, and indicates the relationship existing between items of data. Finally, the procedure division contains the actual commands causing the computer to read, process, and write data. These three divisions merit a more careful introduction than is required by the identification division.

Environment Division. On line 04 in Figure 2-3 may be seen a major component of the environment division. Here a command instructs the computer to "SELECT SALES-TICKET-FILE, ASSIGN TØ IN." This informs the computer that a file, named SALES-TICKET-FILE, is to be processed through a certain data input unit, called IN. This problem assumes IN to be the name assigned to the card reader, as it is in many instances.

A similar command assigns the file called EXTENDED-SALES-FILE to the computer unit named ØU, which is assumed to be a magnetic tape unit. Thus the computer is informed which input-output units are to be used and the files associated with each.

Data Division. This program segment, in turn, tells the computer the appearance of each of the files mentioned above. A code symbol, FD, to the left of the associated name tells the computer that a file is being named. An example of this may be seen on line 07 of Figure 2-3, where the SALES-TICKET-FILE is mentioned.

COBOL PROGRAM SHEET

PAGE 1 3	PROGRAM: SALES ACCØUNTING	SYSTEM	SHEET 1 OF 1
001	PROGRAMMER: MC CAMERØN	DATE	IDENT 73 80

```
SERIAL CONT. A   B
01      IDENTIFICATIØN DIVISIØN.
02      PRØGRAM-ID. SALES-ACCØUNTING.
03      ENVIRØNMENT DIVISIØN.
04      FILE-CØNTRØL. SELECT SALES-TICKET-FILE, ASSIGN TØ IN.
05          SELECT EXTENDED-SALES-FILE, ASSIGN TØ ØU.
06      DATA DIVISIØN.
07      FD  SALES-TICKET-FILE.
08      01  SALES-TICKET.
09          02  AC-NØ                      PICTURE 99999.
10          02  QTY                        PICTURE 99999.
11          02  AMT                        PICTURE 99V99.
12      FD  EXTENDED-SALES-FILE.
13      01  EXTENDED-TICKET.
14          02  ACT-NØ                     PICTURE 99999.
15          02  SALES-AMØUNT               PICTURE 9(7)V99.
16          02  TAX                        PICTURE 999V99.
17          02  TØTAL                      PICTURE 9(8)V99.
18      77  CØNTRØL-TØT  PICTURE 9(10)V99 VALUE ZERØ.
19      PRØCEDURE DIVISIØN.
20      START. READ SALES-TICKET-FILE, AT END GØ TØ FINISH.
21          MØVE AC-NØ TØ ACT-NØ. MULTIPLY QTY BY AMT GIVING
22          SALES-AMØUNT. MULTIPLY SALES-AMØUNT BY .03 GIVING TAX.
23          ADD SALES-AMØUNT, TAX GIVING TØTAL. ADD TØTAL TØ CØNTRØL-TØT.
24          WRITE EXTENDED-TICKET. GØ TØ START.
25      FINISH. DISPLAY CØNTRØL-TØT. STØP RUN.
```

FIG. 2-3.

The code symbol 01 on line 08 of the same figure, preceding the name SALES-TICKET, indicates to the computer that within the SALES-TICKET-FILE are to be found records called SALES-TICKET. This relationship is implied by the symbols and the order in which the names are written.

In turn, 02 symbols on lines 09 through 11 indicate that data items named as shown exist within the record called SALES-TICKET. Each data name is followed by a PICTURE clause, which shows the computer how many characters of data exist in each field. In this definition a 9 indicates a data position, and a V tells the computer to assume the existence of a decimal point. The exact nature of these symbols is explored in detail later and is not important at this point.

On line 18 an item named CØNTRØL-TØT may be seen to have the symbol 77. This indicates that this bit of data does not belong to a record or file, but instead exists apart from all other data elements.

Procedure Division. This is divided into two "paragraphs," named START and FINISH. In the first, to be seen on line 20 of Figure 2-3, may be seen the command, "READ SALES-TICKET-FILE, AT END GØ TØ FINISH." This instructs the computer to read a record from the named file. Finally, when no more records are available, the computer is to go to the FINISH paragraph for its remaining instructions.

Other commands in the START paragraph are in a form so similar to regular clerical instructions that they may be understood without elaborate explanation. It should be noted that all fields in the output record are filled with data. The contents of data item AC-NØ are moved to data item ACT-NØ. Other fields are filled by computations. CØNTRØL-TØT, used to accumulate all billed amounts, is increased by the amount of this billing. The output record is written, and the computer is instructed to return to START and repeat the process.

Eventually, the FINISH paragraph will be executed. Here the total of all billed sales is displayed for control purposes, and the computer is told to stop operations by the final command, "STØP RUN."

This short COBOL program and the equally abbreviated explanation are by no means complete. Several steps essential to an operative program have been omitted in the interests of clarity. However, one may observe from this the kinds of information furnished the computer by the program, and the general flow of data as they come to the machine through an input device, are manipulated and prepared for output, and are finally written through some other unit. Other parts of this text are devoted to a comprehensive explanation of the nature of the COBOL language.

DATA ORGANIZATION

The very short programming example above contains several references to data organization. In it may be found references to files, records, independent data elements, and other data items. This serves to point up the fact that COBOL is a data-processing language, and that an understanding of the nature and organization of data is indispensable to its proper use.

Organization of Grouped Data

"Grouped data" are those bits of data which form a part of a logical data organization. This includes most data used in input and output. Data forming a part of a group are organized into a sort of hierarchical structure.

The broadest class of data is the file, which refers to all data of a general type. Within the file is found a record, containing data on a particular item. Records, in turn, consist of data groups and data elements, which represent explicit facts comprising the record.

Files. A COBOL file is a collection of data of like kind used for data input or output. It may be thought of as similar to a typical file of office information, or as similar to an accounting ledger. Thus a COBOL file might consist of data on personnel, or standard manufacturing costs, or accounts receivable. The programming example above contains two files, one with sales tickets for input, and one output file with extended tickets.

In electronic data processing, a file may be represented by a reel of tape, by a deck of punched cards, or even by a set of printed information.

Files are used in COBOL in a manner somewhat different from their ordinary employment. A COBOL file may be the source of information used as input, or it may contain output data, but not both. It is not feasible to read data from a COBOL file, process it, and return it to its source. Instead, most data-processing procedures call for reading data from one or several files, processing, and writing in one or more new files.

Records. Within the file exist records which contain data of a certain nature pertaining to a particular thing. The thing might be an event, such as all information pertaining to a certain sale (as in the programming example discussed above), or it might be an item of accountability, such as an employee, an item of inventory, a particular accounts receivable account, or some fixed asset. The kind of information depends on the nature of the file, of course; within this, the record will represent all pertinent data applicable to the particular thing.

The programming example cited two records, each existing within a different file. One record, called SALES-TICKET, is found in the file named SALES-TICKET-FILE. The other record, called EXTENDED-TICKET, exists within the file called EXTENDED-SALES-FILE.

A file may contain many records, just as a ledger may contain many accounts. All records in a file contain the same kind of data, although the data themselves will quite probably be different on each record.

Data Groups and Elements. Of course, records contain data which may be found in groups or as elements.

A data element, sometimes called a data item, is a discrete fact not capable of further subdivision. For example. the record above called SALES-TICKET may be seen in Figure 2-3 to contain such data elements as account number, quantity sold, and unit sales price.

Data groups are sets of associated data elements. This definition includes records, which are a special kind of data group. Other data groups are introduced in Chapter 3.

The distinction between data groups and data elements is largely one of definition, for few bits of data cannot be further subdivided. The chief value in the group as a record subdivision is that it permits data to be grouped for ease in processing. The distinction between group and element is not too important at this point but will become significant when the detailed aspects of COBOL are considered later.

Independent Data Elements

Virtually all data read in comes as a part of a record through a file; thus, by definition, data belong to a group (unless the record consists of a single data element). A small amount of data may exist independent of any group, however. CØNTRØL-TØT, the data item used for accumulation of all billings in the example above, is an illustration of such an independent item. Inasmuch as all parts of the computer's memory to be used must be defined in the data division, independent items are frequently required for computations and control totals.

Naming Files, Records, and Data

A clerk is not given data to be used when he is instructed in a certain task; instead, the data which will be used later are referred to by name. In the problem above dealing with the processing of sales tickets, the clerical instruction is given to "Take this file of sales tickets ... calculate total sales ... calculate sales tax as 3 percent of the sales amount ...." Thus the clerk is not given the file at this time, nor does he select a record and make the required computations. At the time of instruction, symbolic reference is made to data, by using data names. Later the clerk will obtain the actual file, withdraw records, and proceed to carry out his instructions.

Thus may be seen the difference between programming and executing. The first is an instructional step, wherein commands are created. The second, or execution, phase involves carrying out the instructions.

The same scheme is used in systems development and programming for electronic data processing. Programs—sets of computer instructions—are created which refer to files, records, and data elements by name. Data for execution are not introduced in this phase at all.

Later, when the program is executed, mention of the file name tells the computer which of its input-output devices is to be used in reading or writing data. Referencing a record by its record name causes all data pertaining to a particular unit to be given attention. Mention of a data item permits use of this particular bit of information.

Rules for Assigning Names. Each file, record, and data group and element must have a name. Once assigned, a name must always be used just as it was assigned, for computers cannot ordinarily recognize approximations. For example, the name CASH-ACCØUNT could never be written in any other way (as, for instance, CASH-ACCT).

Each name must be different from all others or be capable of becoming unique by qualification. In the processing of sales tickets above, both the input and the output records contain the account number. In the former, it is referred to as AC-NØ, while in the output record the item is called ACT-NØ. If the same name were used to designate the account number in more than one record, the computer would have no way of knowing which was which and would be unable to execute the program.

Rules for forming file, record, and data names are the same. They are set out below:

1. The name should not be a word reserved for use by the COBOL language (see Appendix A (pages 222-23) for a list of such reserved words). One easy way to avoid restricted words is to use data names containing a hyphen.

2. It may contain from 1 to 30 characters.

3. The name may consist of letters or numbers or hyphens. It must contain at least one letter, and the first or last character may not be a hyphen.

4. The name may not contain spaces. The hyphen is used in place of a space.

5. It is convenient to assign names suggestive of the item's nature.

Examples of Names. Any name may be used within these limits. For example, it might be appropriate to call a file of customer addresses the ADDRESS-FILE, and its records ADDRESS-RECØRD. CUST-NAME might be a name suitable to the data element representing the customer's name, STREET might be used as the COBOL name of the street field, etc.

Of course, it is not necessary to use names so suggestive of the item's nature. Any of the names below would be suitable for files, records, data groups, or elements:

A14	431-C
NEW-MASTER-FILE	CUSTØMER-NAME
ØLD-MASTER-RECØRD	ACCUMULATED-DEPRECIATIØN
ACCØUNT-1234	

Conversely, the following would not be acceptable names:

ACCT-REC*CØNTRA	(contains an illegal character.)
X52.3	(Contains an illegal character.)
1234	(File, record, and data names must contain at least one alphabetic character.)
BLØCK	(COBOL word.)
ACCUM DEPREC	(Spaces are not allowed.)
SUM-1234-	(Neither the first nor the last character may be a hyphen.)

KINDS OF DATA

COBOL recognizes two basic kinds of data. One, called variable, may assume different values depending on the program or values read from records. The other, called constant, is assigned a value which never changes.

Variable Data

Most data elements are variable. Different values are assumed, arising from items read in or computed. The element is always represented in the program by its data name, rather than by the value itself.

Any data item referred to by name rather than by its value is a variable. Thus all items in records are variables, as is any independent item whose value changes.

COBOL recognizes three types of variables: numeric, alphabetic, and alphameric. Numeric variables used in computation may consist only of the numerals 0-9, and an assumed decimal place and sign if required. Alphabetic variables may contain only the letters A-Z, and the space. On the other hand, alphameric variables may contain any character in the COBOL set. Differences in these types of variables will be ignored at this point but will be considered at length in Chapters 5 and 6.

Constant Data

It is possible to build into a program values which never change. When this is done, the value is referred to as a constant, and it may never be altered.

Named Constants. Constants may be set up and given a name in the program's data division, and then referred to by name in the procedure division. For example, the name PI might be associated with the numeric value 3.1416; henceforth in the program the quantity could be referenced by using its name. Inasmuch as the method of establishing named constants is somewhat technical, their existence is mentioned here only in the interest of completeness. These will be explained in detail in a subsequent chapter.

Figurative Constants. These are constants assigned a value by the COBOL language itself. While the language in its fullest form includes several such constants, only two will be used in this text.

One figurative constant is the word ZERØ, which may also be spelled ZERØS or ZERØES, or it may be represented by the numeral 0. Whenever this term is used, the COBOL language assigns a value of zero to the data item to which it refers. An example of this constant's use may be seen in Figure 2-3, line 18. The program's structure makes it essential that the data item CØNTRØL-TØT contain only zero at the beginning of the run. For this reason the clause VALUE ZERØ is assigned the data element; this, in turn, assigns the value zero at the outset of the program but does not interfere with subsequent accumulations.

The other figurative constant found in frequent use is represented by the word SPACE, or SPACES. When this term is employed, the data item to which it refers will be cleared of all value and contain only spaces.

Literals. It is possible to introduce values to a program by specifying the value itself, rather than its data name. For example, the program considered earlier in this chapter requires that the data item TAX be calculated as .03 of the item called SALES-AMØUNT (see Figure 2-3, line 22). The .03 is used here as a literal; that is, it is "literally" present in the program. Thus a literal is a bit of data which is itself present in the program's procedure division, rather than being represented by a data name.

Literals are of two general types. These are introduced below.

Numeric Literals. These consist of numerals, with an optional decimal point (.) and minus sign (-). The .03 in the example above is a numeric literal.

In forming numeric literals, the following rules are observed:

1. The literal may have as few as one or as many as 18 numerals. (Count does not include decimal point or sign.)

2. A decimal point (.) may appear to the left of all numerals, or between two numerals, as required. However, if the number is whole (that is, an integer), the decimal point is omitted.

3. The literal is left unsigned if it is positive. If negative, the sign is shown as the left-most character, without leaving a space between it and the literal's next symbol.

4. Only numeric literals may be used in arithmetic.

Certain examples of numeric literals are given below:

1965

10

1

3.1416

2.00007

-.25

-25.5

Numeric literals are frequently used to introduce a constant quantity to a computation. For example, if a tax rate remains fairly stable, it may be created in the program, rather than entering through data input. The present social security rate is 4.2 percent. Thus a command such as "MULTIPLY GRØSS-PAY BY .042 GIVING SØCIAL-SECURITY" would cause the variable data element GRØSS-PAY to be multiplied by the numeric literal .042, resulting in the computation of the social security tax amount.

Nonnumeric Literals. A nonnumeric literal is any statement enclosed in single quotation marks (') and may consist of any character available in COBOL, except the quotation mark itself. Thus a number becomes a nonnumeric literal simply by enclosing it in quotation marks. The nonnumeric literal may contain as many as 120 characters, including spaces. Several examples of nonnumeric literals follow:

'ITEM DESCRIPTIØN'

'AUGUST 24, 1966'

'-25.5'

'ANY ERRØR MESSAGE'

Nonnumeric literals are used chiefly in setting up communications from the program to the computer operator or in providing headings in printed statements. In programming, it is possible to specify tests of data or results at various points. If the program is not proceeding as desired, a message can be displayed for the operator. By varying these through nonnumeric literals, it is possible to know the exact nature of the failure.

QUESTIONS AND PROBLEMS

1. What is the relationship between the environment, data, and procedure divisions of a COBOL program?

2. When the computer encounters a READ command in the procedure division, how does it know which of its input-output units to activate?

3. How does the computer know how many characters of an input record to associate with a particular data name?

4. How does the computer know to which family of data a data element belongs?

5. How can a computer recognize that a data item does not belong to any family of data?

6. a) What is a file, as the term is used in COBOL?

   b) Mention several files which might be used in the following data-processing operations of a manufacturer:

      (1) Inventory accounting

      (2) Processing accounts receivable

      (3) Processing accounts payable

      (4) Writing dividend checks

      (5) Preparing employee tax forms at the end of the year

7. a) What is a COBOL record?

   b) What might be the contents of the following records:

      (1) Cash receipts

      (2) Weekly wage withholding for employees

      (3) Accounts receivable balances

      (4) Sales of a particular inventory item

      (5) Standard cost information pertaining to the use of a certain raw material

8. What is the difference between data names and data?

9. "A list of unpaid vouchers payable is prepared daily. This shows the date of the run, the voucher date and voucher number, the amount owed at gross, any discount allowed, the amount owed at net, the payment date required for taking the discount, and the final payment

date. This list is prepared with data from two sources. One is a magnetic tape containing information from purchase orders and receiving reports. This shows the number of units ordered and the number of units received. The other source is a magnetic tape containing information on invoices received. This shows the number of units for which we are billed and all other information required on the voucher run. The current date is input daily as a separate item."

Instructions: List each file referred to in the above quotation, and show what records it contains and the contents of each record. Then, list any independent data element mentioned.

10. Why is the word RECØRD not acceptable as a data name? In what capacities might the word be acceptable in COBOL programming or execution?

11. List the errors, if any, in the following COBOL data names:

    a) ITEM 1

    b) INPUT

    c) RECØRD-NØ

    d) FILE-A

    e) FILE623

    f) UNIT-14.8

    g) ALPHA.-NAME

    h) REC.

    i) PRICE-$

    j) -22

CHAPTER 3

COBOL DATA-MANIPULATIVE LOGIC

An electronic computer has very few capabilities which are controlled by its program. Under program control, a computer can be made to read data, transfer data within its memory from one location to another, do arithmetic, compare quantities, and emit output, or write. Commands are also available which cause the program to do special things, such as interrupt a sequence of commands and jump into another sequence. These instructions were introduced in the example in Chapter 2.

These instructions—read, move data, compute, branch, and write—are the basic operations of the computer. Each must be performed as a separate step in the program; for example, the computer cannot read and perform arithmetic in the same command, nor can it compare and write simultaneously. The above list represents discrete capabilities.

A program is a system of these capabilities, combined in appropriate form, designed to achieve certain ends. Programming logic is predicated on the fact that these capabilities represent the full range of the computer's accomplishments, but that these can be performed very quickly and in any combination desired to yield a very sophisticated instruction system.

Use of the computer requires careful study of the problem at hand and then the creation of a scheme for its solution. A typical problem is so large that it is impossible to write a polished program without preliminary logical design. This designing of a logical structure for the program is called flow-charting or diagramming. Material in these chapters on COBOL logic will be introduced in the context of the flow chart, because here the restraints and requirements of COBOL may be seen without concern as to technicalities.

Standard COBOL instructions will be introduced in simplified form as they are discussed. In these, words written in capitals are COBOL words and are a required part of the command. Other words, written in small letters, represent data which must be supplied by the programmer. For example, in the command "MØVE data-name-1 TØ data-name-2," a typical command, the words MØVE and TØ are required as such, while data-name-1 and data-name-2 indicate that the programmer is to insert data names here.

This chapter introduces the data manipulation computer commands, that is, those commands which actually cause data to be processed by control of the program. These include instructions causing the computer to read data, relocate memory contents, perform arithmetic operations, and write. As will be seen in Chapter 4, certain other commands are concerned with control of the computer proper; these will be referred to as "processor" instructions.

DATA INPUT COMMANDS

Data processing usually begins with the computer's acceptance of data from some external source. Input forms—frequently punched cards or magnetic tape—are loaded in one of the computer's several data input devices. Then, when input commands are executed, these forms are "read" and their contents transferred to the computer's memory.

Opening Files

Actually, before a file may be used for either input or output purposes, it must be "opened." This is accomplished by a special command which names the file and indicates whether it will be used for data input or for data output.

The basic command is as follows:

ØPEN INPUT file-name-a, file-name-b, ..., ØUTPUT file-name-c, file-name-d,...

All files may be opened in a single command, and they need be opened only once in the entire program. This command must be given before reading from or writing into the file is attempted, however.

As an illustration of the ØPEN command, assume that in a certain program the MASTER-FILE and DETAIL-FILE contain information to be read, and the CØST-FILE, NEW-MASTER, and VARIANCE-FILE are files which are to be written. The command opening all of these would be:

ØPEN INPUT MASTER-FILE, DETAIL-FILE, ØUTPUT CØST-FILE, NEW-MASTER, VARIANCE-FILE.

The process of opening need not be repeated in the program, no matter how many times READ or WRITE commands refer to the files. After all reading and writing are completed, the files are closed, as will be seen in the next chapter.

The READ Command

After being opened, the contents of a file may be read by a command of the following general nature: "READ file-name." This command instructs the computer to read the record next in sequence from the specified file.

The contents of the entire record are thus read and transferred to the computer's memory, from which each data element is subsequently available by reference to its data name. It should be noted that while the command cites the file from which reading is carried on, it is a record which is actually read. All the data elements contained in the record are transferred into memory with a single READ instruction.

The READ command is destructive. With each execution, it erases the contents of any record previously read from the same file, and the contents of the new record are substituted. Therefore, many records in a given file may be read with a single READ command.

A READ command may be given at any point in a program. It may be the program's first command, or it may appear after several other instructions. A program may contain as many READ statements as necessary, and the same file may be referred to by as many different commands as necessary, whenever appropriate.

Illustration of the READ Command. As an example of the effect of the READ command, assume that sales records, given the COBOL name SALES-RECØRD, exist within a file called the SALES-FILE. Each record occupies a separate punched card. Data elements are assigned certain card columns, or fields. The card appears as in Figure 3-1. Its contents, and the number of columns occupied by each field, are set forth in Table 3-1 with the data name associated with each element. If these cards are placed in the computer's card read hopper, when the READ command is encountered in the program one card will be read and its contents transferred to the computer's memory.

Table 3-1

Description of Contents	Field	Data Name	Assumed Contents
Date of transaction	1-6	DATE	081766
Customer name	7-26	CUS-NAME	JØHN WHITE
Customer number	27-31	C-NUM	10245
Trade class	32-33	TC	04
Inventory	34-47	INV-DATA	---
Number	34-40	INV-NØ	6040302
Discount class	41-42	DIS-CLASS	10
Cost per unit	43-47	UNIT-CØST	01000
Salesman	48-56	SALESMAN	----
Number	48-54	SLS-NØ	2044012
Commission class	55-56	CØM-CLASS	01
Number of units sold	57-60	NØ-UNITS	0025
Sales price per unit	61-64	UNIT-PRICE	0150

Each file has a space allotted to it in the computer's memory, corresponding in size and field construction to the data elements within the record. Each field has a data name associated with it in memory; these names are assigned by the programmer. A data name, then, is really the memory address at which that bit of data is stored. It represents a variable, in that with each READ command the contents of the memory area can be changed.

In schematic form the reading process may be thought of as shown in Figure 3-2. Execution of the READ command moves the contents of the record from the read-in position into memory. By inspection of Figure 3-2, it may be seen that after the command is executed, the exact contents of the first card (assumed to be as listed in Table 3-1) are to be found in the memory of the computer. From now on in the program, data will be referred to by data names.

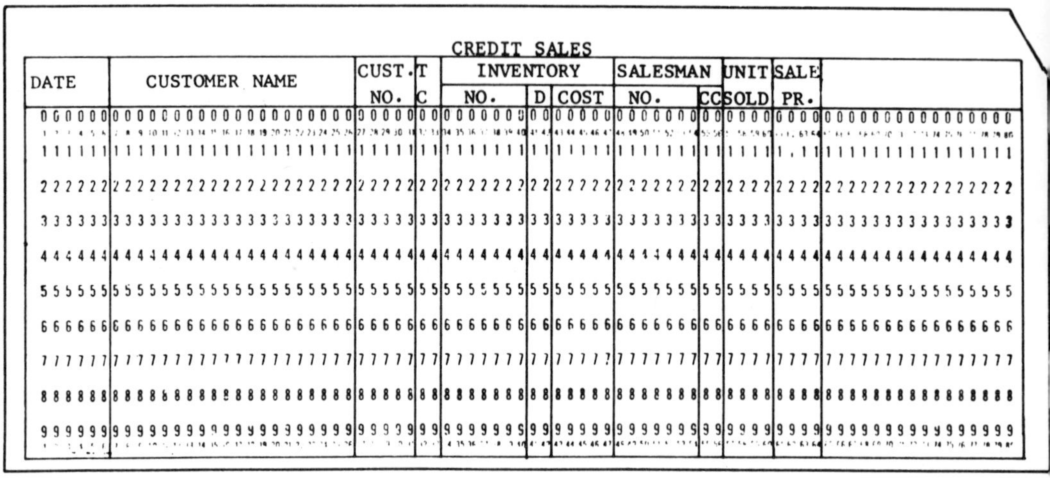

FIG. 3-1. A Sales Record Card

Diagramming the ØPEN and READ Commands. The ØPEN and READ commands are symbolized in flow chart terms by rectangles containing the command title and the name of the file involved. Thus the command to ØPEN and then READ a record from the SALES-FILE would appear as shown at left below.

Of course, to use the ØPEN and READ commands by themselves would be a rather meaningless program. However, for example, we may assume that we wish to pass the contents of all cards through the computer's memory; a flow chart representing this would appear as shown at right below.

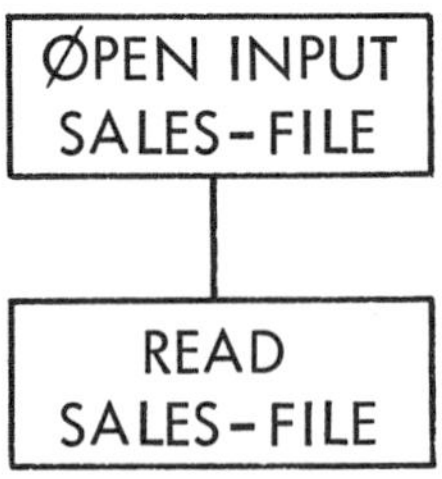

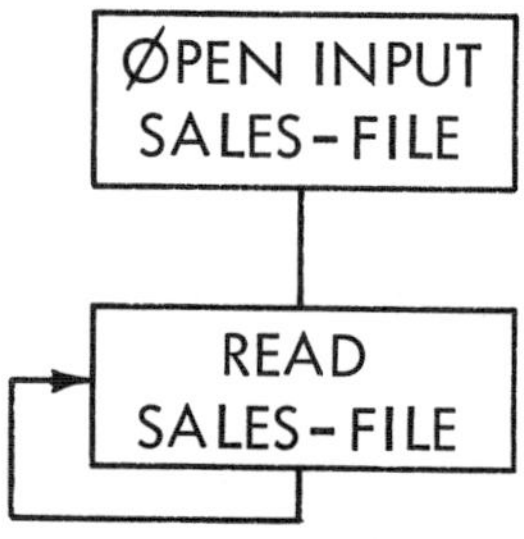

The arrow returning from the bottom of the READ command to its side indicates that the command, once executed, is to be performed again and again. As may be seen the ØPEN command is to be executed only once.

Nothing in this flow chart indicates how this program is to end. It simply shows that the computer is to read a record from the input file, then another, then another, and so on until no more input records are available in the input unit. Each record read would erase the contents of its predecessor, and at the end the computer's memory would contain only the contents of the last record read.

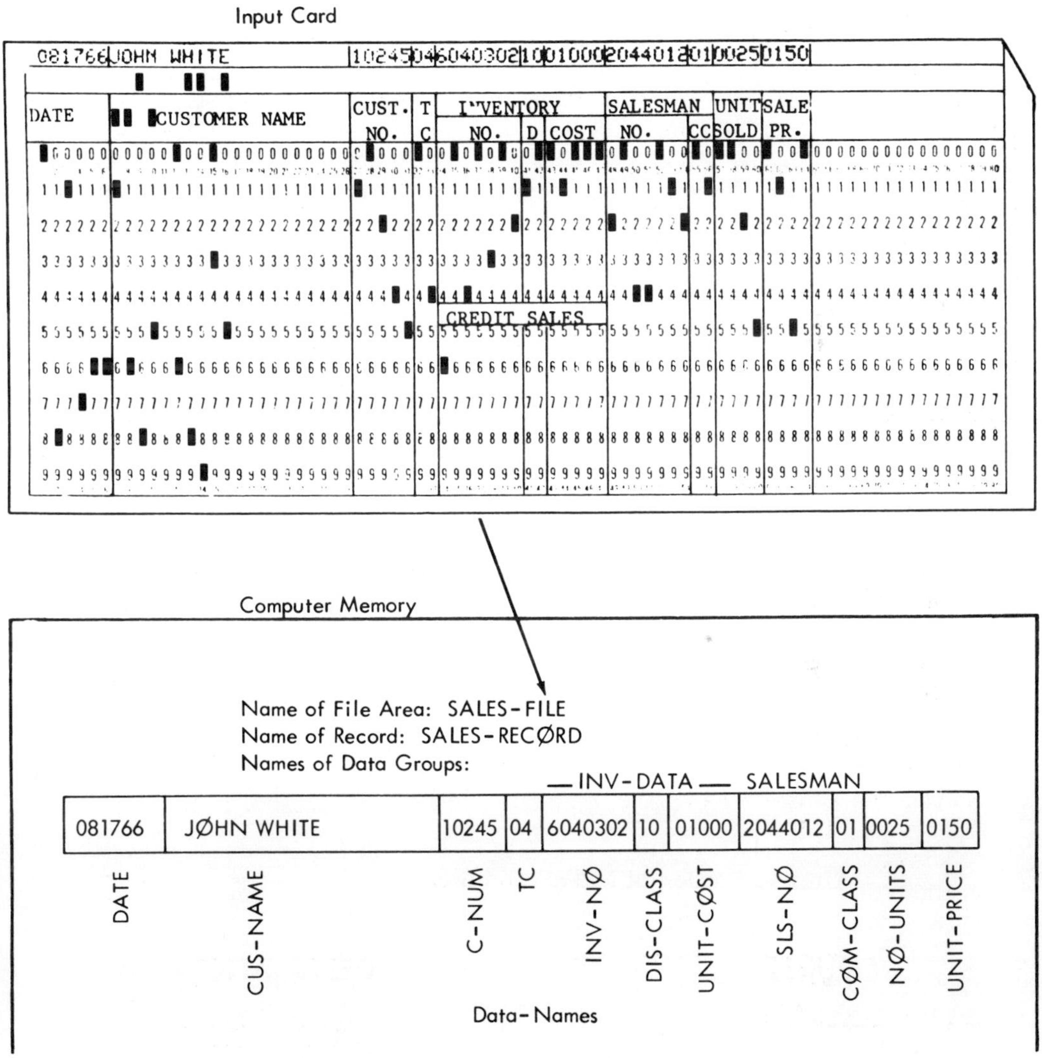

FIG. 3-2. Effect of the READ Command

THE "MØVE" COMMAND

The MØVE command instructs the computer to retrieve data stored in its memory at the location specified by one data name and move it to another location specified by a second data name. The instruction is of the general form

MØVE data-name-1 or literal TØ data-name-2.

The MØVE command really instigates a copying operation, in which data stored at one location in the computer's memory are copied over in another location. This does not destroy the original data but simply causes the information to exist in two parts of the computer's memory.

Execution of the MØVE command does destroy all data stored at the location to which the data are moved, however. This effect is illustrated in Figure 3-3. The contents of a storage location named SØURCE-A are being moved to another storage location, called DESTINATIØN-A. The contents of DESTINATIØN-A before execution of the MØVE command are assumed to be the number 12345. After the MØVE command has been carried out, this location has been cleared of its original contents and now contains the number 00001.

Even though the value stored at SØURCE-A is smaller than that stored at DESTINATIØN-A, the MØVE command completely replaces the latter. When the MØVE instruction is executed, the contents of the location to which data are being transferred are first erased; then new data are moved in.

Instruction: MØVE SØURCE-A TØ DESTINATIØN-A.

1. Before execution of MØVE command:

2. After execution of MØVE command:

FIG. 3-3. Effect of the MØVE Command

Moving Data Elements. The copying ability of the MØVE command may be illustrated in connection with the READ instruction. As discussed above, the READ command causes a record of input data to be brought into the computer's memory. Data will be found in memory in the same sequence they maintain in the input record. Any data element or data group may be moved from this input area to another part of the computer's memory. If, for example, it is desired to move the contents of the memory input area known as C-NUM to another memory location known as CUS-NUM, this could be signaled by the following:

```
MØVE
C -NUM →
CUS-NUM
```

This would not change the data stored at C-NUM in any way but would simply copy it at another memory location, CUS-NUM. In Figure 3-4, where all examples of the MØVE command are illustrated, this move is indicated as No. 1.

Moving Groups or Records. By the same token, a data group or an entire record may be moved from one memory location to another. When data are moved at the group or record level, their arrangement is not changed from that at the source.

Example 2, Figure 3-4, shows the movement of all the contents of data group SALESMAN to a new area known as SALESMAN-INFØ. In example 3 the entire SALES-RECØRD is moved to a new area called DATA-FRØM-MØVE.

Except in certain circumstances, data are not read out of a computer's memory from the same positions they were read into it. Instead, a movement of data from input area to output area occurs and may include a rearrangement of data elements or groups. Note that in example 4 the contents of the SALES-RECØRD are moved to an area known as ØUT-RECØRD, but the fields in the latter are not in the same order as they were in the source record.

In example 4 a program consisting of several steps is indicated. Fields in the ØUT-RECØRD are to be filled by selecting certain input data. The operations to be performed are as follows:

a) Move the contents of DATE to ØUT-DATE.

b) Move the contents of CUS-NAME to ØUT-NAME.

c) Move the contents of the data group INV-DATA to ØUT-INV.

d) Move the contents of NØ-UNITS to ØUT-UNITS.

e) Move the contents of UNIT-PRICE to ØUT-PRICE.

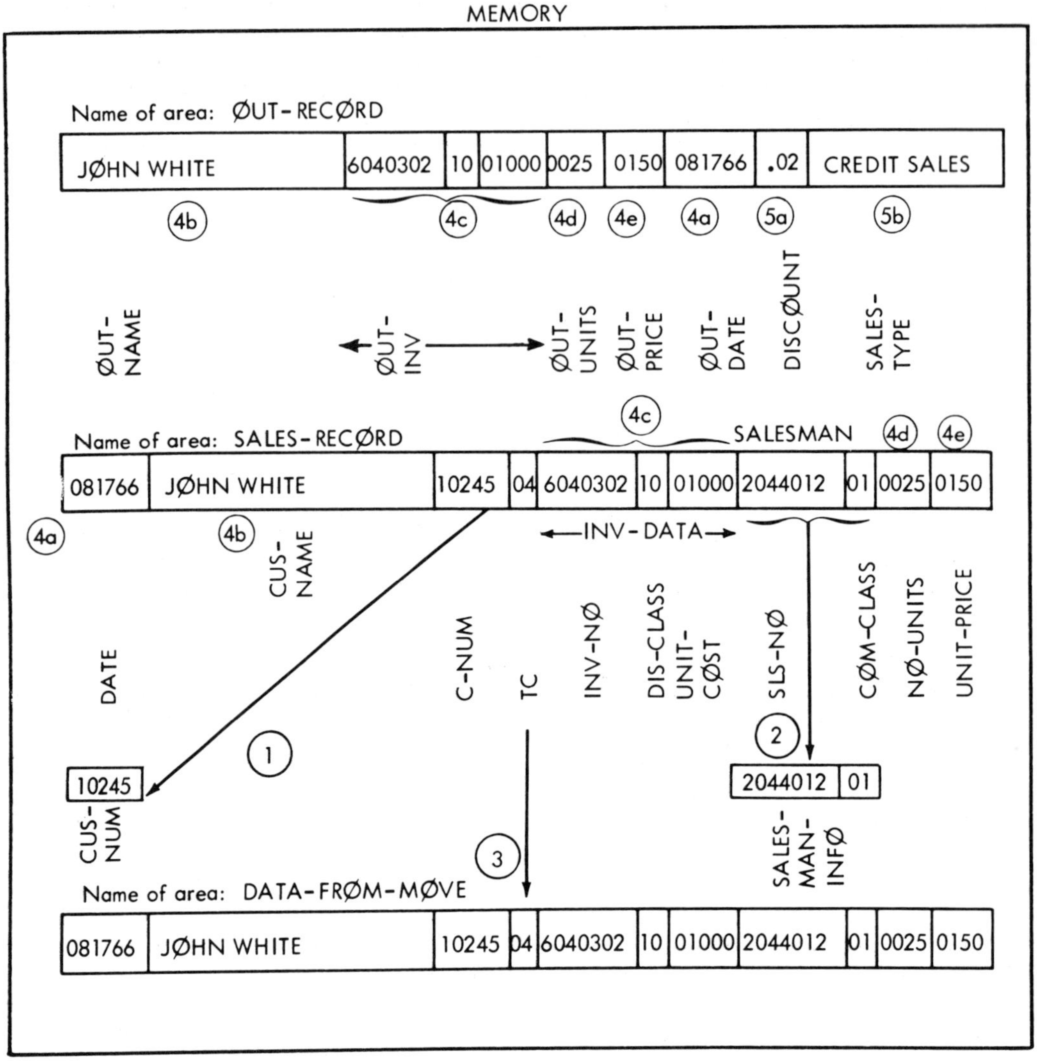

FIG. 3-4. Examples of the MØVE Command

Since these 5 operations are independent, they may be written in any order. The flow chart representing these steps is shown in Figure 3-5. A careful review of example 4 in Figure 3-4 will indicate that the data have not necessarily been moved into corresponding positions in the new record, and that not all data have been moved. Each of these conditions is quite acceptable and is subject to the requirements of the particular problem.

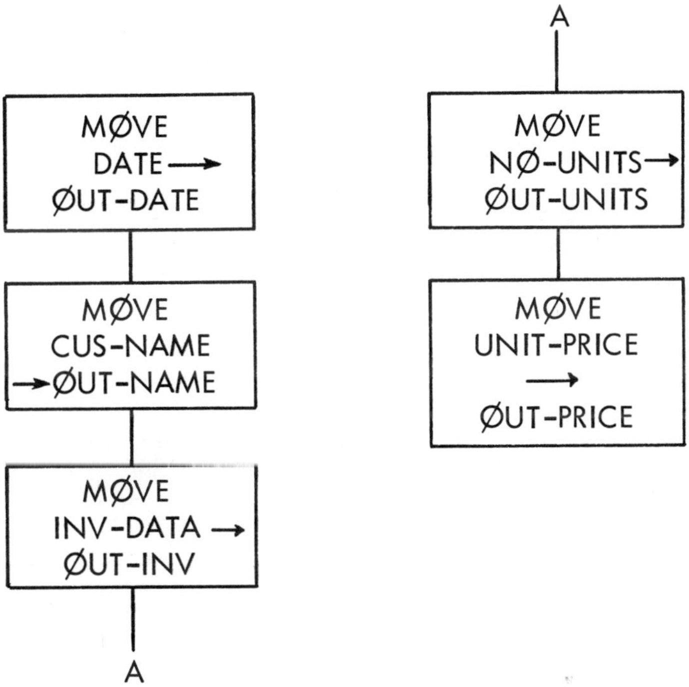

FIG. 3-5

Moving literals. It is possible to create data in the program itself by moving a literal to a storage location. This is accomplished by a step which specifies "MØVE literal TØ data-name." The literal involved may be numeric, in which instance the number itself is shown; or it may be nonnumeric, the literal being enclosed in quotation marks.

This version of the MØVE command is quite useful when data required in output are not read in through the input record.

Examples of this instruction are presented in Figure 3-4. Example 5, filling a part of the data group called ØUT-RECORD, illustrates the effect of moving numeric and nonnumeric literals into memory areas. In example 5a the command "MØVE .02 TØ DISCØUNT" is illustrated. Example 5b shows the effect of the command "MØVE 'CREDIT SALES' TØ SALES-TYPE." Note that in the latter case the nonnumeric literal, but not the quotation marks in which it is enclosed, is moved to the destination area.

Moving Figurative Constants. Figurative constants, introduced in Chapter 2, may also be used in MØVE commands. For example, when a data item is to be set to zero, either the command "MØVE 0 TØ DATA-ITEM," or "MØVE ZERØ TØ DATA-ITEM" will serve. By the same token, if a data item is to be blanked out, the command "MØVE SPACE TØ DATA-ITEM" will load all positions of the data item with blanks.

In neither instance does it matter how many positions the data item has, nor is the singular or plural form of the noun required. All positions of the data item will be set to the designated constant, regardless of the noun form.

DATA OUTPUT COMMANDS

Two COBOL commands cause data to be emitted, or written. One instruction causes data to be written rapidly, one record at a time. The other is used to write out short messages on the computer's low-volume output unit, frequently a typewriter. The commands are introduced in the following order.

The WRITE Command

The results of a computer's computations and other activities are not known unless some sort of output is arranged. This is commonly done by use of the WRITE command, in which a record, prepared in memory, is transmitted to the appropriate output unit, which may be a printer, a card punch, a magnetic tape, or some other device. Execution of the instruction does not erase the written-out data in memory. This remains undisturbed until new data are transferred to the field.

This command is of the nature "WRITE record-name." It references the name of the output record, in contrast with the READ command, which references the name of the input file. These commands should be carefully considered and this difference remembered, inasmuch as many programming errors result from improper referencing.

Ordinarily, the record written out is not the same as that read in. Data manipulation must usually occur before output is ready for use. Therefore, COBOL provides that the memory output area should be different from the input area. For the moment, it will be assumed that even if an input record were to be copied intact as output, it would be necessary to go through the routine shown in Figure 3-6.

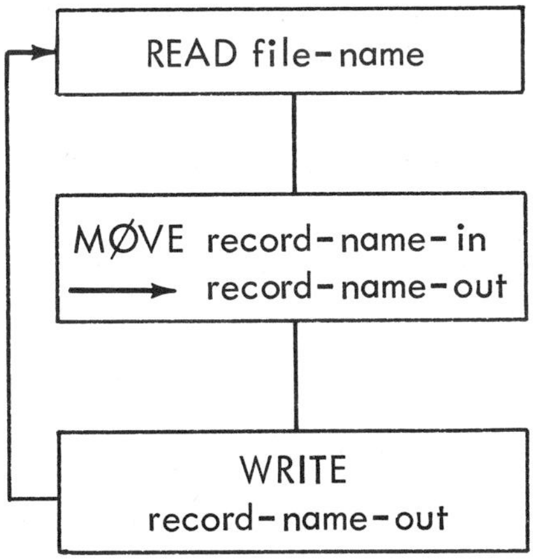

FIG. 3-6

The DISPLAY Command

Most electronic data processors have a slow output unit, such as a typewriter, for writing out such monitoring and control information as error messages, control totals, and the like. A special output command is used with these devices. It is of the nature:

DISPLAY literal or data-name.

The DISPLAY command may be used to write a message, in which case a numeric or nonnumeric literal is set up in the write command. The instruction may also be used to display the contents of a particular storage address, by referencing the data name of the element desired.

Examples of this command's use will not be shown in this chapter, because the basic instructions covered thus far do not lend themselves to use of the DISPLAY command. However, the next chapter will mention several instances in which the instruction may be used to advantage.

EXTENDED ILLUSTRATION

To illustrate the use of the ØPEN, READ, MØVE, and WRITE commands, the example used previously in the chapter is employed once more. Assume that input records of the type illustrated in Figure 3-1 are to be processed. They are to be read; and certain data are to be extracted, moved to an output area, and written. The input file is called the SALES-FILE; in it are input records called SALES-RECØRD. Output is to be processed through a file called ØUT-FILE; it contains records named ØUT-RECØRD.

The data items to be extracted from the input record, and their names in the output record, are as follows:

Data in Input Record	Data in Output Record
DATE	ØUT-DATE
CUS-NAME	ØUT-NAME
INV-DATA	ØUT-INV
NØ-UNITS	ØUT-UNITS
UNIT-PRICE	ØUT-PRICE

It may be seen by referring to Figure 3-4 that this portion of the illustration is the same as the moves in example 4.

The output record is to contain two literals in addition to the data items enumerated above. The data item DISCØUNT is to contain the numeric literal .02, and the data item SALES-TYPE is to contain the non-numeric literal 'CREDIT SALES.'

The modified record is then to be written out. Operations are to continue until all records are processed.

Program Analysis

In considering the above problem, it becomes apparent that four basic operations must be performed—OPEN, READ, MØVE, and WRITE. Furthermore, it is obvious that they must be executed in this sequence, for data may not be read in before opening files, nor moved until read in, and cannot be written before they are moved to the write-out section of memory.

It matters little in what order the data items are moved into the output record. It makes slight difference if the literals are moved before the input data, or which input fields are moved before others (although, as will be seen presently, the program can be shortened somewhat by careful location of the MØVEs).

Simple Flow Chart

A flow chart representing the required program might appear as shown in Figure 3-7. The four basic parts have been labeled A, B, C, and D for identification. The logic of this flow chart is sound, in that reading is accomplished prior to data movement, and this occurs before attempting to write.

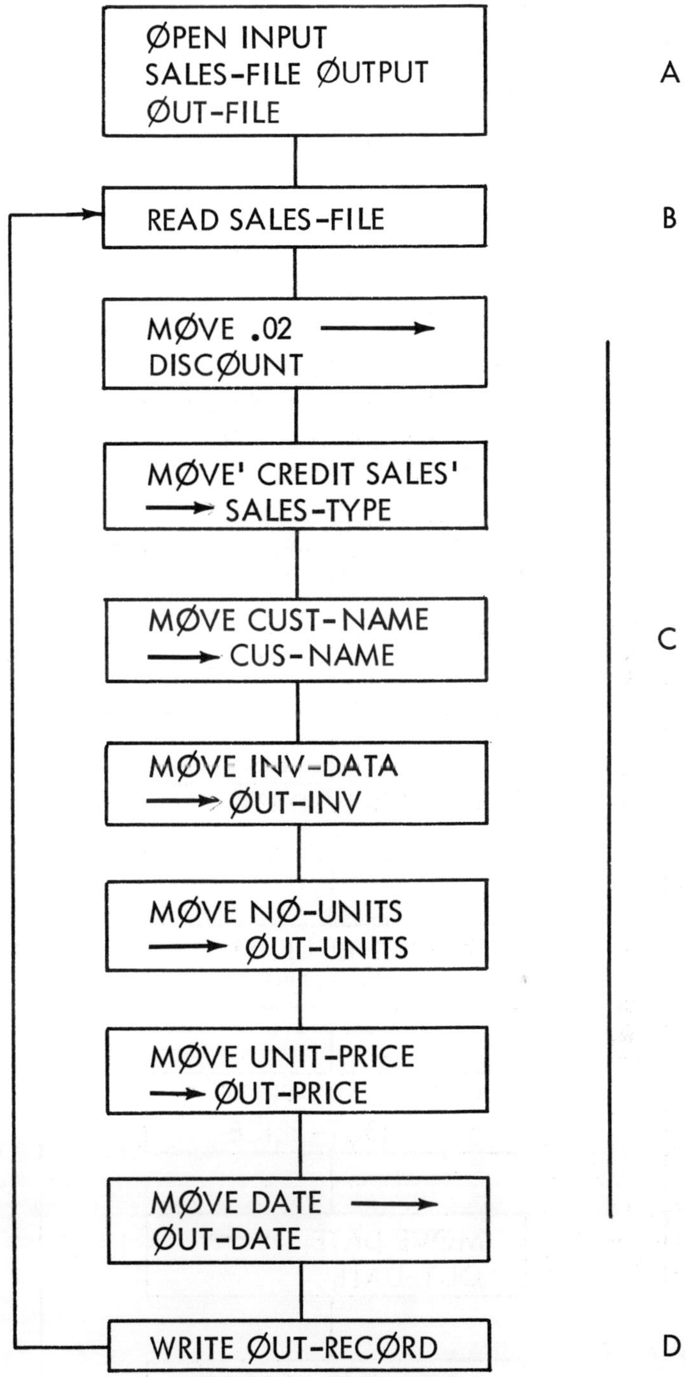
ØPEN INPUT SALES-FILE ØUTPUT ØUT-FILE
A
READ SALES-FILE
B
MØVE .02 → DISCØUNT
MØVE' CREDIT SALES' → SALES-TYPE
MØVE CUST-NAME → CUS-NAME
C
MØVE INV-DATA → ØUT-INV
MØVE NØ-UNITS → ØUT-UNITS
MØVE UNIT-PRICE → ØUT-PRICE
MØVE DATE → ØUT-DATE
WRITE ØUT-RECØRD
D

FIG. 3-7

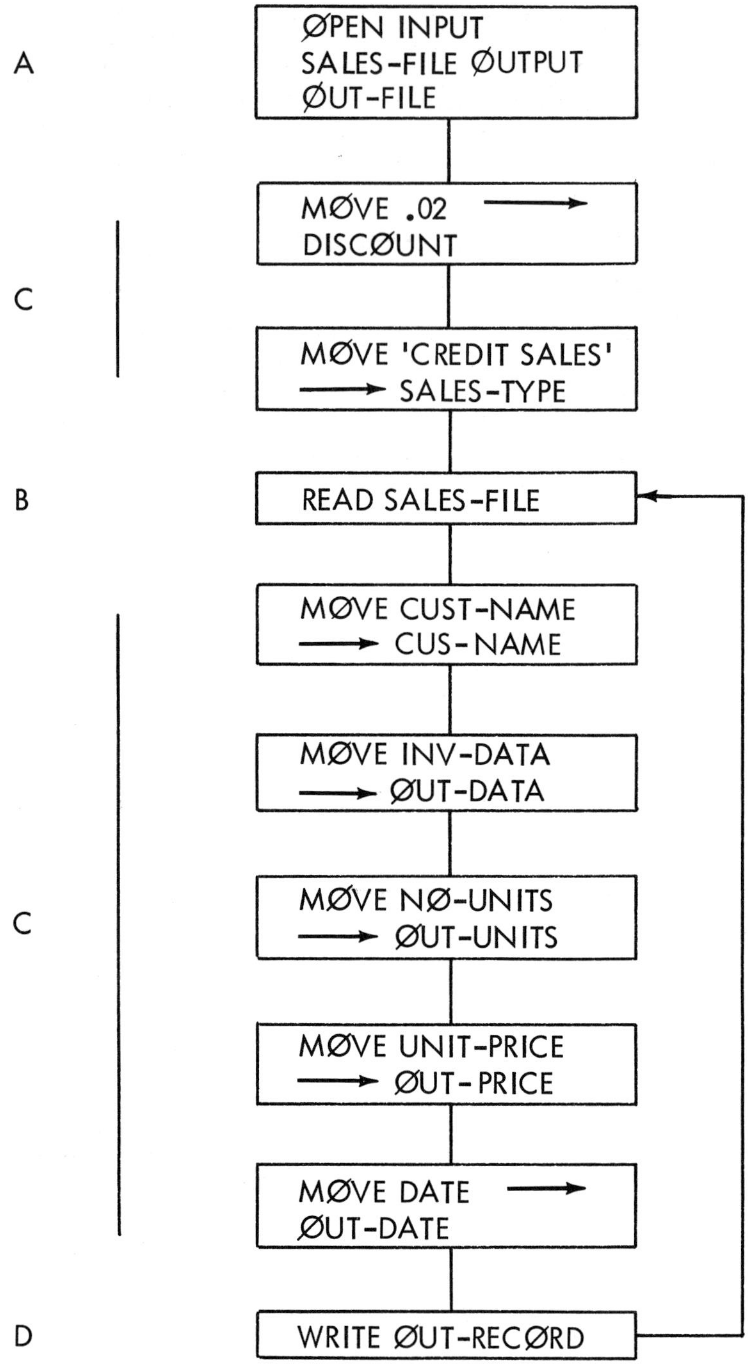
A
ØPEN INPUT SALES-FILE ØUTPUT ØUT-FILE
C
MØVE .02 → DISCØUNT
MØVE 'CREDIT SALES' → SALES-TYPE
B
READ SALES-FILE
C
MØVE CUST-NAME → CUS-NAME
MØVE INV-DATA → ØUT-DATA
MØVE NØ-UNITS → ØUT-UNITS
MØVE UNIT-PRICE → ØUT-PRICE
MØVE DATE → ØUT-DATE
D
WRITE ØUT-RECØRD

FIG. 3-8

A More Sophisticated Approach

A review of the WRITE command's characteristics might suggest a slightly better way of organizing the solution to this problem. It may be recalled that the WRITE instruction is nondestructive; that is, it does not erase the contents of the record it transmits. At the same time, the literals moved into output areas are to be the same on all output records. Therefore, they may be moved into output before the READ command, and the program need never return to them. The data elements moved in, the numeric literal .02 and the nonnumeric literal 'CREDIT SALES,' will not be erased after their initial move and will therefore appear in all output records.

This modification may be seen in the flow chart in Figure 3-8. The return arrow indicates that the program never returns to the two initial MØVE commands after they are executed once, but cycles through the READ instruction, the movement of changeable data from the newly read record to the output area, and the writing of the new output record.

EXERCISES

1. When must the ØPEN command appear?

2. Does execution of the READ command erase the former contents of the read-in memory area?

3. Does the READ instruction contain the file name or the record name? How many data are read when the command is executed?

4. Does the WRITE instruction contain the file name or the record name? How many data are written when the command is executed?

5. A memory location named STUDENT contains the data element JØHN PAUL JØNES. Give the command to move your name to this location. Show the contents of STUDENT before and after execution of the MØVE.

6. The input file named IN-FILE contains a record called IN-RECØRD. This record consists, in turn, of a single data element called IN-DATA. This presently contains the number 0123456.

   a) Give the command necessary to read in a new data element.

   b) Show the contents of IN-DATA before and after execution of the READ command, assuming that the new value read is 0000099.

7. The Ajax Company wishes to use the computer for processing its records of raw material purchases. At present, purchases are being punched into cards, which appear as shown in Figure 3-9 (fields are numbered across the bottom for reference).

Additional information pertaining to data input, data names to be used, and the contents of the first input record are provided in Table 3-2. The aggregate of raw material purchase records is to be called the PURCHASE-FILE, and the records are to be known as the PURCHASE-RECØRD.

RAW MATERIALS

DESCRIPTION	NO.	DATE	REFERENCE		INV. NO.			PR	NO.	COST			
			P.O.	INV.	CL	GR	ITEM		UNITS	INVOICE	FGT.	TAX	
1	2	3	4a	4b	5a	5b	5c	6	7	8a	8b	8c	

FIG. 3-9

Instructions:

a) Prepare a sketch of computer memory showing the PURCHASE-RECØRD after the first record is read. Show all group and data names, and the contents of memory locations, in a manner similar to that used in Figure 3-4.

b) Add to your sketch the results of a command moving the entire contents of the PURCHASE-RECØRD to a new record, known as the ØUTPUT-RECORD. This exists within a file called MAT-BAL.

c) Add to your sketch the results of a command moving the data group REFERENCE to a memory area known as STØRAGE-1.

d) Add to your sketch a new memory area known as STØRAGE-2, containing data elements FIELD-1, FIELD-2, FIELD-3, and FIELD-4. Show the results of the following commands:

(1) The contents of data location VENDØR are moved to FIELD-1.

(2) The nonnumeric literal 'RAW MATERIALS' is moved to FIELD-2.

(3) The contents of data location FREIGHT are moved to FIELD-3.

(4) All data in the data group PUR-CØST are moved to FIELD-4.

e) Prepare a flow chart to depict the following processing routine: Raw materials records are to be read. Data are to be moved as in items a, b, c, and d, above. The area known as ØUTPUT-RECØRD, in the MAT-BAL file, is to be written out. The area known as STØRAGE-2 is to be displayed. The process is to be repeated for an indefinite number of input records.

Table 3-2

Field No.	Field Contents	Field Size—Characters	Memory Data Name	Contents of First Record
1	Name of item purchased	20	DESC	AJAX STØCK
2	Supplier code	5	VENDØR	40223
3	Date received	6	DATE	082166
4a	Purchase order number	6	PCH-NØ	643382
4b	Invoice number	5	INVØICE	72884
5a	Inventory class number	2	CLS	41
5b	Inventory group number	3	GRØUP	211
5c	Inventory item number	4	ITEM	4207
6	Purpose of purchase	2	PURPØSE	01
7	Number of units received	5	UNITS	00100
8a	Invoice cost	7	INV-CØST	0010000
8b	Freight charge	6	FREIGHT	000500
8c	Tax on purchase	5	TAX	00100

Notes:

1. Items 4a and 4b belong to the data group REFERENCE and supply reference data.

2. Items 5a, 5b, and 5c belong to the data group INV-NØ and together make up the inventory number.

3. Items 8a, 8b, and 8c belong to the data group PUR-CØST and together make up the delivered cost of the purchase. In each field the decimal point is assumed to lie two places from the right, so that each field expresses its amount in dollars and cents. (Thus the invoice cost shown is $100.00).

8. A memory field called AREA-1 now contains the number 250. What will its contents be after execution of the following command: "MØVE 50 TØ AREA-1?

9. What is wrong with the following command: "MØVE AREA-X TØ 400"?

10. What may the DISPLAY command be used to write?

ARITHMETIC COMMANDS

The electronic computer is essentially a calculating machine and, as such, uses the arithmetic instructions as its "working" commands. COBOL offers two kinds of arithmetic statements. One type permits a single arithmetic manipulation in each statement. The other allows a statement to be created which uses as many arithmetic steps as desired, in any combination. These are considered separately below.

Simple Arithmetic Commands

Basic arithmetic includes the operations of addition, subtraction, multiplication, and division. Simple commands are provided for each of these. In the commands certain connectives — the comma, and AND — may be used, but are not required.

Simple Addition. In the simplest kind of addition, one or more literals or the contents of data names may be added to the contents of another data name. The sum is stored at the last position, destroying whatever value was previously found there. This command is of the general nature "ADD data-names and/or literals TØ data-name-n," where one or more data elements or literals may be added to the last data element.

This sort of addition may be seen in the following illustration. Assume that two memory positions, AREA-A and AREA-B, contain the following:

AREA-A	AREA-B
25	50

If the command "ADD AREA-A TØ AREA-B" is given, the following will result:

AREA-A	AREA-B
25	75

It may be seen that the contents of AREA-A remain undisturbed. The old contents of AREA-B have been added to the contents of AREA-A, and the sum has been stored back at AREA-B. This, as may be seen, destroys the old quantity stored at AREA-B.

Another version of the same command adds a numeric literal to the value stored at a data name. If, for example, the command "ADD 20 TØ AREA-A" were executed, to AREA-A's old contents, 25, would be added 20, making the new value of AREA-A 45.

This command may involve more than two factors. For example, assume that the three memory locations shown below contain indicated quantities:

AREA-X	AREA-Y	AREA-Ƶ
100	50	55

The command "ADD AREA-X, AREA-Y TØ AREA-Ƶ" would leave AREA-X and AREA-Y unchanged, but would set AREA-Ƶ, the sum area, to 205.

In this command a comma or the word AND may be used as a connective between values in the list being summed. For example, it would be appropriate to give the command "ADD AREA-Y, 25, AND AREA-Z TØ AREA-X," which would result in the storage of 380 (50 + 25 + 205 + 100) at AREA-X. This shows the use of a numeric literal in the list of items being summed as well as the connectives.

This command developes the <u>algebraic sum</u> of the items being accumulated. Thus the command "ADD -75 to AREA-X" would now cause the sum, 305, to be stored at AREA-X, assuming its contents to have been 380. If AREA-Z contained the amount -55 and AREA-Y 50, the command "ADD AREA-Z TØ AREA-Y" would cause the algebraic sum, -5, to be stored in the latter area.

At this point the exact technique of writing commands is not too important. However, to avoid forming improper coding habits, certain general rules of statement creation should be noted. First, any words in capitals (such as the words ADD and TØ in the command above) are required, and substitutes therefor are not permitted. Second, it should be noted that the last element in a series in the ADD command (the item appearing after the TØ) must be the name of a data element rather than a literal, because the answer will be stored in this location.

<u>The GIVING Option</u>. Inasmuch as the programmer frequently wants his sum stored in a new location, thereby avoiding the destruction of one of his factors, the ADD command has another form. In this type of simple addition the command causes two or more elements—data names or literals—to be added, and the sum is stored in a new location. Assume the following for purposes of illustration:

AREA-A	AREA-B	AREA-C	AREA-D
25	10	40	72

The command "ADD AREA-A, 50, AREA-B AND AREA-C GIVING AREA-D" would cause the former contents of AREA-D to be erased, although not used in the computation, and the sum stored therein. In this example, AREA-D would contain the value 125 (25 + 50 + 10 + 40) after the command's execution. Note carefully the difference in the two kinds of simple addition commands. These two command types are used for each arithmetic operation.

1. The command "ADD (literals and data-names) TØ data-name-n" includes data-name-n as a factor in developing a sum. The sum is stored at data-name-n, erasing previous contents.

2. The command "ADD (literals and data-names) GIVING data-name-n" does not include data-name-n as a factor, although the sum is stored in that location and erases previous contents.

3. The key to the kind of addition command used lies in the choice of the word TØ or GIVING. Pay careful attention to the use of these words in the formation of all addition instructions.

ADD Exercises. Given below are data names and values to be used in the unrelated exercises. The amounts are to be used as shown in developing a sum. Show the command required for each exercise and the sum which would be developed.

Data Name	Value
A	20
B	-15
C	4.5
D	25

1. Add the values of A, B, and C, and store their sum at C.
2. Add the values of A, B, and C, and store their sum at D.
3. Add 12, -24, A, B, and C, and store their sum at A.
4. Add A and 25, and store the sum at A.
5. Add C and 1, and store the sum at D.
6. Add B and 1, and store the sum at B.

Simple Subtraction. Simple subtraction, like simple addition, may be performed by one of two commands, depending on the desired location of the remainder. In one form, "SUBTRACT data-names and/or literals FRØM data-name-n," the remainder is stored at the address of the minuend. In the other, "SUBTRACT data-names and/or literals FRØM (data-name or literal) GIVING data-name-n," the remainder is stored at the address given by data-name-n, which is not ordinarily a factor in the computation. Subtraction produces the algebraic remainder.

For illustrations of these basic subtraction commands, assume the following data names and values:

Data Name	Value
W	10
X	-5
Y	20
Z	25

Illustration 1: Note that the basic difference between the two versions of subtraction commands is found in the presence of the GIVING phrase in the second. For example, if X is to be subtracted from Y and the remainder stored at Y, the command "SUBTRACT X FRØM Y" would be given. After execution, Y would have as its value the remainder, 25. If it is desired to retain values of X and Y intact, the second version of the command would be used: "SUBTRACT X FRØM Y GIVING Z." X and Y would be unchanged by this computation; but the storage of the remainder, 25, at Z would erase its previous contents.

Illustration 2: A series of items—data names and/or literals—may be subtracted from a minuend in a single step. For example, the command "SUBTRACT X AND 10 FRØM Y" would leave Y a value of 15 (20 - [-5 + 10]).

Illustration 3: The computer performs arithmetic algebraically. Thus the command "SUBTRACT 25 FRØM Y" would cause -5 to be stored at Y as the remainder. With this value of Y, if the command were given to "SUBTRACT Y FRØM X," a remainder of zero would result.

SUBTRACT Exercises. Given below are data names and values to be used in the unrelated exercises. The amounts are to be used as shown in developing a remainder. Show the command required for each exercise and the remainder which would be developed.

Data Name	Value
A	10
B	-5
C	20
D	45

1. Subtract A from C, storing the remainder at C.

2. Subtract A from C, storing the remainder at D.

3. Subtract A from C, storing the remainder at A.

4. Subtract A and 15 from C, storing the remainder at C.

5. Subtract A, B, and 10 from D, storing the remainder at C.

6. Subtract B from A, storing the remainder at C.

7. Subtract C from B, storing the remainder at B.

8. Subtract B and -50 and A from C, storing the remainder at D.

9. Subtract -2 from B, storing the remainder at B.

Simple Division. The two simple division commands are very similar in nature to the addition and subtraction instructions already discussed. The basic command form is "DIVIDE data-name-a or literal INTØ data-name-b." If the command is written in this fashion, the quotient is stored at data-name-b (the dividend's location) when it is developed.

However, the GIVING option is available, permitting the command to be written as "DIVIDE data-name-a or literal-1 INTØ data-name-b or literal-2 GIVING data-name-c." The quotient will now be stored at data-name-c.

Several illustrations of these simple division commands are provided below. In each, the following data values are used:

Data Name	Value
A	10
B	5
C	-2
D	14
E	2

<u>Illustration 1</u>: The quotient may be stored in the location of the dividend or elsewhere, as desired:

The command "DIVIDE B INTØ A" stores the quotient, 2, at A.
The command "DIVIDE B INTØ A GIVING E" stores the quotient, 2, at E.

In either event the former contents of the quotient location are destroyed.

<u>Illustration 2</u>: It is not possible to divide a series of divisors into a single dividend in all versions of COBOL; therefore, it is best to assume that it is never possible. Thus, to find the quotient of D divided by the sum of B and E, two steps are required:

```
ADD B TØ E.
DIVIDE E INTØ D.
```

The quotient, 2, would be stored at D.

<u>Illustration 3</u>: Standard algebraic sign rules are followed. For example, the command "DIVIDE C INTØ A" stores -5 at A as the quotient. Likewise, the command "DIVIDE -2 INTØ C" stores 1 as its quotient, at C.

<u>DIVIDE Exercises</u>. Given below are data names and values to be used in the unrelated exercises. The amounts are to be used as shown in developing a quotient. Show the command required for each exercise and the quotient which would be developed.

Data Name	Value
P	-4
Q	12
R	10
S	5

1. Divide S into R, storing the quotient at R.

2. Divide S into R, storing the quotient at P.

3. Divide Q by 3, storing the quotient at S.

4. Divide Q by P, storing the quotient at P.

5. Accumulate the values R, S, and 9, storing the sum at S. Then, divide this into Q, storing the quotient at R.

6. Divide P by -2, storing the quotient at Q.

7. Accumulate P and 7, dividing the sum into Q and storing the quotient at S.

8. Subtract P from Q, dividing the remainder into R and storing the quotient at S.

9. Divide the sum of R and 6 by the sum of Q and P, storing the quotient at R.

10. Divide the remainder of P less Q by the sum of P and -4, storing the quotient at S.

Simple Multiplication. Two simple commands are also available for multiplication. The first is of the form "MULTIPLY data-name-a or literal BY data-name-b." The product is stored at data-name-b, erasing the multiplier formerly stored there.

The second simple multiplication command is of the form "MULTIPLY data-name-a or literal-1 BY data-name-b or literal-2 GIVING data-name-c." This stores the product at a new location, data-name-c. This, of course, erases whatever was previously stored at that position.

The multiplication commands follow standard sign rules in development of the product. The computer also treats the decimal point in appropriate fashion.

A quantity may be multiplied by itself, giving its square. For example, the command "MULTIPLY A BY A GIVING B" would compute A^2, storing this value at B. Of course, other powers could be obtained in a similar fashion, but the process is not so efficient as a command to be introduced shortly.

MULTIPLY Exercises. Use the following data names and values in the independent exercises. In each, show the command or commands required and the resultant product.

Data Names	Value
A	2.5
B	.75
C	-4
D	-.8
E	6

1. Multiply A by B, storing the product at A.

2. Multiply A by 40, storing the product at A.

3. Multiply D by -10, storing the product at C.

4. Multiply the sum of A and B by 2.1, storing the product at D.

5. Divide the sum of B and C by D; then, multiply the quotient by A. Store the product at A.

6. Multiply the sum of A and C by 10, storing the product at D.

7. Subtract C from A, and multiply the remainder by the sum of D and 25. Store the product at B.

8. The area of a circle is calculated as pi (3.1416) times the radius squared. Calculate the area of a circle of radius A, storing the product at B.

9. Jones, Brown and Green are estimating the area of a rectangular plot of land (found by multiplying length times width). Jones and Brown walk off different parts of the land's length. Jones finds his part to be of length A; Brown finds his part to be of length E. The total length, therefore, is A + E. Green estimates the width to be approximately 60 percent of A. Calculate the area, storing the product at E.

10. The area of a triangle is found by multiplying height by base and dividing by 2. Calculate the area of a triangle with a height equal to 1.5 times A and a base equal to three quarters of E. Store your answer at E.

Summary of Simple Arithmetic Commands

Characteristics. The simple arithmetic commands have several common characteristics. The most important of these are:

1. Except for the ability to sum the subtrahend in a SUBTRACT command, each command can execute only one kind of arithmetic.

2. Signs of factors are treated in appropriate algebraic fashion.

3. Decimal points are appropriately aligned.

4. Arithmetic symbols may not be used; the words ADD, SUBTRACT, MULTIPLY, and DIVIDE must be written out.

The Commands. Each arithmetic operation is represented by two commands; one storing the results of computation at the location of a factor, the other storing results at a new location. These are listed as commands A and B below:

1. Addition:

   A. ADD (literals and/or data-names) TØ data-name-n.

   B. ADD (literals and/or data-names) GIVING data-name-n.

2. Subtraction:

   A. SUBTRACT (literals and/or data-names) FRØM data-name-n.

   B. SUBTRACT (literals and/or data-names FRØM (literal or data-name) GIVING data-name-n.

3. Division:

   A. DIVIDE (literal or data-name) INTØ data-name-n.

   B. DIVIDE (literal or data-name) INTØ (literal or data-name) GIVING data-name-n.

4. Multiplication:

   A. MULTIPLY (literal or data-name) BY data-name-n.

   B. MULTIPLY (literal or data-name) BY (literal or data-name) GIVING data-name-n.

In each of the above, the result is stored at the location called data-name-n.

Using Simple Arithmetic Commands

Arithmetic Commands are but one more kind of computer instruction and are used in conjunction with READ, MØVE, and WRITE commands to form a computer program. There are no absolute rules governing the order in which these are used; this depends entirely on the logical requirements of the problem. In a typical read-manipulate-write situation, however, the order of activity usually requires first the reading of an input record.

MØVE and arithmetic commands are not usually dependent on one another and so may ordinarily be written in any sequence. Some arithmetic computations may be predicated on others, and this will naturally govern the order in which computational instructions are written. Writing can occur only after the output record has been filled with data through calculations or moves.

Extended Illustration

The interplay between computer commands introduced thus far may be illustrated by continuing the previous example. Figure 3-2 shows an input record, SALES-RECØRD, containing data on credit sales existing within the file, SALES-FILE. Data in this record have been assigned data names. These names, together with illustrative data, are as shown in Table 3-3.

Table 3-3

Data Description	Data Name	Illustrative Data
Transaction date	DATE	081766
Customer's name	CUS-NAME	JØHN WHITE
Customer's account number	C-NUM	10245
Trade class	TC	04
Inventory number of articles sold	INV-NØ	6040302
Discount class	DIS-CLASS	10
Cost per unit	UNIT-COST	01000 (decimal point assumed three places to left)
Salesman's number	SLS-NØ	2044012
Commission class	CØM-CLASS	01
Number of units sold	NØ-UNITS	0025
Sales price per unit	UNIT-PRICE	0150 (decimal point assumed two places to left

Problem Requirements. 1. An output record called ØUTPUT-RECØRD, in the ØUT-FILE, is to be prepared for each input record. This is to consist of the data shown in Table 3-4.

Table 3-4

Data Description	COBOL Name
Customer name	NAME
Transaction date	T-DATE
Number of units sold	UNITS-SOLD
Sales price per unit	U-PRICE
Sales price for transaction	SALES-PRICE
Sales tax	SALES-TAX
Total transaction charge	TØTAL-PRICE

2. A count of the number of records is to be made. This will be stored in the data item called RCD-CNT. Also, the total number of units sold is to be accumulated as TØT-UNITS and the total of all transaction charges as TØTAL-CHARGES. These three totals will not be written out in this illustration because the necessary commands have not been introduced. Chapter 4 discusses the display of such control information.

Problem Analysis. Study of the above requirements indicates that certain output fields may be filled by moving data from the input record, while other elements must be calculated. Among the former are the following:

Customer name

Transaction date

Number of units sold

Sales price per unit

Items to be calculated are as follows:

Items in the output record:

Sales price for transaction—this will be computed as the product of price per unit times the number of units sold.

Sales tax—this will be computed as 3 percent of sales price.

Total transaction charge—to be calculated as the sum of sales price and sales tax.

Control totals:

Record count—the accumulation of 1 for each record processed.

Total number of units sold—the accumulation of all NØ-UNIT fields.

Total of all transaction charges—the accumulation of all TØTAL-PRICE fields.

Control Implications. When electronic computers are used in data processing, the matter of accuracy becomes very important. One phase of accuracy measurement, or control, involves determining that the proper number of input records has been read and that certain machine-prepared totals agree with amounts calculated before submitting data to the computer. For this reason, typical computer procedures involve the accumulation of control amounts.

This process is symbolized in the illustration by the preparation of a record count, the accumulation of the number of units sold, and the determination of the total transaction amount for all transactions. The record count is simply a step in the process of ascertaining that the proper number of records is processed. The accumulation of units sold (called TØT-UNITS in this illustration) provides an example of a "hash total"—that is, a total which is meaningless insofar as the data processed are concerned, but one which may be used for control. If this same total is obtained by noncomputer means before submitting data to the computer and the man- and machine-prepared totals agree, the number of units reported as sold in all transaction records is probably accurate.

The sum of all transaction charges (called TØTAL-CHARGES) is prepared for much the same reason. This amount may be compared with other computations made elsewhere, such as with total charges to accounts receivable, and one more indication of accuracy is thereby gained.

Logical Flow Chart. A flow chart for this processing situation may appear as in Figure 3-10.

After opening the files, the program proceeds to a READ command. Data elements are then moved from the input record to the output record. No special comments are required, inasmuch as these MØVE commands are similar to those explained previously.

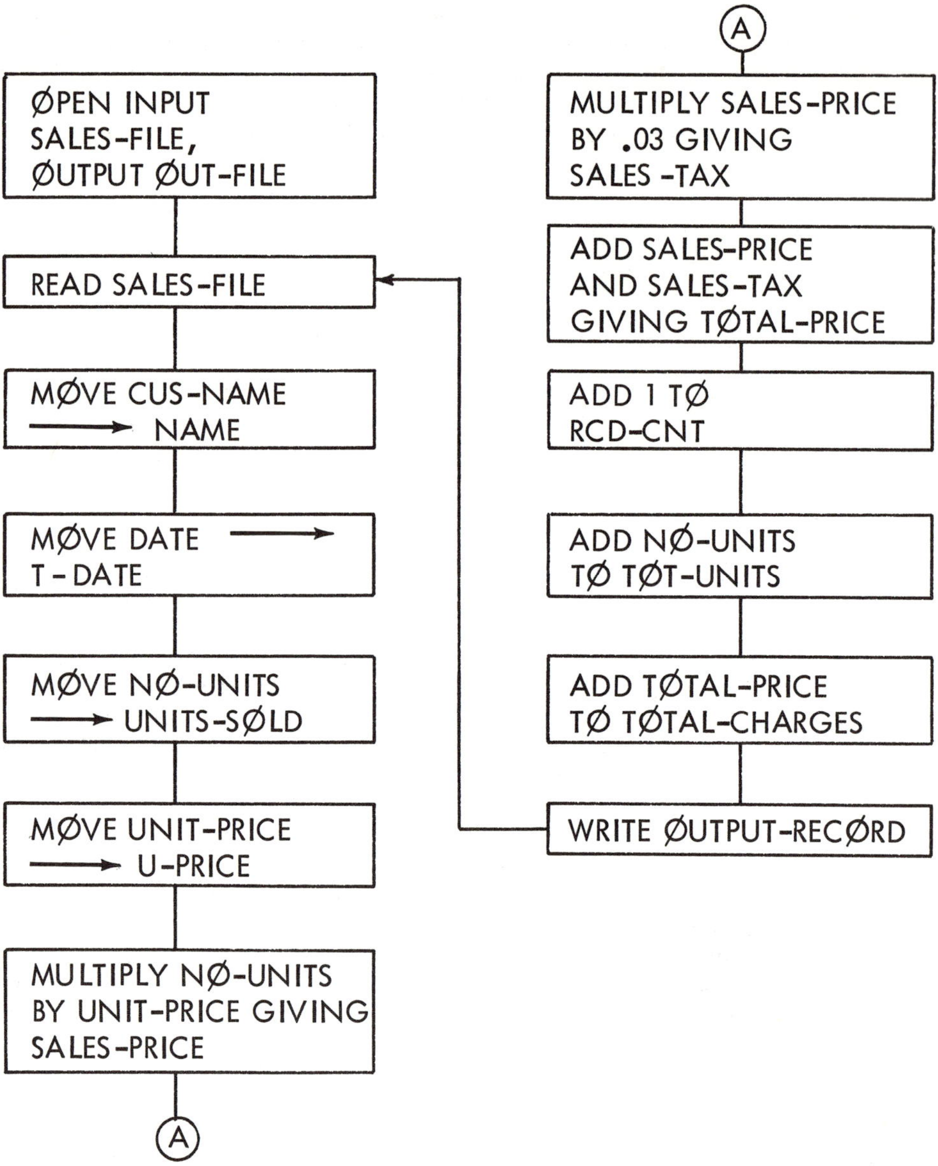

FIG. 3-10. Logical Flow Chart

Data are then calculated as required to fill certain data elements in the output record. It may be seen that SALES-PRICE is needed in the computation of SALES-TAX; therefore, it must be calculated first. Since both SALES-PRICE and SALES-TAX are used in the computation of TØTAL-PRICE, the latter cannot be calculated until both factors are available. We shall find later that it is often impossible to use output data in computations, and that factors such as SALES-PRICE and SALES-TAX must be calculated and stored in a special area; but for the moment, this refinement is ignored.

Control totals are then accumulated. These steps could come at any point in the program after reading and computing SALES-PRICE. It is convenient to include them just before writing the output record, however.

After filling the output record through computation and MØVE commands, it may be written. The program is then to return, read another input record, and repeat the process. The only portion of the program not repeated is the step where the files are opened.

Comprehensive Arithmetic Command

A command is available in COBOL which permits the combination of arithmetic operations in almost any fashion in arriving at a solution. The general form of this instruction is "CØMPUTE data-name = (any combination of literals, data names, and operational symbols necessary to express the desired computation)." The only COBOL word required is CØMPUTE. A single data name is given to the left of the equal sign (=), and the results of the computation will be stored here. The right-hand side of the command may consist of any formula.

Operation Symbols. This command uses standard arithmetic symbols, rather than the arithmetic words employed by those discussed previously. The operational words ADD, SUBTRACT, MULTIPLY, and DIVIDE may not be used with the CØMPUTE instruction. The symbols which are used and their meaning are listed below:

Symbol	Operation
+	Addition
-	Subtraction
/	Division
*	Multiplication
**	Exponentiation

The only symbols not commonly used are the asterisk (*) for multiplication and the double asterisk (**) for exponentiation.

Using Operation Symbols. In the CØMPUTE command, operational symbols are used just as they are in regular arithmetic. For example, a program command to add the quantities represented by data names A and B, the sum to be stored at data name TØT-AB, would appear as follows:

"CØMPUTE TØT-AB = A + B." This means exactly the same as "ADD A AND B GIVING TØT-AB."

Unlike the simple arithmetic commands, the CØMPUTE instruction may combine several arithmetic operations. In the extended illustration above, data element SALES-TAX was calculated as 3 percent of SALES-PRICE; the latter had to be calculated first, however, as the product of NØ-UNITS and UNIT-PRICE. If the CØMPUTE command is used, SALES-TAX may be calculated in a single step, as follows:

CØMPUTE SALES-TAX = (NØ-UNITS * UNIT-PRICE) * .03. [1]

Data element NØ-UNITS was assumed to have a value of 25, and UNIT-PRICE a value of 1.50, in the first record. Therefore, SALES-TAX will be calculated as .03 of (25 times 1.50), or $1.13.

The exponentiation symbol (**) is used to obtain the whole or fractional power of an item. To raise data element A to the third power and store the result at A-PØW, for example, the command "CØMPUTE A-PØW = A ** 3" would be written. By the same token, the square root of A could be found by the command "CØMPUTE A-PØW = A ** .5," the third root by the command "CØMPUTE A-PØW = A ** .33," and so forth. The item raised to a power may be a data element, a literal, or a complex formula.

<u>Evaluating the CØMPUTE Command</u>. The CØMPUTE command, technically of the nature "CØMPUTE data-name = expression" really means "Evaluate the expression, and store its result at the data name specified." Certain matters in the computer's method of processing must be explained before the expression's evaluation can be clearly understood.

The general evaluation of the expression is from left to right. However, if parentheses are used, that part of the expression in the parentheses will be evaluated first, still working from left to right. If several sets of parentheses are used, evaluation is from the inner to the outer set.

The left-to-right evaluation sequence is also broken by the hierarchy assigned arithmetic operations. According to this, exponentiation occurs first, followed by multiplication and division, then by addition and subtraction. Multiplication and division occupy the same hierarchical level, as do addition and subtraction.

Thus the order of evaluation may be summarized as follows—left to right, with priority of operation recognized as shown below:

1. Material in parentheses (inner to outer set)
2. Exponentiation (**)
3. Multiplication and division (* and /)
4. Addition and subtraction (+ and -)

---

[1] Parentheses are used for readability. They are allowed, but not necessary, in this statement.

If the order in which arithmetic operations are normally performed is not satisfactory, parentheses may be used to change the order. For example, if X is to be computed as $\frac{A + B}{C + D}$, the simple command "CØMPUTE X= A+ B/C + D" will not suffice. However, inclusion of the numerator and denominator in parentheses will cause addition to occur before division, resulting in correct computation. The proper command thus appears as "CØMPUTE X = (A+B)/(C + D)."

Parentheses may be used even when they are not required if they make the expression more easily understood.

The only limit on the CØMPUTE command's use is found in the fact that it always derives a single answer. To illustrate this limitation, assume that the following items are read in an input record: UNITS, representing the number of inventory units purchased; UNIT-CØST, representing the cost per unit; and DISCØUNT, representing the quantity discount rate applicable. With this information, it is possible to compute directly the net cost of the purchase by the command

CØMPUTE NET-CØST = (UNITS * UNIT-CØST) - (DISCØUNT * (UNITS * UNIT-CØST)).

In the process of arriving at NET-CØST, this computation also derives the total cost and amount of discount. However, these amounts are not available to the programmer, because the computer does not save them. Thus, if these amounts are desired, they must be computed separately. <u>It may be said that since the CØMPUTE command derives only one answer, a different instruction must be used for each answer desired.</u>

The following illustrations are designed to demonstrate some of the uses of the CØMPUTE command. Inasmuch as the computer is basically a calculating device, this command may be said to lie at the very heart of the instrument's utility.

<u>Illustration 1</u>: The following data elements are available in this payroll computation:

ST-HØURS, representing the number of straight-time hours worked
PM-HØURS, representing the number of premium hours worked
RATE, representing the pay rate for straight-time hours

<u>Problem:</u> Compute the amount of total pay (TØTAL-PAY) as the sum of straight-time pay and premium pay, where premium hours are paid for at 1.5 times the regular rate.

<u>Solution:</u> TØTAL-PAY may be calculated in a single step, as follows:

CØMPUTE TØTAL-PAY= (RATE * ST-HØURS)+(1.5 * RATE * PM-HØURS).

Parentheses are not required but are included for readability.

Illustration 2: The following data elements are available for computing the mean and standard deviation:

N, representing the number of items summed
SUMX, representing the sum of the X values
SUMXS, representing the sum of the X-square values

Problem: a) Compute the mean, as SUMX divided by N.

Solution: CØMPUTE MEAN = SUMX/N.

b) Compute the standard deviation as $\sqrt{\frac{SUMXS - \frac{SUMX^2}{N}}{N - 1}}$.

Solution: The standard deviation may be calculated in a single computation, as follows:

CØMPUTE STD = ((SUMXS - (SUMX ** 2/N))/(N - 1)) ** .5.

Illustration 3: The number of arrangements, or permutations, of a group of n different objects is n factorial, written as n!.

Problem: Determine how many different ways a group of 5 objects can be arranged.

Solution: CØMPUTE PERM = 5 * 4 * 3 * 2 * 1.

Illustration 4: Find the deviation of actual cost from standard cost, where ACT is the actual cost per unit, STD the standard cost per unit, and U the number of units.

Solution: CØMPUTE DEV = (ACT * U) - (STD * U).

Illustration 5: Problem: Increase the value of factor A by 1.

Solution: CØMPUTE A = A + 1.

QUESTIONS AND PROBLEMS

1. Why is the CØMPUTE command included in COBOL, when the other arithmetic instructions are available?

2. Can the product be stored in the memory location formerly occupied by the multiplier when the CØMPUTE command is used? Illustrate, multiplying A by 3.

3. Give a CØMPUTE command which will calculate A as B raised to the fifth power.

4. Give a CØMPUTE command which will calculate A as the square root of the sum of B and C.

5. In inventory control a formula for finding the optimum lot-size inventory orders is given as $\not{O}PT = \sqrt{\frac{2DC}{US}}$, where D represents the demand for the item for a given time, in units; C represents the cost of placing an order; U represents the item's per unit cost; and S represents the cost of carrying the item in inventory, expressed as a percentage of its cost per unit. Write a COBOL command which will compute the optimum lot size, ØPT.

6. The Ajax Company wishes to process its inventory purchase records on an electronic computer. Prepare a diagram of the necessary procedure. Input records, known as PURCHASE-RECØRD, exist in the PURCHASE-FILE, and contain the data shown in Table 3-5. (Test data are shown to the right of data names.)

Table 3-5

	Item Description	Data Name	Test Data
1.	Name of item purchased	DESC	AJAX STØCK
2.	Supplier code	VENDØR	4022
3.	Data received	DATE	082166
4.	a) Purchase order number	PCH-NØ	643382
	b) Invoice number	INVØICE	72884
5.	a) Inventory class no.	CLS	41
	b) Inventory group no.	GRØUP	211
	c) Inventory item no.	ITEM	4207
6.	Purpose of purchase	PURPØSE	01
7.	Number of units received	UNITS	00100
8.	a) Invoice cost	INV-CØST	0010000
	b) Freight charge	FREIGHT	000500
	c) Tax on purchase	TAX	00100

Notes:

1. Items 4a and 4b belong to the data group REFERENCE and supply reference data.

2. Items 5a, 5b, and 5c belong to the data group INV-NØ and comprise the inventory number.

3. Items 8a, 8b, and 8c belong to the data group PUR-CØST and comprise the delivered cost of the purchase. In each field, the decimal point is assumed to lie two places from the right.

Problem requirements:

a) Input data are to be read, and an output record (ØUT-RCD, in the ØUT-FILE) is to be prepared and written. The output record is to contain the data shown in Table 3-6.

Table 3-6

Item Description	Data Name
Name of item purchased	ITEM-DESC
Reference data (purchase order and invoice numbers)	ØUT-REF
Inventory number	INVEN-NUM
Number of units received	NØ-UNITS
Total cost	TØTAL-CØST
Cost per unit	UNIT-CØST
Sales price per unit	UNIT-SALES
Sales value of order	ØRDER-SALES

Most of the required output information may be moved intact from the input record. However, certain calculations must be made. These are as follows:

(1) Total cost is the sum of invoice cost, freight charge, and tax on purchase.

(2) Cost per unit is the total cost divided by the number of units received.

(3) Sales price per unit is taken to be 150 percent of unit cost.

(4) Sales value of the order is 150 percent of total cost.

b) In addition to preparing data for output, totals of the following amounts are to be calculated from all input records:

Invoice cost: Total to be known as TØT-INV.
Freight charge: Total to be known as TØT-FGT.
Tax on purchase: Total to be known as TØT-TAX.

c) Using the test data provided, give the computed values for TØTAL-CØST, UNIT-CØST, UNIT-SALES, and ØRDER-SALES.

7. Draw a flow chart to process the payroll data shown in Table 3-7, computing gross pay, social security taxes, and net pay. More than one input record is to be processed, and an output record is to be prepared for each.

Table 3-7

Item Description	Data Name	
	Input*	Output*
Employee name	NAME-IN	NAME-ØUT
Pay rate	PAY-RATE	
Hours worked	HØURS	
Gross pay		GRØSS-PAY
Social security tax		SS-TAX
Net pay		NET-PAY
File names	IN-FILE	ØUT-FILE
Record names	IN-RCD	ØUT-RCD

*The presence of a data name indicates that these data appear, or are to appear, in the indicated record. Employee name, for example, appears in both the input and the output record, while hours worked appear only in input and gross pay is shown only in output.

Notes:

1. Employee name is to be moved to the output record.

2. Gross pay is to be calculated by multiplying pay rate times hours worked.

3. Social security tax is 4 percent of gross pay.

4. Net pay is gross pay less social security tax.

8. Draw a flow chart to process the sales data shown in Table 3-8, eliminating excise taxes from the sales prices indicated therein. More than one input record is to be processed, and an output record is to be prepared for each.

Table 3-8

Item Description	Data Name	
	Input	Output
Name of inventory item	NAME-IN	NAME-ØUT
Sales price marked	SALES-PRICE	
New sales price		NEW-PRICE
Excise tax eliminated		TAX-ØFF
File names	IN-FILE	ØUT-FILE
Record names	GROSS-RCD	NET-RCD

Notes:

1. Inventory item name should be moved to the output record.

2. The excise tax included in the old price was 10 percent of sales price before tax.

3. As input records are processed, the following values are to be accumulated:

a) Old sales prices, including excise taxes, in a data element called T-SALES.

b) Excise taxes eliminated from sales prices, in a data element called T-TAX.

c) Sales prices, after elimination of excise tax, in a data element called NET.

9. Draw a flow chart to process the sales records in Table 3-9, calculating therefrom the sales commission owed. More than one input record is to be processed, and an output record is to be prepared for each.

Table 3-9

Item Description	Data Name	
	Input	Output
Salesman's number	S-NØ	MAN-NØ
Sales price, including excise tax	SALES-PRICE	
Sales price, excluding excise tax		NET-PRICE
Commission earned		CØMM
File names	SALES-FILE	CØM-FILE
Record names	SALES-RCD	CØM-RCD

Notes:

1. The salesman's number should be moved to the output record.

2. The sales price shown includes a 10 percent excise tax. Commissions of 15 percent are based on sales prices excluding excise tax.

3. NET-PRICE is SALES-PRICE less excise tax.

4. The amount of commission earned is to be accumulated from all output records, in a data element called TØT-CØM.

10. Draw a flow chart to process the notes receivable records shown in Table 3-10, calculating the approximate amount of accrued interest as of December 31. All notes are less than one year old.

Table 3-10

Item Description	Data Name	
	Input	Output
Note identification number	NØTE-ID	NØTE-REC-NØ
Month of creation, in numbers*	DATE	
Interest rate	RATE	
Face of note	AMØUNT	NØTE-AMØUNT
Amount of accrued interest		INTEREST
File names	NØTES	AC-INT
Record names	NØTE-RCD	INT-AMT

*For example, March would be represented as 03, June as 06, etc.

Notes:

1. The note's identification number and its face amount should be moved to the output record.

2. In computing interest, the month of the note's creation is excluded.

3. The life of the note for interest computation purposes may be obtained by subtracting the month of its creation from 12. Thus a note signed in March would be 9 (12 - 3) months old.

4. The total amount of interest accrued is to be accumulated in a data element called TØTAL-INTEREST.

11. Draw a flow chart for computing depreciation by the units-of-output method. More than one input record is to be processed, and an output record is to be prepared for each. (See Table 3-11.)

Table 3-11

Data Description	Data Name	
	Input	Output
Asset description	ASSET	DESC
Cost	CØST	
Estimated scrap value	SCRAP-VAL	
Depreciation taken previously	DEPREC-TAKEN	
Estimated units of output	EST-ØUTPUT	
Units produced this period	UNITS-PRØD	UNITS-MADE
Depreciation per unit		DEP-UNIT
Depreciation for this period		CUR-DEPREC
Accumulated depreciation, including this period		TØTAL-DEPREC
Undepreciated cost		CØST-BAL
File names	ØUTPUT-FILE	DEP-FILE
Record names	ØUTPUT-RCD	DEP-RCD

Notes:

1. Asset description and units produced are to be moved to the output record.

2. Depreciation per unit is computed by subtracting scrap value from cost and then dividing by estimated units of output.

3. Depreciation for this period is derived by multiplying the depreciation per unit by the number of units produced.

4. Accumulated depreciation through the current period is the sum of depreciation taken previously and depreciation for this period.

5. Undepreciated cost is the difference between cost and the total depreciation taken through the current period.

6. As asset records are processed, the amount of depreciation taken currently is to be accumulated in a data element called TØT-DEP.

12. Draw a flow chart for computing depreciation by the declining-balance method. More than one input record is to be processed, and an output record is to be prepared for each. (See Table 3-12.)

Table 3-12

Item Description	Data Name	
	Input	Output
Asset description	ASSET	ASSET-NAME
Use life	LIFE	USE-LIFE
Cost	CØST	CØST-ØUT
Scrap value	SCRAP	SCRAP-ØUT
Depreciation taken—total	ACCUM-DEPT	A-DEP-ØUT
Current depreciation		CUR-DEP
Book value	BØØK-VAL	NEW-BØØK-VALUE
File name	ASSET-FILE	DEPREC-FILE
Record name	ASSET-REC	DEPREC-REC

Notes:

1. The amount of depreciation to be taken is R * Carrying Value, where $R = 1 - \sqrt[n]{S \div C}$, where S is scrap value, C is original cost, and n is the number of years of useful life. The nth root of a value, X, may be expressed as $(X)^{1/n}$, or X raised to the 1/n power.

2. Book value is cost less depreciation taken. This is the same as carrying value.

3. The first four input fields are to be moved unchanged to the output record.

4. Depreciation taken in the input record is prior depreciation. To this should be added current depreciation in calculating the output amount.

5. NEW-BØØK-VALUE is to be calculated as cost less total depreciation taken.

13. Draw a flow chart for computing depreciation for 1967 by the sum-of-the-year's digits method. More than one input record is to be processed, and an output record is to be prepared for each. (See Table 3-13.)

Table 3-13

Item Description	Data Name	
	Input	Output
Asset description	ASSET	ASSET-NAME
Year of acquisition	YR-ACQ	
Estimated useful life	USE-LIFE	
Cost	CØST	CØST-ØUT
Scrap value	SCRAP	
Depreciation taken to date	ACCUM-DEP	NEW-ACCUM-DEP
Current depreciation		CUR-DEP
Asset book value		BØØK-VAL
File name	ASSET-FILE	DEPREC-FILE
Record name	ASSET-REC	DEPREC-REC

Notes:

1. Asset description and cost are to be moved to the output record.

2. The denominator of the year fraction in a sum-of-the-year's-digits computation may be calculated as $\frac{n(n+1)}{2}$, where n is the useful life of the asset. This should be calculated in a separate computation and the amount called DENØM.

3. No depreciation is taken on an asset in the year of acquisition. Therefore the years expired since an asset was acquired are the difference between its year of acquisition and the current year. For example, 6 years (1967 - 1961) have elapsed since an asset was acquired in 1961. The numerator of the year fraction can then be found by subtracting this from (asset life + 1).

4. Current depreciation is to be calculated as the year fraction times (cost less scrap value).

5. New accumulated depreciation is to be the amount of accumulated depreciation read in, plus depreciation for the current period.

6. Asset book value is cost less new accumulated depreciation.

14. Draw a flow chart for calculating unit costs. More than one input record is to be processed, and an output record is to be prepared for each. (See Table 3-14.)

Table 3-14

Item Description	Data Name	
	Input	Output
Time period	TIME	PERIØD
Fixed costs for period	FIXED-CØSTS	
Number of units manufactured	NØ-UNITS	
Variable cost per unit	VAR-CØST	UNIT-VAR-CØST
Fixed cost per unit		UNIT-FIXED-CØST
Total cost per unit		UNIT-TØTAL-CØST
File name	CØST-FILE	ØUT-FILE
Record name	CØST-REC	ØUT-REC

Notes:

1. Time period and variable cost per unit are to be moved to the output record.

2. The firm gathers its fixed manufacturing costs in a single amount but apportions its variable costs to production during each production period.

3. Fixed costs per unit are to be calculated and then added to variable unit costs to arrive at total unit costs.

15. Draw a flow chart for adjusting account balances by relative index numbers. More than one input record is to be processed, and an output record is to be prepared for each. (See Table 3-15.)

Table 3-15

Item Description	Data Name	
	Input	Output
Account name	ACCØUNT	ACCT
Amount	AMØUNT	ØRIG-AMT
Index number of originating period	INDEX	
Amount, adjusted by index nos.		ADJ-AMT
File names	RAW-DATA	ADJ-DATA
Record names	ACT-BAL	ADJ-BAL

Notes:

1. The first input record does not contain data on a real account. In the space INDEX, this record contains the index number for the current year. This record should be read and the index number moved out of the input area to an area called CUR-INDEX.

2. Original amounts are to be adjusted to current index equivalents by multiplying them by a fraction, the numerator of which is the index of the current year, the denominator being the index of the originating period.

3. Accumulate the following for all accounts:

   TØT-CØST, the total of all original amounts
   TØT-ADJ, the total of all original adjustments
   TØT-NEW, the total of all adjusted account balances

16. Given the coordinates of 2 points on a straight line, X1 and Y1, X2 and Y2, the slope of the line, S, may be found as follows:

$$S = \frac{Y2 - Y1}{X2 - X1}$$

Draw a flow chart for computing the slope, given a single input record INPUT-REC, in input file INPUT-FILE, containing data elements X1, X2, Y1, Y2. Display the answer, S.

17. Draw a flow chart for computing budget allowances and variances under the conditions shown in Table 3-16. More than one input record is to be processed, and an output record is to be prepared for each.

Table 3-16

Item Description	Data Name	
	Input	Output
Account title	ACCØUNT	ACCT
Fixed budget allowance	BASE	
Incremental percentage	PCT	
Amount of actual expense	ACT-EXP	
Amount of budget allowance		ALLØW
Variance		VAR
File names	EXP-FILE	VAR-FILE
Record names	AMT-RCD	VAR-RCD

Notes:

1. The first input record will not contain data on an expense item but will contain the amount of sales in the BASE field. This should be moved to a data area named SALES.

2. For all data records:

   a) The account title is to be moved to the output record.

   b) The budgetary allowance for each expense is expressed in two amounts: a fixed amount, called BASE, and an incremental amount to be calculated as a fraction of sales. This is to be computed for each expense by multiplying PCT by SALES. The base and increment together comprise the amount of the budget allowance.

   c) The variance is the difference between the budget allowance and the amount of actual expense.

   d) As records are processed, the following data should be accumulated:

      Amount of actual expense, in TØT-ACT
      Amount of budget allowance, in TØT-BUD
      Amount of variance, in TØT-VAR

18. Draw a flow chart for analyzing cost variances. More than one input record is to be processed, and an output record is to be prepared for each. (See Table 3-17.)

Table 3-17

Item Description	Data Name	
	Input	Output
Job Number	JØB-NØ	JØB-NUM
Standard labor pay rate/hour	S-RATE	
Standard labor hours/unit produced	S-HRS	
Standard labor cost/unit produced	S-CØST	S-UNIT-CØST
Actual labor rate/hour	A-RATE	
Number of units produced	UNITS	P-UNITS
Hours worked	HØURS	
Actual unit cost		A-UNIT-CØST
Actual job cost		ACT-CØST
Labor rate variance		RATE-VAR
Labor efficiency variance		EFF-VAR
Standard cost		STD-CØST
File names	CØST-FILE	VAR-FILE
Record names	CØST-RCD	VAR-RCD

Notes:

1. Job number, standard labor cost per unit, and number of units produced should be moved to the output record.
2. Actual unit cost may be calculated by dividing the number of units produced into the product of the actual labor rate times the hours worked.
3. Actual job cost may be calculated as the actual labor rate per hour times the hours worked.
4. The labor rate variance for the job may be calculated by multiplying the difference between actual and standard rates by the hours worked.
5. The total efficiency variance may be found by determining the difference between hours worked and the number of hours which should have been required and then multiplying this by the standard labor rate per hour.
6. The following variance data are to be accumulated for all records processed:

    Amount of rate variances, in TØT-RATE
    Amount of efficiency variances, in TØT-EFF
    Amount of total variance, in TØT-VAR

CHAPTER 4

COBOL CONTROL LOGIC

All computer activities discussed thus far have concerned data manipulation—reading, moving, writing, or calculating. This chapter introduces certain computer control operations—steps which make the electronic computer a "thinking machine" and which permit it to perform quite impressive feats of logic.

SIMPLE CONTROL COMMANDS

Several control commands are quite simple. One is known as an unconditional branch and governs the flow of program logic. Another causes the computer to print a message and to pause pending operator action. Others are concerned with activities required at the termination of a program.

Unconditional Transfer

A COBOL program is ordinarily executed in the same order used in reading English—from left to right, top to bottom. By the same token, flow diagrams are generally meant to be read from top to bottom. However, it is frequently necessary to interrupt this reading sequence; as, for example, when a record has been processed and the program is to return and process another. This sequence interruption is effected by a command called an unconditional transfer.

In COBOL the unconditional transfer is written as "GØ TØ procedure-name," where "procedure-name" is a subdivision of the program. In diagramming, the command is represented by an arrow running from one point in the program to another command not next in sequence. Thus, it might appear as follows:

A

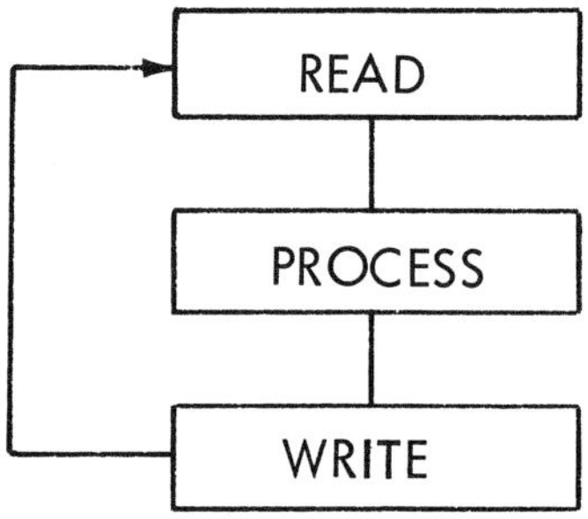

The arrow (A) leading from the end of the program to the beginning symbolizes the presence of the unconditional transfer. It may be seen that this command has been used in almost all the programs illustrated thus far, although it was not specifically mentioned.

Terminal Commands

Certain actions must be taken near the end of a program. These may be referred to as terminal commands.

The CLØSE Command. First may be mentioned the CLØSE command, used to close all files prior to termination of a program. Its function is to write end labels on magnetic tapes, to rewind tapes, and the like. The instruction is very similar to the ØPEN command, except that the type of file (input or output) is not mentioned.

To illustrate the CLØSE instruction, assume that a certain program has used three files; FILE-A and FILE-B for data input and FILE-C for output. The proper CLØSE instruction in this instance would be "CLØSE FILE-A, FILE-B, FILE-C."

The files may be listed in any order; and as pointed out above, their status as input or output files is not mentioned. Once closed, a file will no longer accept a READ or WRITE command unless it is reopened by repeating the ØPEN instruction.

The STØP RUN Command. Every program must eventually reach the point where there is nothing more to be done. This point is known as a logical terminal. A program may have more than one way of ending, meaning that it has more than one logical terminal.

The last statement at the end of a logical path is of the form "STØP RUN" and serves as the logical terminal. When this statement is reached and executed, the computer is released from this particular program. Thus, care must be taken to be sure that the instruction is not encountered prematurely. It is equally important to see that each program path leads to a STØP RUN command, because failure of the program to do so will cause a serious logical error. One of the major values derived from diagramming a program is realized by tracing logic paths to see that every one has a logical conclusion and that this conclusion is represented by STØP RUN.

Making the Computer Pause. It is sometimes desirable to cause the computer to stop temporarily as it executes a program. A pause of this nature may be useful when errors are encountered, such as improper input data or the computation of a logically impossible amount. The program may also be stopped during testing so that test data results may be verified.

No matter what the reason for causing the pause, it is executed by a command very similar to the STØP RUN. This command is of the nature "STØP literal," where the literal may be any numeric or nonnumeric literal desired. Quite frequently, some message will be included here which indicates the reason for the stop.

Execution of this command causes the computer to cease operations. The program can be restarted by the operator by pressing the START button on the computer console. When this is done, the program continues, executing the next instruction. Thus, this STØP command and the STØP RUN differ greatly, in that the former permits the program to be restarted, while the latter does not.

The instruction "STØP literal" is similar to the DISPLAY command discussed previously, in that the designated literal will be displayed on the computer's low-volume output device. However, the DISPLAY statement permits the writing of either literals or the contents of data names, while this version of the STØP instruction is restricted to the writing of literals. Furthermore, execution of the DISPLAY command does not interrupt the computer's running. Each command therefore has its unique place in the COBOL instruction set.

CONDITIONAL STATEMENTS

All computer programs discussed thus far have been relatively simple, because all commands lay along a single logical path. In a typical real-world situation, however, a number of alternatives exist and must be allowed for. The computer's usefulness would be seriously limited if it were not able to allow for alternative courses of action.

Electronic computers do have the ability to test data and select one course of action from numerous alternatives, through the use of conditional statements. These commands do not process data; instead, they evaluate data in one of several possible ways and then send the program along one of two paths according to the results of the test.

All major COBOL conditional statements are binary in nature; that is, they allow testing with two possible results. If the data inspected meet the stipulated criteria, the program proceeds along the TRUE path set up by the conditional statement; if not, it proceeds along the FALSE path. Thus the data must satisfy the test in all its particulars, or results are considered false. While this may appear at first glance to restrict the computer's decision making rather severely, in fact many tests may be combined to approximate a quite sophisticated set of logical choices.

Conditional commands are quite simple in nature and may therefore be introduced quite easily. To use them effectively is another matter, however. Data-processing situations are generally quite complex and are often typified by a maze of alternatives. The usefulness of the computer as a data processor depends on its ability to recognize these alternatives and act properly; this, of course, depends in turn on the design ability of the programmer. Conditional statements are the very heart of computer control. Successful computer utilization demands that the programmer use them with discretion and imagination.

Because of the nature of the problem inherent in conditionals—their ease of understanding and difficulty of utilization—the major part of this chapter is devoted to examples of their use. These are drawn from various areas of possible computer application. While by no means exhaustive, the examples contain special applications of the conditional. They should be studied carefully before attempting this chapter's problems.

SPECIALIZED CONDITIONALS

Several kinds of conditionals are present in COBOL. Two of these have very special uses and will be introduced first. The others are used in the general logic of the program.

The AT END Conditional

It is often desirable to execute some special routine when all input records have been read and processed. For example, control totals are frequently accumulated from data read in or calculated; and after all records are processed, these totals are used to ascertain that all records were transmitted. Files must also be closed. Such operations are known as terminal routines.

To use these requires that the program follow one path while input records are still available, but transfer to another path when no more records may be read. The READ command causes this conditional transfer.

The complete READ command is as follows: "READ file-name AT END any imperative command...." If a record is available for reading when the READ command is executed, the AT END conditional is ignored, including the imperative commands which make up a part of the conditional. However, if a record is not available, the AT END path is followed. Thus the AT END clause is a type of conditional. If further reading is possible, the FALSE branch is followed; when reading is complete, the computer branches to the TRUE path.

The use of this conditional may be seen in the following situation: Assume that a number of records (called SALES-RCD) in the SALES-FILE are to be processed and that each record contains the following data:

Description	COBOL Name
Account number	AC-NØ
Number of units sold	UNITS
Unit sales price	PRICE

Output records, called SALES-LIST, are to be prepared in a file named ØUT-FILE. One output record, showing the account number (ACCT) and the sales amount (AMØUNT), is to be prepared for each input record. In addition, the sum of all sales (TØT-SALES) is to be accumulated, and a record count (REC-CNT) is to be made. Each of these is to be displayed after all input records are processed.

A flow chart symbolizing the program appears in Figure 4-1. As long as input records are available, data are prepared for the output record, and the sum of all sales is accumulated. Control is then transferred to the READ command, and the process is repeated.

However, when an input record is not available for reading, the program no longer proceeds along the main processing path. Instead, it is transferred by the AT END conditional to the logical branch calling for display of total sales and the record count, files are closed, and the program is terminated.

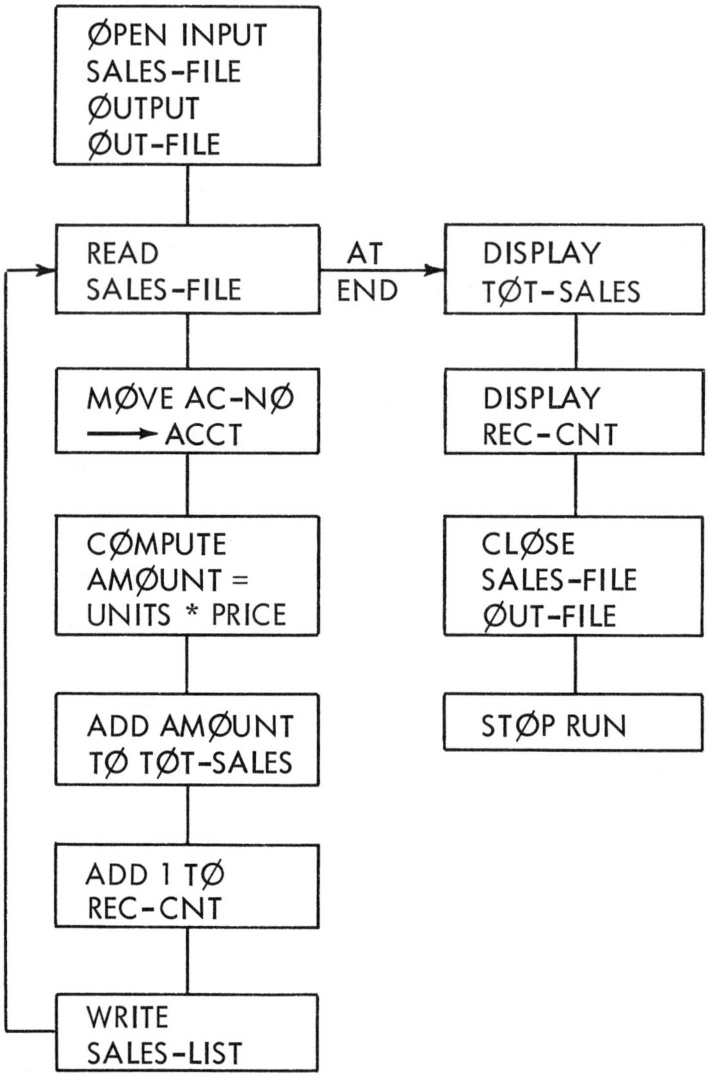

FIG. 4-1 The AT END Conditional Illustrated

Any amount of data processing may be effected in the AT END branch. In fact, some problems may require the major computations to be made only after all data are read. For example, assume that an unknown number of records in the IN-FILE contain a field called AMØUNT. It is desired to compute and display the mean of this value. (Note that an output file is not required in this problem.)

It is obviously impossible to find the mean of the values until they have been summed. Furthermore, the number of values is unknown until the last amount is read. Therefore, the flow chart for solution of the problem appears as shown in Figure 4-2.

After initializing, which consists of opening files, a loop is entered wherein records are read, quantities accumulated in an area called SUMX, and a record count (N) is maintained. When no more input records are available, control is transferred through the AT END conditional to that part of the program which computes the mean, displays it, and terminates the program. This sort of routine is frequently encountered in computer utilization.

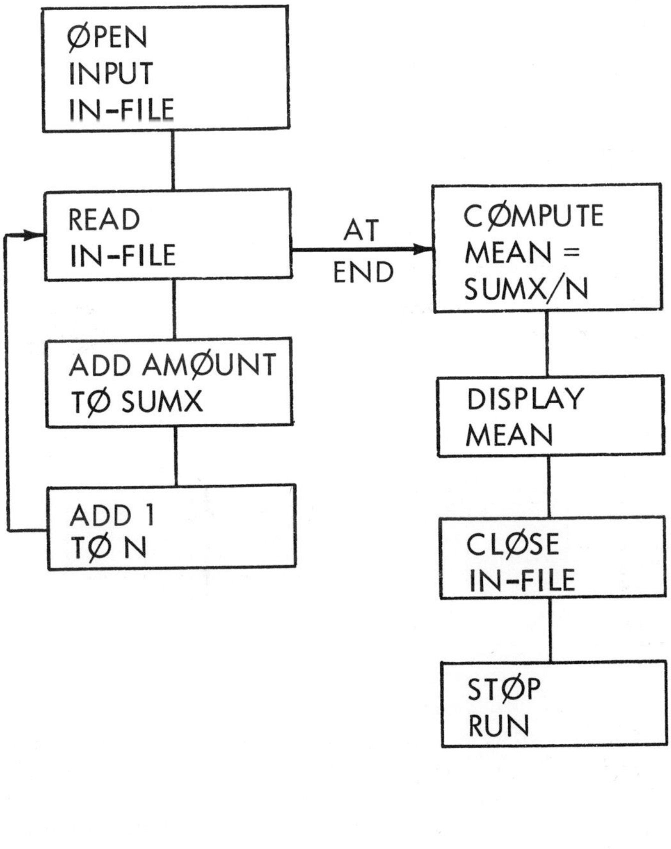

FIG. 4-2

The SIZE ERRØR Conditional

The computer has the use of only that segment of its memory which has been defined by COBOL, and the fields are only as large as required by the same definition. It is therefore possible that the result of an arithmetic computation might be larger than the field size allowed for its storage.

To illustrate this situation, assume that a data field, called A, is of size XXXVXX, where X denotes a numeric position and V the assumed decimal point. It now contains the value 875V00. The command "ADD 200 TØ A" is given. Execution of this causes the computer to attempt development of the sum 1075V00, but this is impossible, because the field size only permits three digits to the left of the decimal point. Therefore the sum overflows the solution field, and an improper answer (075V00) occurs.

This very serious programming error may be averted by use of the SIZE ERRØR conditional. This conditional may be used with any arithmetic command. In contrast with the AT END conditional, it is not required but may be used or not, at the programmer's option. Thus, if there is any chance that an overflow might occur upon execution of an arithmetic statement, the SIZE ERRØR option should be used. If overflow is impossible, the conditional may be omitted.

Writing the SIZE ERRØR Conditional. This option, if used, is written as part of its associated arithmetic command. The TRUE branch, followed if an overflow occurs, contains first any desired imperative command and then whatever instructions are appropriate. For example, if A and B are to be summed, and an error message is to be printed in the event of an overflow, the commands would appear as "ADD A TØ B ØN SIZE ERRØR STØP 'SUM OF A AND B CAUSED ØVERFLØW'." This group of commands would be diagrammed as follows:

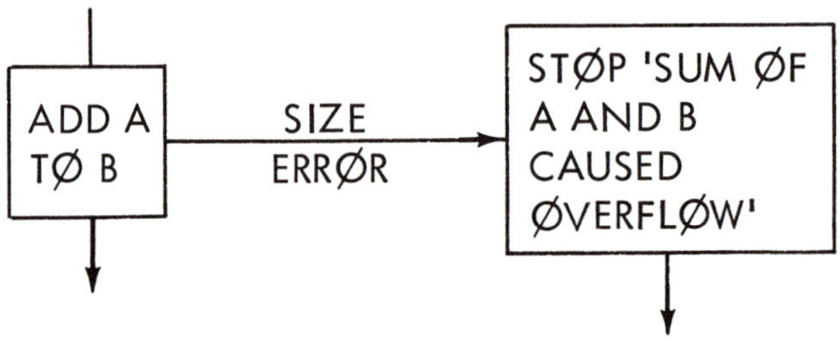

Execution of SIZE ERRØR. So long as an overflow does not occur, the program is executed as reported when describing arithmetic statements. Should overflow occur, however, several significant processing changes take place. First, the contents of the result field are left as they were before execution of this arithmetic step was attempted. Second, progress of the program is diverted from its regular channel into the SIZE ERRØR branch. In this branch the programmer may specify any appropriate corrective steps.

Example of SIZE ERRØR. In illustrating the AT END conditional, a situation was cited wherein sales amounts were calculated by multiplying sales price by the number of units sold. To illustrate the use of the SIZE ERRØR option, assume that data field UNITS is of size XXX and that data field PRICE is of size XVXX. Assume further that data field AMØUNT in the output record is of size XXXVXX and that sales are of such a nature that none are ever made for more than $999.

A flow chart depicting the use of the SIZE ERRØR option under these circumstances is illustrated in Figure 4-3. Should the quantity calculated

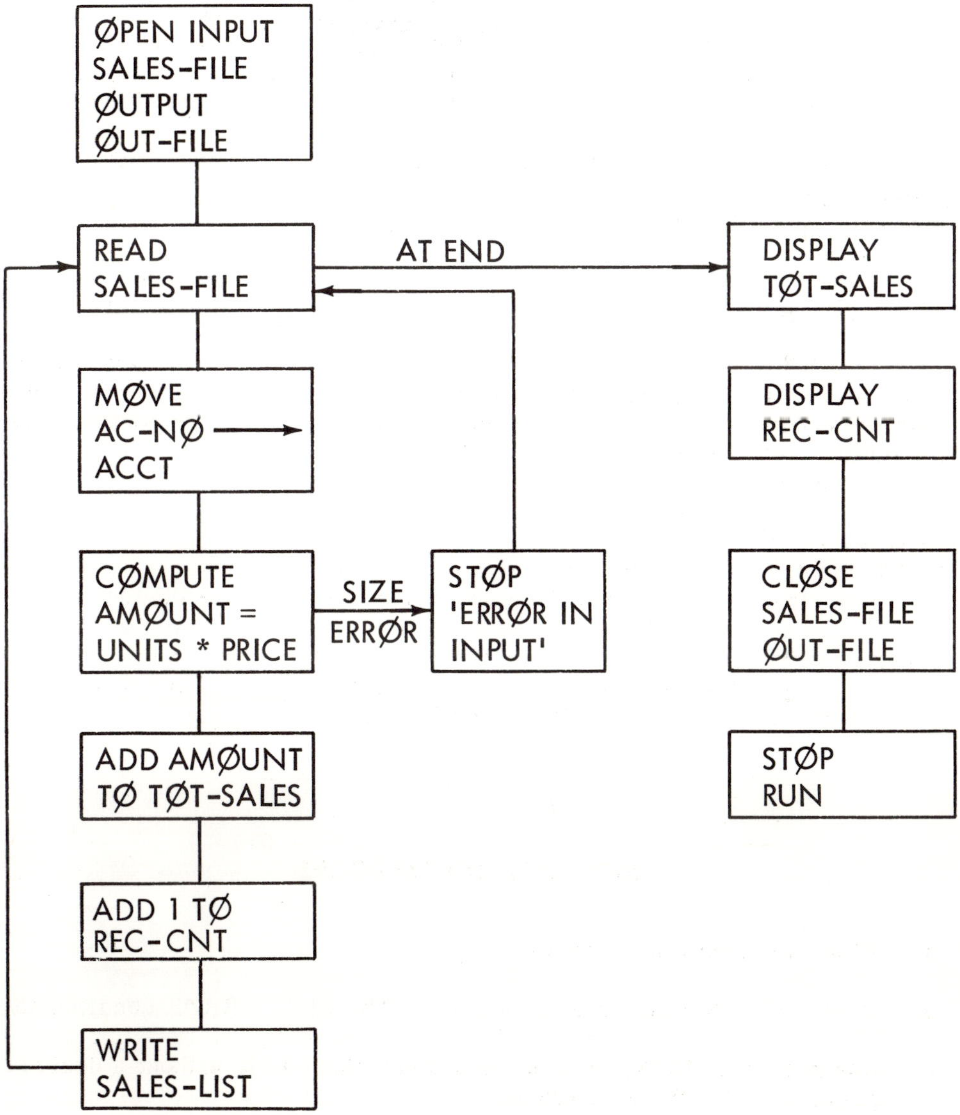

FIG. 4-3. The SIZE ERRØR Conditional Illustrated

as AMØUNT attempt to overflow the memory location, the location's contents will remain undisturbed, and the program will branch, causing the computer to print the designated error message and pause for operator intervention.

To illustrate the effects obtained by using or omitting the SIZE ERRØR option, assume that REC-CNT is 112, AMØUNT is 104V66, and TØT-SALES 14022V20 when record number 113 is read, reporting sales of 900 units at 8V00 per unit. AMØUNT will be computed as 7200V00 and will obviously overflow the field.

If the SIZE ERRØR option has been specified, the attempted overflow will be detected and prevented. AMØUNT will remain with its contents of 104V66, the error message will be printed, and operations will cease. On the other hand, if SIZE ERRØR has not been specified, the overflow will cause AMØUNT to assume a value of 200V00—the most significant digit being lost in the overflow. This will be added to TØT-SALES, causing a wrong total of 14222V20, and the record count will be increased to 113. Operations will continue, and nothing will show that a very serious error has been committed.

When programs permit the reintroduction of data, care must be taken to see that cumulative fields are not improperly affected. In the illustration above, for example, suppose that the command "ADD 1 TØ REC-CNT" appeared before AMØUNT was computed. This would mean that if AMØUNT caused an overflow, the record would be rejected for data computation purposes but would be included in the record count. The control total would thus be invalidated.

Summary

Note that neither conditional introduced thus far executes a data-processing command. They neither read, move, write, nor perform arithmetic. Their function is simply to provide the beginning of an alternative path in the program. What is done on this path depends entirely on the imperative commands which follow the branch.

QUESTIONS AND EXERCISES

1. What is a conditional expression?

2. Is the AT END conditional optional? The SIZE ERRØR conditional?

3. Assume that SUMX, defined as a four-place field without a decimal point, contains the value 7845.

   a) What will be printed as a result of executing the following program segment?

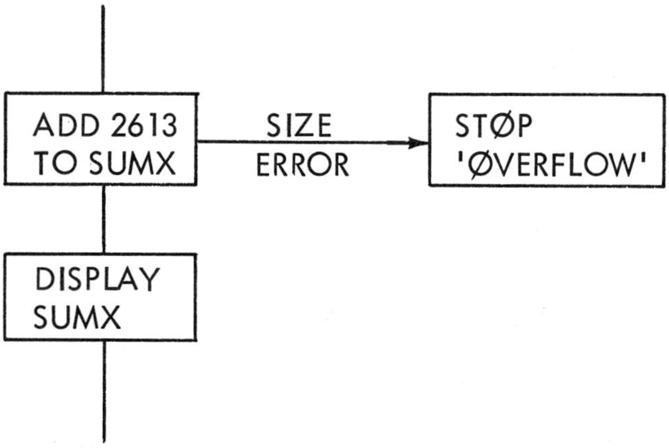

b) What value will be stored at SUMX?

c) What would be printed, and what value would be stored at SUMX, if the SIZE ERRØR option had not been exercised?

4. Draw a flow chart for the processing of data shown in Table 4-1. Sales records are to be read through the input file, and the output record described below is to be prepared and written for each. The program is to process more than one record. Input and output files and their contents are given in Table 4-1.

Table 4-1

Item Description	COBOL Name
Input file	SALES-FILE
Input record	SALES-REC
Contents of input record:	
Item number	ITEM-NØ
Item name	ITEM-NAME
Sales price per unit	UNIT-PRICE
Number of units sold	NØ-UNITS
Output file	EXT-FILE
Output record	EXT-RCD
Contents of output record:	
Item name	I-NAME
Sales amount	S-AMT
Sales tax	TAX
Total amount	TØTAL

In the output record, S-AMT is to be calculated by multiplying UNIT-PRICE and NØ-UNITS. TAX is to be computed as 3 percent of S-AMT. TØTAL is the sum of S-AMT and TAX. ITEM-NAME is to be moved to the output record as I-NAME.

A record count called RCD-CNT is to be kept as an independent data element. Also, sales amounts, sales tax, and total amount are to be accumulated from all records as the independent data elements TØT-SALES, TØT-TAX, and TØT-AMT, respectively.

When the last input record has been processed, the record count and the three control totals are to be displayed. Files are then to be closed, and processing is to be terminated.

Computation of S-AMT and TAX may cause an overflow. If either overflows, a suitable error message is to be printed, and processing is to pause and then return to read another record. Care must be taken to see that no cumulative total has been updated in such a way as to be in error if an overflow condition develops.

5. The equation of a straight line providing the best fit for a set of data may be found by solving the following simultaneous equations:

$$\text{I.} \quad \Sigma Y = Na + b\Sigma X$$
$$\text{II.} \quad \Sigma XY = a\,\Sigma X + B\,\Sigma X^2$$

Solution is effected by first multiplying the first equation by a fraction, the numerator of which is ΣX (coefficient of a in the second equation), and the denominator of which is N (coefficient of a in the first equation); second, subtracting the second equation from the first to eliminate a; third, solving the remaining equation for b; and fourth, solving for a in either of the original equations by substitution of the actual b value.

Instructions: A group of input records of unknown number is available, each containing a value of X (called X) and a value of Y (called Y). The record is named IN-RCD and is in the IN-FILE.

a) Prepare a program for reading these records and accumulating all required data. These data include:

Data Description	Data Name
Sum of Y values	SUMY
Number of records	N
Sum of X values	SUMX
Sum of product of X and Y	SUMXY
Sum of X's squared	SUM-X-SQ

b) After all records have been read, the straight line is to be fitted, as described above. If possible, prepare the program for this solution; if you cannot, simply indicate where computation is to take place. Display your computed values of a and b. Note: You may ignore problems of overflow in your program.

GENERAL CONDITIONAL STATEMENTS

The conditionals desribed above are linked to another command and are therefore rather restricted in application. The COBOL instructional set includes a conditional statement, however, which may be used at almost any time and brings much discretionary ability to the language.

The IF Statement

This conditional command is known as the IF statement. It exists as a conditional sentence, where the term IF is followed by the condition set forth. If the condition is met, the program follows one branch of instructions. If conditions are not met, a different program branch is followed. The former is called the TRUE branch; the latter is the FALSE branch.

As an illustration of the IF statement and an introduction to its use, suppose that an amount QUANT has been accumulated and is to be tested to determine its size. If QUANT is greater than 1,000, the program is to proceed to a computation called BIGGER; if not, it is to proceed to a computation called SMALLER. This would be diagrammed as shown in Figure 4-4. It is assumed that BIGGER and SMALLER are parts of a rational program; inasmuch as they are not pertinent to the IF statement proper, they are only alluded to in the diagram.

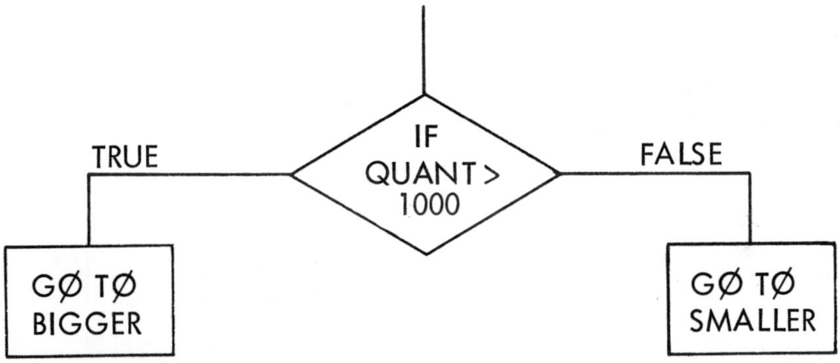

FIG. 4-4

The IF statement is ordinarily symbolized in flow-charting by the diamond, as in Figure 4-4. The condition is set out as shown. Then, provision must be made for the program if the statement is true, and if it is false. Obviously, both conditions must be possible, or the statement would be unnecessary.

As may be seen, a single conditional statement provides for only two possibilities: true and false. These statements may be combined to permit any number of possible choices, however. This may be seen if the previous example is expanded. Suppose that QUANT is to be evaluated in the following manner:

If less than 100, go to VERY-SMALL.

If 100 or more, but less than 500, go to SMALL.

If 500 or more, but less than 1,000, go to MEDIUM.

If 1,000 or more, but less than 1,500, go to LARGE.

If 1,500 or more, go to VERY-LARGE.

This is represented by the diagram in Figure 4-5.

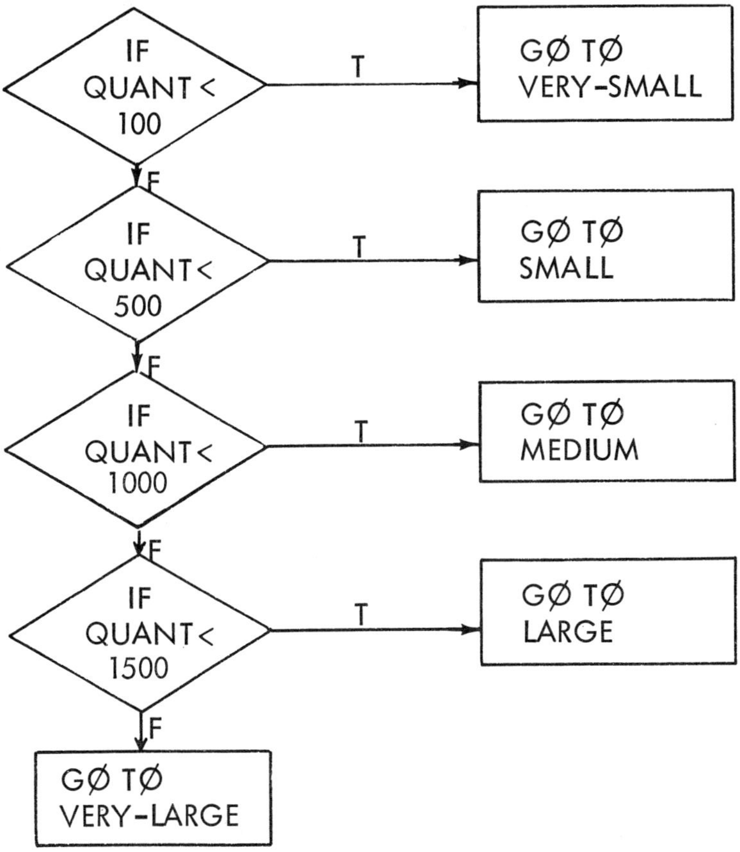

FIG. 4-5

It may be seen that five conditions are tested in four conditional statements. In each instance except the last, a false response is tested further while a true response is transferred, until the size is found by a process of elimination. Thus may a binary conditional be transformed into a conditional with many possible responses.

Kinds of Conditional Tests

The IF statement can make various kinds of tests. It can test the relative magnitude of two values, as seen in the examples above; it can test data fields to see whether they are alphabetic or numeric; or it can test the status of certain computer devices called sense switches. The most significant kinds of tests are introduced below.

The Relation Test. This test may be used to determine the relative size of two items, which may be numeric literals, data names, or formulas. In the examples above, the contents of a data name were tested against a literal or a series of literals. In a similar fashion, the contents of one data name may be tested against the contents of another, arithmetic expressions may be tested against other arithmetic expressions, or any combination of these may be used.

Three relations may be tested. These are:

> GREATER THAN (symbolized in flow charts as >), wherein the IF conditional is true if the first value is algebraically larger than the second;
>
> EQUAL (symbolized in flow charts as =), wherein the IF conditional is true if the first and second values are algebraically equal; and
>
> LESS THAN (symbolized in flow charts as <), wherein the IF conditional is true if the first value is algebraically smaller than the second.
>
> The opposite of each of these may be obtained by using NOT. Thus:
>
> NOT GREATER is the opposite of GREATER.
>
> NOT EQUAL is the opposite of EQUAL, and
>
> NOT LESS is the opposite of LESS.

Relational Illustrations

Several illustrations of the IF conditional command are presented below, making use of relational conditionals. The first three commands are simple and are included to provide a clearer understanding of the instruction's nature. Other more sophisticated commands are also presented with a view toward illustrating the kinds of things one may do with relationals. Of course, the examples are only suggestive of the very great power of this command.

Simple Illustrations. For the following simple illustrations, assume that the data names below contain the values shown:

Data Name	Value
A	10
B	2
C	-25
D	7
E	-5

1. Comparison of two data names: If A is less than C, calculate TØT as 2C + D. If not, calculate TØT as 2E. This would be diagrammed as shown in Figure 4-6. Of course, A in the test data shown is not algebraically less than C, so the condition is false. The program would then proceed to compute TØT to be -10.

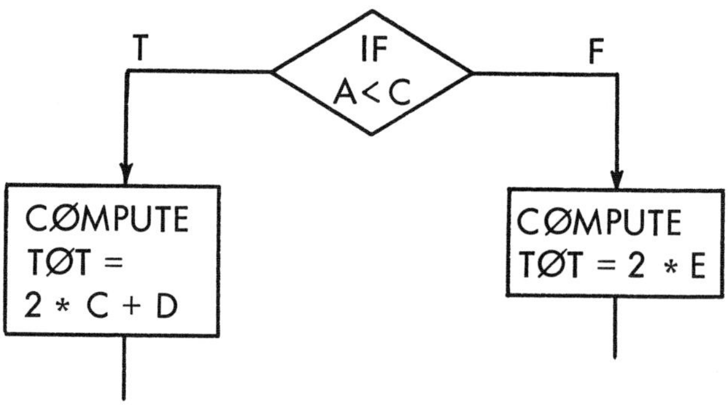

FIG. 4-6

2. Comparison of two formulas: If (2E + C) is equal to (D + B), compute TØT as 4AB; if not, compute TØT as E - 7. This would be diagrammed as shown in Figure 4-7.

$$2E + C = -35$$
$$D + B = 9$$

Therefore the condition is false, and TØT will be calculated as E - 7.

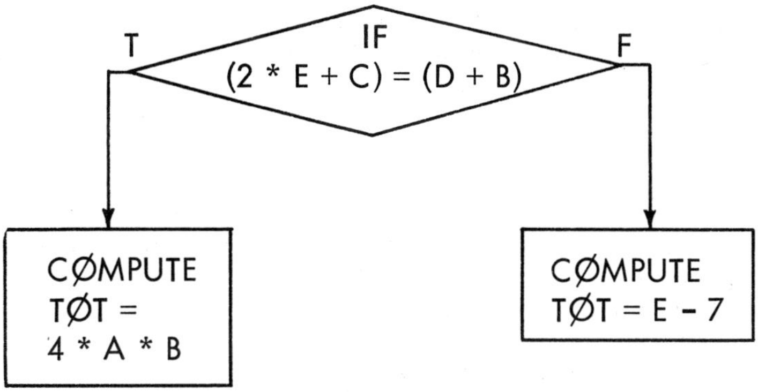

FIG. 4-7

3. More than one comparison: If A is greater than B but less than 2D, go to PATH-A; if not, go to PATH-B. This involves two relational tests and may be diagrammed as shown in Figure 4-8.

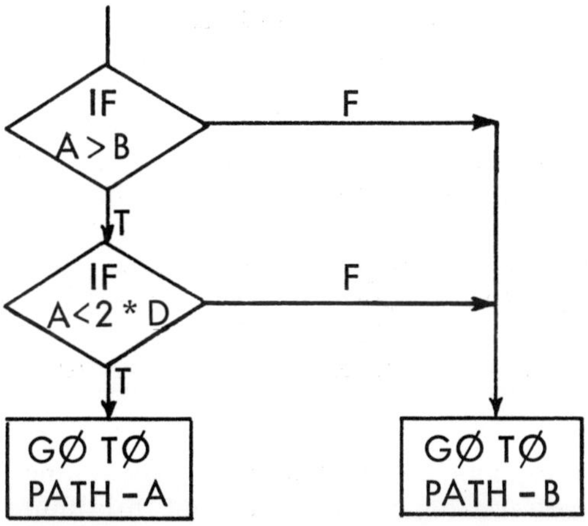

FIG. 4-8

This illustration shows again that by using more than one test, several conditions may be explored. The entire statement may be considered true only if both conditions are met. It will be seen later that connectives may be used to link conditionals, making it possible to write more than one conditional in a single expression.

Illustrations of More Sophisticated Use. The brief illustrations above set out the basic nature of the IF statement and its use with relational conditionals. In the illustrations to follow, some slightly more complex situations are explored, and the versatility of the IF statement and relational conditional is suggested.

1. Use in checking a counter: Conditionals are often used to count the number of times a program repeats itself, perhaps modifying the program at certain points. For example, assume that a problem requires reading records from the X-FILE, each of which contains an amount called AMT. These values are to be summed in groups of 25 and each sum (TØT) is to be printed. The total of the last group (which might not contain 25 records) is also to be printed, together with a count of the number of records in the group.

This problem requires that a count (CNT) of incoming records be kept and checked to see if the twenty-fifth record has been read. If so, the cumulative total is to be written, the field is to be reset to zero, and reading is to be continued. If not, the amount is to be accumulated, and reading is to continue. This problem could be diagrammed as shown in Figure 4-9.

The field called CNT is used to keep track of the number of iterations performed, by adding 1 to the field with each iteration and checking to see when CNT = 25. When CNT = 25, the total is printed out, and data fields used for accumulating TØT as well as for counting are reset to zero. On other iterations the fields are not reset.

Care must be taken in organizing problems of this sort. It is quite easy to miscount records, or to fail to include one in the sum, if iterative accumulation and test steps are improperly located.

2. Testing a "reminder." A program may require that the computer be able to recognize one of several possible states existing with regard to a certain item. In this, a numeric code is often used to designate the state and is tested by the conditional to control computer operation.

For example, assume that a firm processing inventories electronically stores on-hand balances and minimum reorder points. When the balance falls below the reorder point, an order is to be placed; however, only one order should be outstanding at a time, and so the program should not continue to report an item as requiring ordering if an order has been placed. Thus the computer must be able to recognize whether or not the need for ordering has been previously reported and, if so, not report it again. This can be done by using a "reminder."

Assume that input is handled through the INV-FILE, with each inventory item occupying a record called the INV-RCD. This contains ITEM, the inventory number; BAL, the on-hand balance; RØP, the reorder point; and ØRDER, indicating whether an order is outstanding. This will contain a 1 if order is outstanding or a 0 if not.

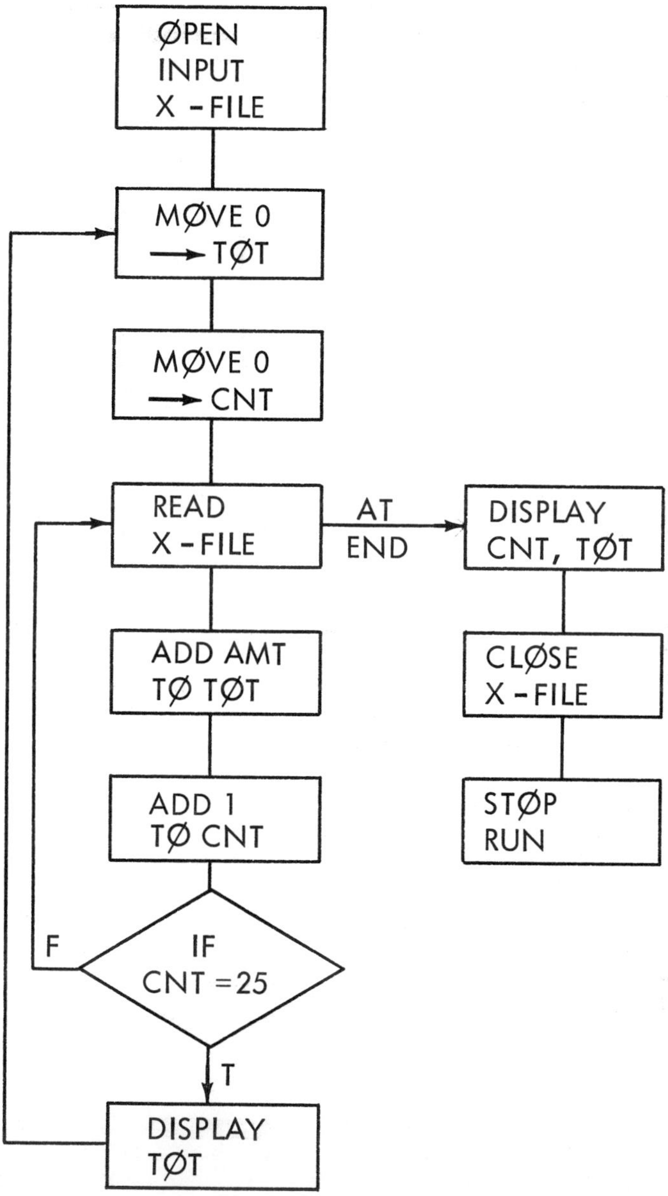

ØPEN
INPUT
X -FILE
MØVE 0
→ TØT
MØVE 0
→ CNT
READ
X-FILE
AT
END
DISPLAY
CNT, TØT
ADD AMT
TØ TØT
CLØSE
X-FILE
ADD 1
TØ CNT
STØP
RUN
F
IF
CNT =25
T
DISPLAY
TØT

FIG. 4-9

Output, through the ØRDER-FILE, ØRDER-RCD, is to contain the inventory number (NUM).

A flow chart for processing these records might appear as shown in Figure 4-10.

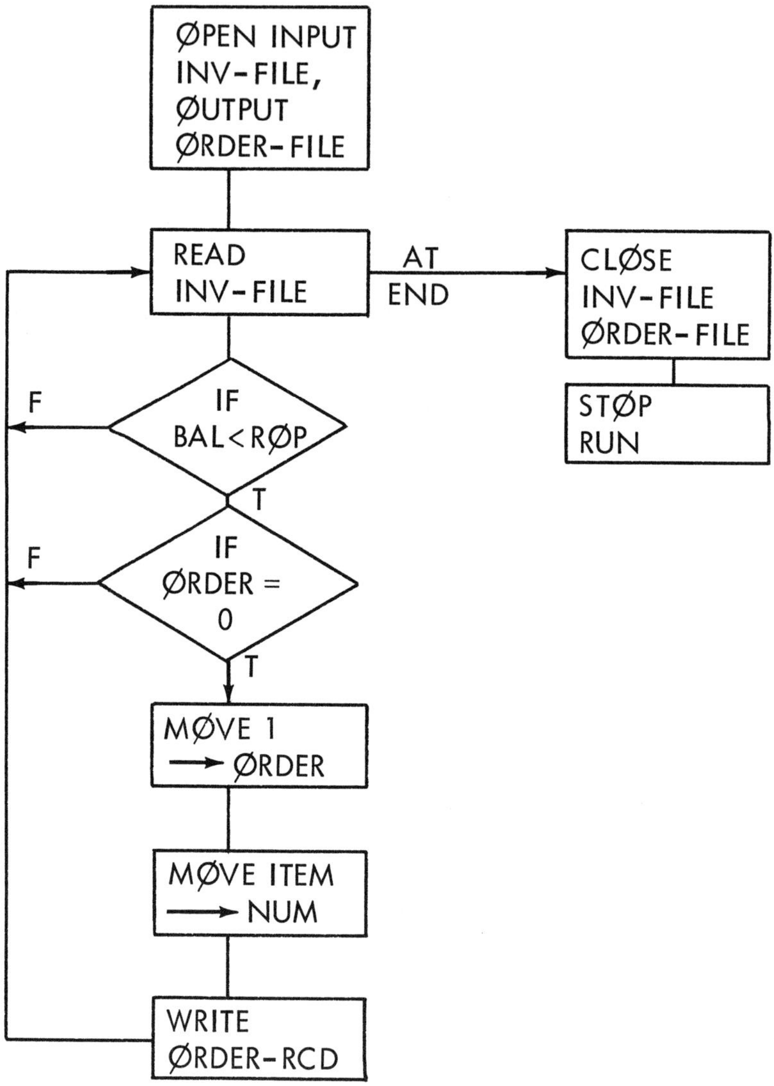

FIG. 4-10

Records are first tested to see whether the on-hand balance is less than the reorder point. If so, an order record is not written immediately, but the order indicator is instead tested. If this shows an order already to be outstanding, the item is ignored; but if no order has been placed, the signal is changed to show an order, and the item is added to the list for replenishment. The receiving routine, not shown here, would contain provisions for resetting ØRDER to zero when the inventory arrives.

3. Use in record search: Use of the relational test can again be illustrated by assuming that a certain record, containing account data, is to be found and written out of a file as it is read by the computer. In this process a single record, called a "finder," will be read in through one input device and will contain the account number of the file record to be removed. Then the account file will be processed through another input device. As each file record is read, its account number is checked against the account number in the finder. When the account numbers match, the file record is written out, and the program is completed. If the entire file is searched without finding the record, an error is assumed to exist. Assume the following file, record, and data names:

	Finder File	Data File	Output File
File name	FINDER-FILE	ACCT-FILE	ØUT-FILE
Record name	FINDER-RCD	ACCT-RCD	ØUT-RCD
Data name	FINDER-NØ	ACCT-NØ	ØUT-ACCT

Although other data are present in the account records, their description is irrelevant.

A flow chart to perform the file search appears in Figure 4-11.

This problem illustrates several points. The first is that although the AT END conditional has no particular meaning in the READ FINDER-FILE command because it is anticipated that this file will be read only once, the conditional must still be included. In this case the AT END conditional simply transfers to the next command; this is a standard way of complying with the rules of the READ command when the conditional has no real part to play in the program.

A second point to note is that reading is being accomplished from two files. This is not unusual, and many files may be used for either input, output, or both.

This is simply a scanning operation, and no data manipulation is involved. Therefore, if the record read does not meet code number requirements, it is disregarded. When the proper record is found, it is to be written out unchanged.

If all records in the ACCT-FILE have been scanned and the proper one has still not been found, an error exists. This is recognized in a

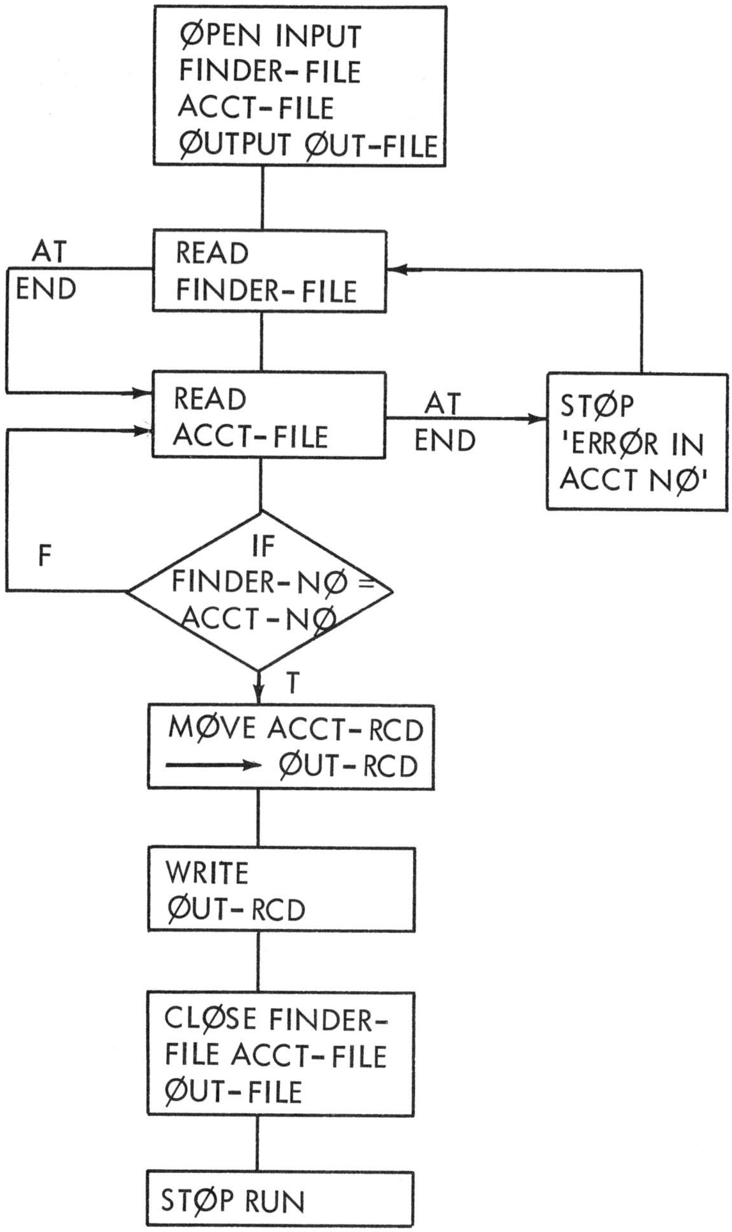
ØPEN INPUT
FINDER-FILE
ACCT-FILE
ØUTPUT ØUT-FILE
AT
END
READ
FINDER-FILE
READ
ACCT-FILE
AT
END
STØP
'ERRØR IN
ACCT NØ'
F
IF
FINDER-NØ =
ACCT-NØ
T
MØVE ACCT-RCD
ØUT-RCD
WRITE
ØUT-RCD
CLØSE FINDER-
FILE ACCT-FILE
ØUT-FILE
STØP RUN

FIG. 4-11

message displayed on an output unit, and the computer is halted for operator intervention.

A final point worth mentioning is that the program's logical terminal does not fall on the path taken when the AT END conditional is found true, but on the regular path. This is quite acceptable if it satisfies the problem's requirements.

4. Ambiguous tests: Logical errors are easily committed when IF statements are used with relational conditionals, particularly if the exact nature of the test to be made is not clearly specified. One of the errors most frequently committed arises out of the improper inclusion or exclusion of limits.

For example, assume that the following instructions are given: If G is between 0 and 5, compute TØT as 4 + D; if not, compute TØT as I - 2. In problems of this sort the exact action to be taken if G equals either limit is unclear. What path should be taken if G = 0? If G = 5?

A generally accepted programming convention indicates that these limits are to be accepted as included; and so, if G is between 0 and 5, inclusive, the statement is taken as true. It is false if G is less than 0 or greater than 5. This being the case, the tests are easier to write if the condition "outside limits" is taken as the true side of the branch. This may be seen by comparing diagrams 1 and 2 of Figure 4-12, the first accepting "inside limits" as true, the latter based on the reverse.

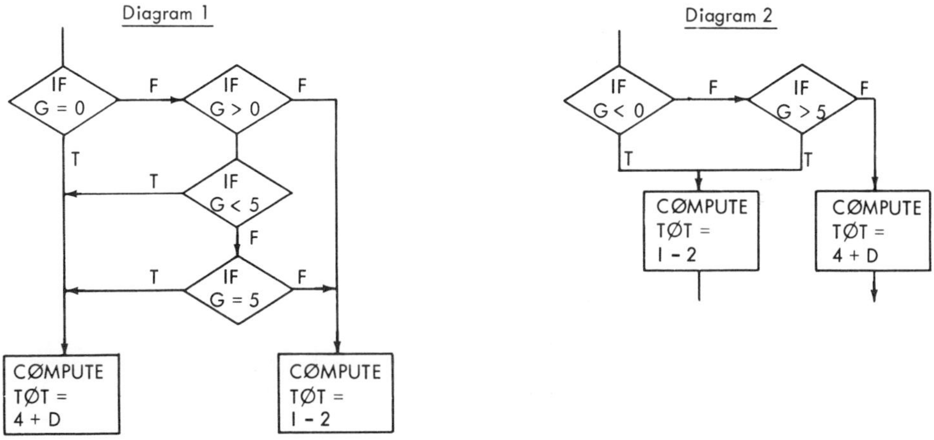

FIG. 4-12

Diagram 1 requires four tests: two at the upper and lower limits, and two to find if G is greater and less than the lower and upper limits, respectively. Diagram 2, by stating the conditionals in such a way that they determine if G is equal to or greater than 0 and equal to or less than 5, performs the same operation in two tests. Of course, the use of NØT would serve the same purpose in shortening the tests.

Sign Condition Tests. Branching statements may be written which test the algebraic sign of a value. Three possible tests are available, and each may be made negative by including NØT. The general form of the test is:

Formula or data-name is { PØSITIVE / NEGATIVE / ZERØ } .

In testing, the appropriate condition is specified. If the formula or data name agrees as to its sign (or zero condition) with the condition, the test is found to be true; if not, it is false. The following examples illustrate the use of the sign condition test:

1. Test FACTØR-A. If found to be positive, go to ADD-TRUE; if not, go to ADD-FALSE.

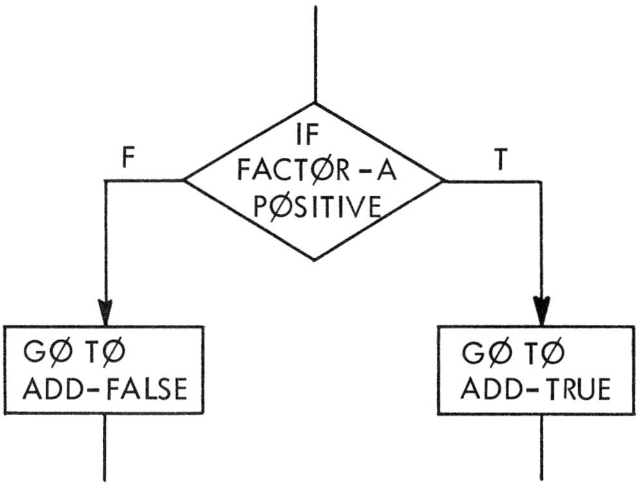

2. <u>Test BØND-WITHHØLD.</u> If zero, go to NØ-BØNDS; if not, go to BØND-DEDUCT.

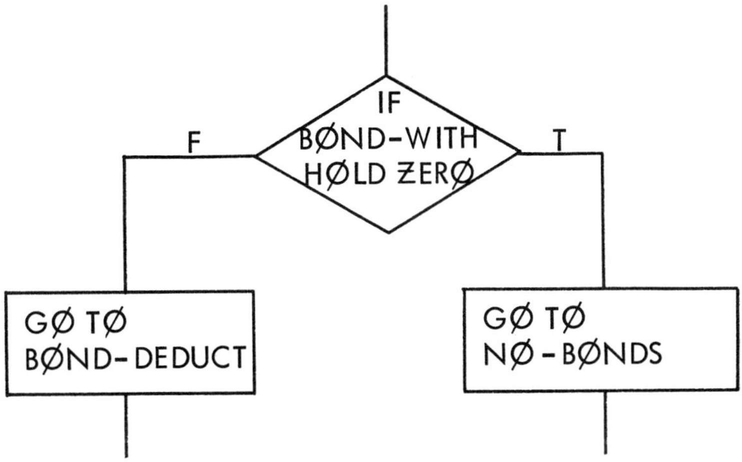

3. <u>Test ØN-HAND.</u> If zero or negative, go to BACK-ØRDER; if not, go to ØRDER-ROUTINE.

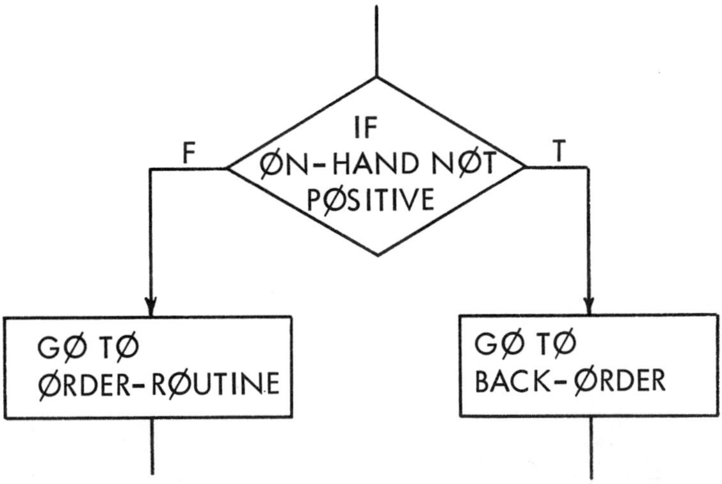

Note that as this test was stated, either one of two conditions would cause a true statement to exist—ØN-HAND might be zero, or it might be negative. It is easier to reverse the test and look for either PØSITIVE or NØT PØSITIVE in a single test than to write the diagram as the condition was set out.

The sign condition test is really a subdivision of the relational test. PØSITIVE is the same as GREATER THAN ZERØ, ZERØ is of course the same as EQUAL ZERØ, and NEGATIVE amounts to the same test as LESS THAN ZERØ. However, the sign condition test is frequently faster to write than its relational counterpart.

Compound Conditionals

As mentioned above, conditional statements may be formed which specify more than one conditional test. These statements are then referred to as compound conditionals. The compound conditional may test a single item, or various items may be made the subject of the tests. Relational and sign tests may be mixed.

Connectives Used with Compound Conditionals. When compound conditionals are constructed, the tests are joined by using either of the connectives AND or ØR. AND used as a connective means that both the tests used must be true for the compound conditional to be true. ØR means that either or both conditionals must be true for the compound conditional to be considered true.

The subject of a compound conditional, once stated, need not be repeated when using relational conditionals so long as it does not change. This is not true if sign conditionals are used.

Compound Conditionals Illustrated. It is assumed in each illustration that reading, writing, and other processing is carried on, but these steps are omitted because they have been described previously.

1. Compound test: Test AGE to find if it is greater than 21 and less than 65. If true, go to IN-LIMIT; if not, go to ØUT-LIMIT.

Using simple conditionals, this situation might be diagrammed as follows:

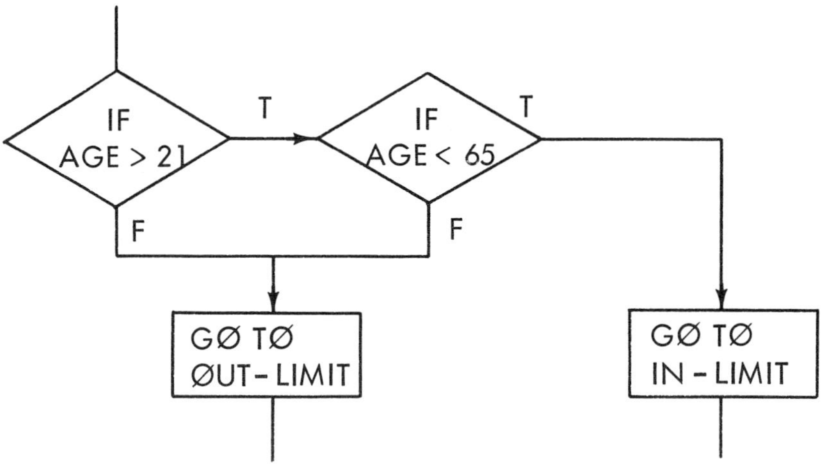

It is much faster and simpler, however, to use a compound conditional, as follows:

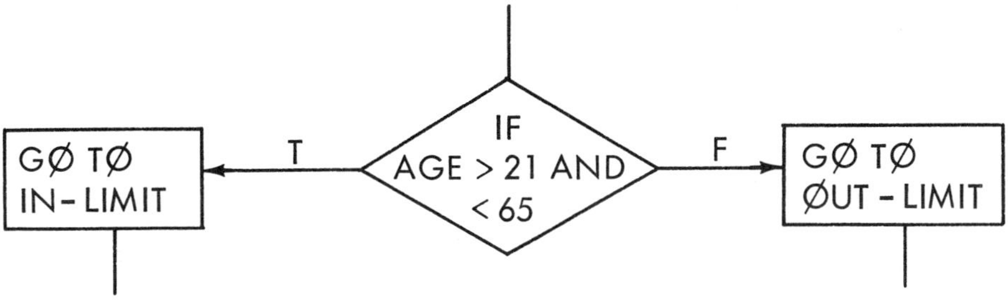

Note that the subject AGE is implied in this conditional, inasmuch as only relational tests are used and the subject does not change.

Two conditions are specified, and the statement is considered correct only if both are met. Therefore the connective AND is used. AGE must be both GREATER THAN 21 AND LESS THAN 65 for the statement to be true.

2. Testing inclusive limits: Relational conditions which state their limits inclusively are more difficult to program than those which expressly exclude the limits, as did illustration 1 above. Suppose the test in No. 1 were worded in this fashion: "If AGE is between 21 and 65, inclusive, go to IN-LIMIT; otherwise, go to ØUT-LIMIT." This could be diagrammed as follows:

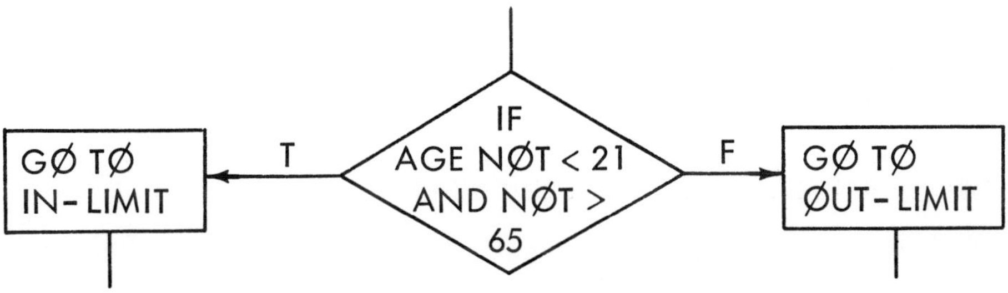

This includes only those AGE data items which are between 21 and 65, inclusive.

The exact meaning of certain relational terms may be seen in this example. "AGE NØT LESS 21" means that the test is true if AGE is 21 or more; it is false if AGE is anything less than 21. "NØT

GREATER 65" means that the test is true if AGE is anything through 65; it is false if AGE is 66 or more.

The tests might also be changed and diagrammed as follows:

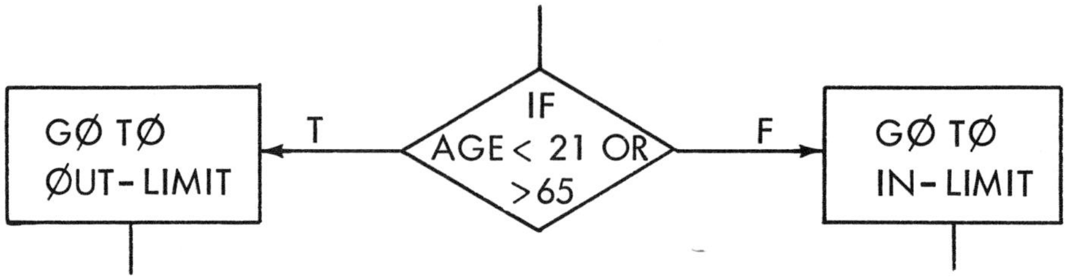

This time, the status of true and false is reversed, and the ØR connective is used. Thus, if either "AGE LESS 21" or "AGE GREATER 65" is true, the statement is considered true, and control is transferred to ØUT-LIMIT. However, if neither is true, AGE must lie between 21 and 65, inclusive, and control is transferred to IN-LIMIT.

3. Testing two data items: Assume that employee records are to be scanned, and a list of all personnel holding college degrees who are older than 45 is to be made. Employee age is recorded in the AGE field by year of birth, and education is recorded in the EDUC field, where a 4 represents a college degree, other educational levels being represented by other code numbers. The employee records (PERS-REC) are in the PERSØNNEL file; the output list is to consist of records called GRADUATE in the ØUT-FILE. This program might be diagrammed as shown in Figure 4-13. Both age and educational requirements can easily be queried in the same conditional statement. Note that age is tested by a simple equation, where the employee's age is found by subtracting his year of birth from the current year.

4. Using the sign conditional: Calculate the amount of income tax (TAX) to be withheld by subtracting 13 times the employee's dependents (DEP) from his gross earnings (GRØSS), and then taking 14 percent of the remainder. If this figure is negative, as it may be when gross pay is small and an employee has a large number of dependents, TAX should be set to zero; otherwise, the program should proceed to an address called UPDATE. This situation, diagrammed as shown below, illustrates the use of the sign test conditional. If TAX is negative at all, its magnitude is unimportant, and the item is set to zero. The computation of TAX is not shown in detail, because it is not essential in the example.

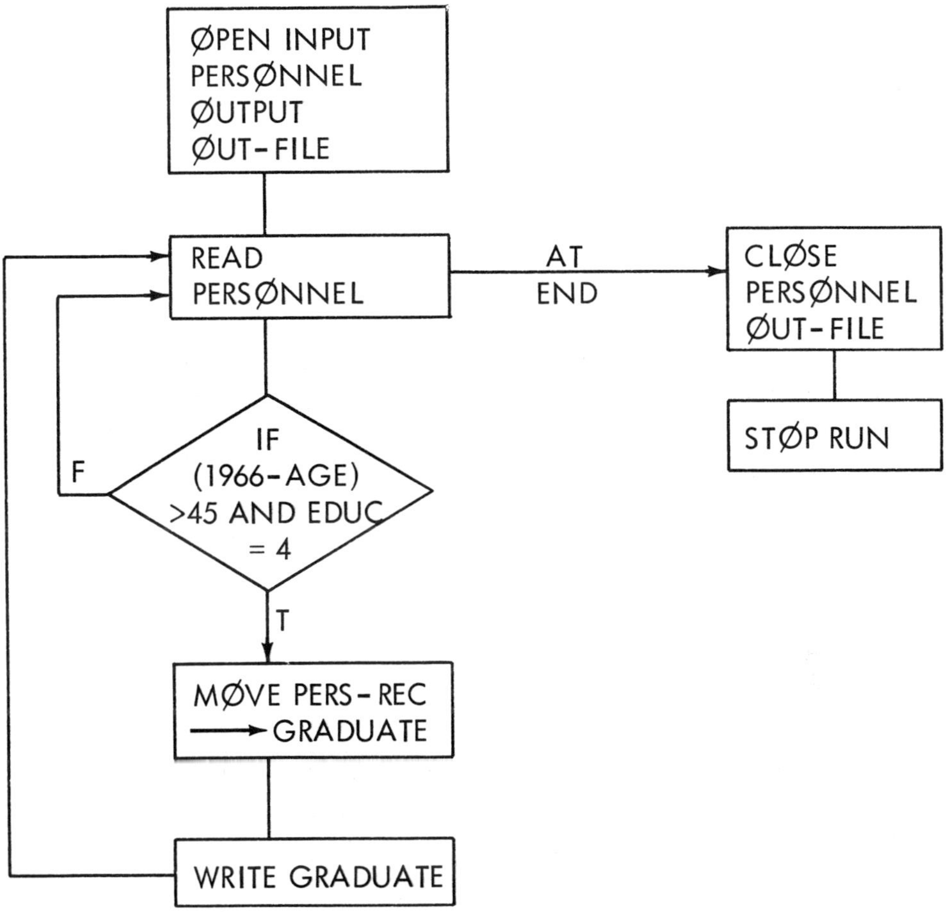
ØPEN INPUT
PERSØNNEL
ØUTPUT
ØUT-FILE
READ
PERSØNNEL
AT
END
CLØSE
PERSØNNEL
ØUT-FILE
STØP RUN
F
IF
(1966-AGE)
>45 AND EDUC
= 4
T
MØVE PERS-REC
GRADUATE
WRITE GRADUATE

FIG. 4-13

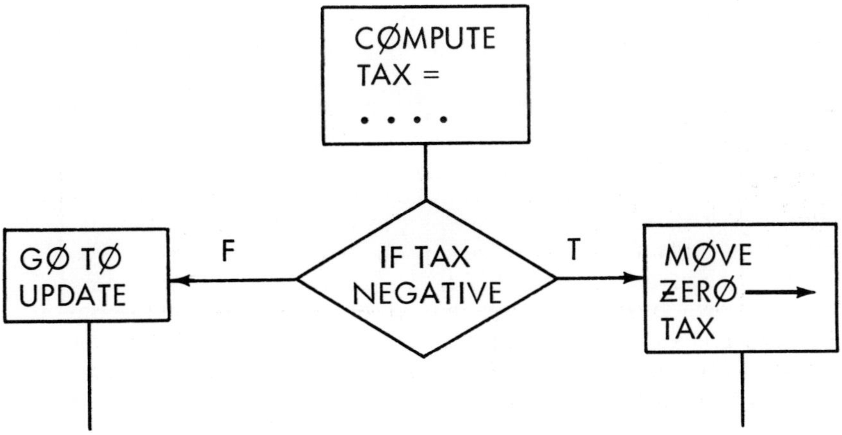
CØMPUTE
TAX =
. . . .
GØ TØ
UPDATE
F
IF TAX
NEGATIVE
T
MØVE
ZERØ
TAX

5. <u>Analyzing complex situations:</u> Assume that the following situation is to be programmed: From an input record containing GRØSS, the amount of pay earned by an employee during this pay period, and YTD-GRØSS, the amount of pay earned by an employee during this year not including the current pay period, the amount of current social security withholding (SØC-SEC) is to be calculated. The current rate of withholding is 4.2 percent, assessed on the first $6,600 earned in the calendar year.

Situation Analysis: One of three conditions may exist with regard to the social security liability of an employee: (a) He may owe nothing, because he has already earned $6,600 or more this year and satisfied his liability; (b) He may owe social security tax on his entire earnings for the current time period; (c) Part of his current pay may be taxable and part nontaxable, because he reaches the $6,600 cutoff this period with a part of his current pay. Each condition must be allowed for in the program.

A series of tests for determining the liability status and calculating social security tax might appear as shown in Figure 4-14.

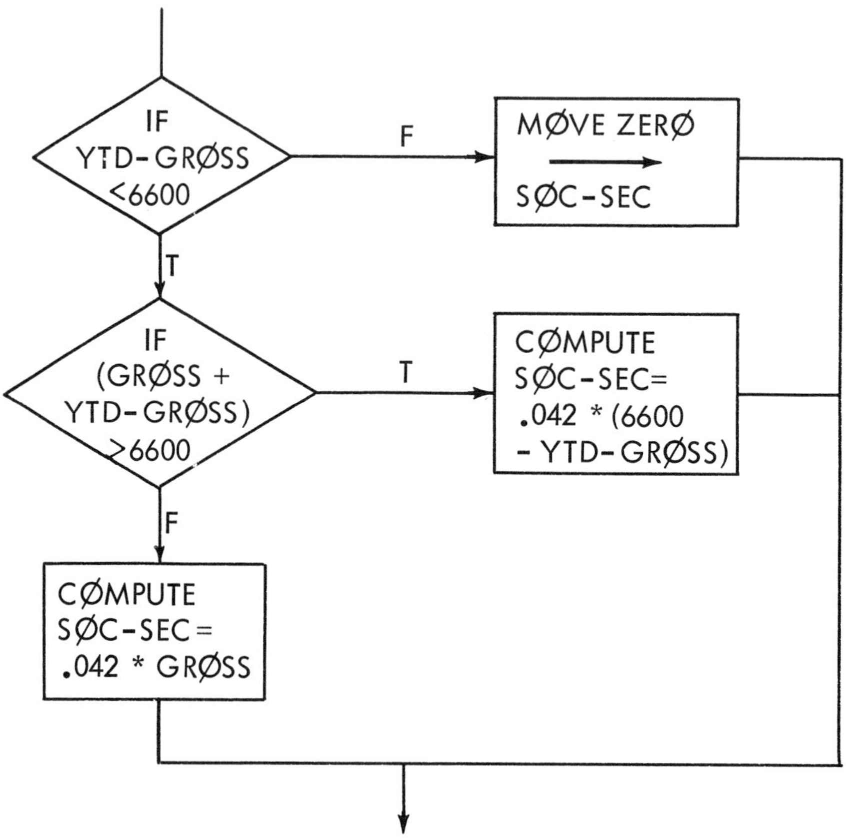

FIG. 4-14

Note that if no social security tax is owed, SØC-SEC is carefully set to zero. Presumably, this field is a part of an output record; if it is not set to zero, it will reflect the amount of social security withheld from the previous employee and cause an erroneous output record to be written. Remember that writing is nondestructive; the simple act of writing a record does not destroy it in memory. Old data are not erased until new data are written in the location.

Summary of Conditionals

The exact effect to be expected of a given conditional may be somewhat unclear at this point, especially when the NØT option is used. Table 4-2 sets out all conditionals introduced so far and details the circumstances which will make the conditional statement follow the TRUE branch as well as test results leading to a FALSE routing.

Table 4-2

If the Conditional Specifies:	To Be TRUE, the Item Must Be:	To Be FALSE, the Item Must Be:
LESS	LESS	EQUAL ØR GREATER
EQUAL	EQUAL	GREATER ØR LESS
GREATER	GREATER	LESS ØR EQUAL
NØT LESS	EQUAL ØR GREATER	LESS
NØT EQUAL	GREATER ØR LESS	EQUAL
NØT GREATER	EQUAL ØR LESS	GREATER
PØSITIVE	PØSITIVE	ZERØ ØR NEGATIVE
ZERØ	ZERØ	PØSITIVE ØR NEGATIVE
NEGATIVE	NEGATIVE	ZERØ ØR PØSITIVE
NØT PØSITIVE	ZERØ ØR NEGATIVE	PØSITIVE
NØT ZERØ	PØSITIVE ØR NEGATIVE	ZERØ
NØT NEGATIVE	PØSITIVE ØR ZERØ	NEGATIVE
Condition-A AND Condition-B	Both Conditional-A AND Condition-B TRUE	Either Conditional-A ØR Condition-B ØR both, FALSE
Condition-A ØR Condition-B	Either Condition-A ØR Condition-B, ØR both, TRUE	BØTH Conditional-A AND Condition-B FALSE

It should be obvious that many programming variations are available in the construction of simple and compound conditionals. Input, output, and arithmetic statements are quite straightforward, and little possibility for change is present. However, many possible sound programming routes may exist in a complex conditional situation. Each programmer should choose the type of logic most reasonable to him and use it consistently. The only general recommendation which may be made is that compound conditionals be kept simple enough to be fully understood. One is quickly lost in a maze of compound conditionals, especially when some terms are made negative by use of NØT, and logical precision is quite likely to suffer.

EXTENDED ILLUSTRATION

Commands introduced thus far—READ, MØVE, WRITE, calculate, and branch instructions—are sufficient for the programming of almost any data-processing situation. This illustration demonstrates the process of instruction combination which is necessary for effective computer utilization, as well as certain programming techniques which are effective in complex situations.

Procedure Requirements

For purposes of illustration, assume that the X Company desires to convert its processing of raw material inventory records to electronic methods. The firm uses the weighted-average method of inventory pricing.

Three files are to be created to replace the raw material ledger. One file will contain data on inventory balances, each different inventory item occupying a different record. A second file will contain records on each receipt of inventory. The third file will be used to record each issuance of inventory.

Records will be stored by inventory number, in ascending sequence. Depending on the activity of the particular item, either receipts, issues, or both may be absent. However, every item carried in stock will have a balance record.

Generally stated, the purpose of the processing run is to update inventory balance records and prepare raw material cost records for cost accounting. This is to be accomplished by reading old balances, adding receipts, deducting issues, and preparing the required output.

Records containing inventory issue data do not contain unit cost information, because the new average cost is not known at the time of issuance. Instead, the new average cost is computed as old balance and receipts records are processed. Then, as issue records are processed, the cost accounting record is prepared by use of the newly computed average cost.

Each balance record is to contain a minimum reorder point. As new balance records are prepared, the quantity on hand is to be compared with minimum balances; and if holdings are deficient, a reorder listing is to be prepared.

Certain amounts are to be accumulated on each run for control purposes. These are the cost amounts of total old balances, total receipts, total issues, and total new balances. These will be accumulated in such a way that if they fail to balance (old balance + receipts - issues = new balance), a processing error will be indicated.

Output Requirements

The general statement of procedure above should be broken down for analysis. In so doing, the output requirements are first enumerated. These may be seen to be:

1. An updated balance record

2. Costed material issues

3. A list of items requiring replenishment

4. Certain control totals

The updated balance record must contain the same fields as the old balance record, for it will become the old record at the next processing. It is assumed that balance records as shown in Table 4-3 are to be used in the procedure.

Note that these records contain much information in addition to the basic financial and control data. The number of postings to the record is kept for control purposes. Year-to-date information is gathered to provide information for analysis of raw material costs and use volume. Finally, both reorder point and reorder quantity are included. The first indicates the level to which stocks may fall before reordering; the second is the standard order quantity.

The balance records of four hypothetical inventory items are also shown in Table 4-3. These, with similar data on receipts and issues, will be used to check the accuracy of the procedure designed to process inventory records.

Other required output records—reorder records and costed issue records—are shown in Table 4-4 as REØRDER-REC and MAT-USED, respectively. These may be seen to be quite simple, the costed issues record showing the item number, job charged, number of units issued, and cost; and the reorder record showing the inventory number and description, and the standard order quantity.

The last output requirement, that of providing control totals, will be satisfied by accumulating old balance amounts in TØT-ØLD-BAL, receipts in TØT-REC, issues in TØT-ISS, and new balance amounts in TØT-NEW-BAL.

Table 4-3

Contents of Balance Records

	Old Balance	New Balance
File name:	MATERIALS-BALANCE	NEW-MAT-FILE
Record name:	BAL-RCD	NEW-BAL-RCD

Data Element	COBOL Name	Test Data 1	2	3	4
Inventory number	NØ-BAL	123	124	127	130
Item description	DESC	PIN	CAP	TAP	SØCKET
Activity counters:					
Receipts	C-REC	3	15	18	10
Issues	C-ISS	14	35	28	25
Year to-date information:					
No. of units received	U-REC	1,050	7,500	18,000	4,000
No. of units issued	U-ISS	1,000	7,200	17,400	3,800
Total cost of receipts	CØST-R	1,600	14,750	31,625	11,800
Total cost of issues	CØST-IS	1,525	14,150	30,575	11,200
On-hand information:					
Number of units	UNITS	50	300	600	200
Total cost of units on hand	T-CØST	$75	$600	$1,050	$600
Cost per unit	U-CØST	$1.50	$2.00	$1.75	$3.00
Reorder point (units)	RØP	100	100	500	150
Reorder quantity (units)	RQTY	350	500	1,000	400

Available Input

The inventory procedure to be designed must satisfy its output requirements from three basic data input sources: the old balance records, inventory receipt records, and inventory issue records. The old balance record has the same content and organization as new balance records and may be seen in Table 4-3.

Receipts data, carried in the REC-RCD record, consist of inventory number, number of units received, invoice cost before freight, and freight cost. Data on inventory issues, carried in the ISS-REC, consist of inventory number, number of units issued, and the production job to which the raw material was issued. Descriptions of those records, including the data names of their contents, may be seen in Table 4-4. Test data representing hypothetical receipts and issues are shown in Table 4-5.

Table 4-4

Contents of Records

	Item Description	COBOL Name
1.	File name	REC-FILE
	Record name	REC-RCD
	Record contents:	
	Inventory number	NØ-REC
	Number of units received	UNITS-REC
	Invoice cost before freight	INV-CØST
	Freight charge	FGT
2.	File name	ISS-FILE
	Record name	ISS-REC
	Record contents:	
	Inventory number	NØ-ISS
	Number of units issued	UNITS-ISS
	Production job to which issued	JØB-NØ
3.	File name	REØRDER
	Record name	RECØRD-REC
	Record contents:	
	Inventory number	NØ-ØRD
	Item description	DESC-ØRD
	Standard reorder quantity	QUANTITY
4.	File name	CØST-ACCØUNTING
	Record name	MAT-USED
	Record contents:	
	Inventory number	ITEM
	Production job number	JØB
	Number of units issued	NØ-UNITS
	Cost charged	RM-CHG

Table 4-5

Sample Contents of Receipts and Issues File

Records in receipts file, in order of appearance:

Records	1	2	3	4
Inventory number	123	123	123	130
No. of units received	350	350	350	400
Invoice cost	$560.00	$560.00	$565.00	$1,150.00
Freight charges	65.00	50.00	55.00	75.00

Records in issues file, in order of appearance:

Records	1	2	3	4	5	6
Inventory number	123	123	124	124	130	130
No. of units issued	300	400	150	100	300	200
Production job using	1,014	1,017	1,013	1,014	1,017	1,015

Control Implications

Careful attention must always be paid to the matter of control in systems development. "Control" in this sense means "accurate compliance with decree" and in electronic data processing is accomplished by certain programmed checks to see that accuracy is achieved or errors are disclosed. A few such checks will be built into the illustration; these are typical of techniques commonly used in procedure development.

One control already mentioned is the accumulation and display of cumulative totals. These will be developed in such a way that failure to extend properly will indicate a procedural error. Furthermore, in an actual system, data such as these would be previously accumulated independently of computer operations, and failure of the automated system to produce proper check figures would indicate error.

The SIZE ERRØR option accompanying arithmetic statements is another kind of control used to insure accuracy. This will be used only when old balances are accumulated in the illustration to simplify the flow chart; ordinarily, the option should be used whenever arithmetic occurs which might conceivably cause an overflow.

One new control technique will be illustrated. When files are arranged sequentially, as in this example (that is, the records are in sequential order), a record out of place may be recognized by the fact that an account number will be less than that of the record preceding it. This is referred to as a "step-down" condition and indicates an error. For example, if records 101, 105, 107, and 108 are in a file, and 107 is mislocated, it will cause a step-down before or after it is encountered. Files processed sequentially are checked for this condition, as will be the balance file in the illustration.

Procedure Diagram

A procedure diagram for processing inventory records in conformance with requirements appears in Figures 4-15, 4-16, and 4-17. Of course, there are many procedural variations which also work satisfactorily.

The diagram is divided into blocks for identification and discussion purposes. Each block is discussed briefly below. However, for a full understanding of the procedure outlined, the test data furnished should be traced through the diagram. Only in this way can the performance of the system be seen under various circumstances and an insight into various programming techniques be gained.

Block 1 (Fig. 4-15). Files are opened in this, the initializing phase. Zeros are also moved to three storage locations, BAL-CTRL, NØ-REC, and NØ-ISS. The last two fields are to be used to determine when account numbers change with regard to receipts and issues records, respectively. As a record is read, its account number will be checked with that stored in one of these locations. If the numbers agree, the newly read record must belong to the same account as that processed previously. Should the numbers not agree, however, the new record belongs to another account, and all records of the type being dealt with have been processed for the old account.

The field BAL-CTRL is to be used in checking for a step-down among balance records. The account number of balance records read in will be checked against this element. If the number is not larger, an error is recognized.

All balances are set to zero at the beginning, thus storing sham account numbers in the field. Then, on the first time through the program, this will not match the account number read, and a first-record condition will be recognized.

Block 2 (Fig. 4-15). The major purpose of this block is to read old balance records and see that a step-down has not occurred by comparing the account number of the newly read record with BAL-CTRL. If the current number is not larger, an error message is printed, and the computer stops. If the number is larger, it is moved to BAL-CTRL (where it will be available for comparison when a new record is read), the amount of the old balance is accumulated, and the program continues.

Note that two control checks are made in this block. One, for a step-down, has been previously mentioned. The second checks the accumulated amount of old balances for overflow and writes a suitable error message should the error exist. These are the only control checks made in this program; an actual system would have tests of this type at a number of points. Terminal routines are also included in block 2.

Block 3 (Fig. 4-15). This block contains all procedures related to processing inventory receipts records. It may be noted that the procedure begins by checking inventory numbers in balance and receipts records. Of course, these will not match the first time the test is made, because no receipts record has been read. However, the mismatch leads to another test, where the fact that the inventory number in the receipts record (known to be zero at the start) is less than the number on the balance record (123) causes a receipts record to be read. The program returns to check inventory numbers again; and this time, with the test data, a match is found. Thus the receipts record is processed against its appropriate balance record.

Eventually, a receipts record will be read which belongs to a different balance record. This will be recognized by the fact that the inventory number of the receipts record is greater than its counterpart in the balance record; and so a new unit cost will be computed, and the program will pass on to the processing of issues records.

Block 4 (Fig. 4-16). Issues are processed in this block in much the same manner as the receipts records just discussed. Matching inventory numbers in issue and balance records mean that the records belong to the same item, and so the issue is processed. It will be noted that the record showing raw material costs for cost accounting purposes is prepared in this block.

Block 5 (Fig. 4-16). Encountering an inventory number on an issue record which exceeds the number in the balance record indicates that all transactions in that particular inventory item have been completed, and the program passes into block 5. Here, new balance records are written. Inasmuch as the old balance record has been modified, the WRITE FRØM option is used, thus avoiding moving a great number of items from old to new balance records. This writing option is explained at length in the next chapter.

Block 5 also contains the routine for checking reorder points. Thus reorder points are checked only after all receipts and issues associated with a particular item have been processed. This avoids the possibility of writing multiple reorder notices in cases where several issues occur after the reorder point is passed.

The details of processing receipts and issues records involve straightforward movement and computation of data, and so are omitted from the major flow chart. They are presented in Figure 4-17.

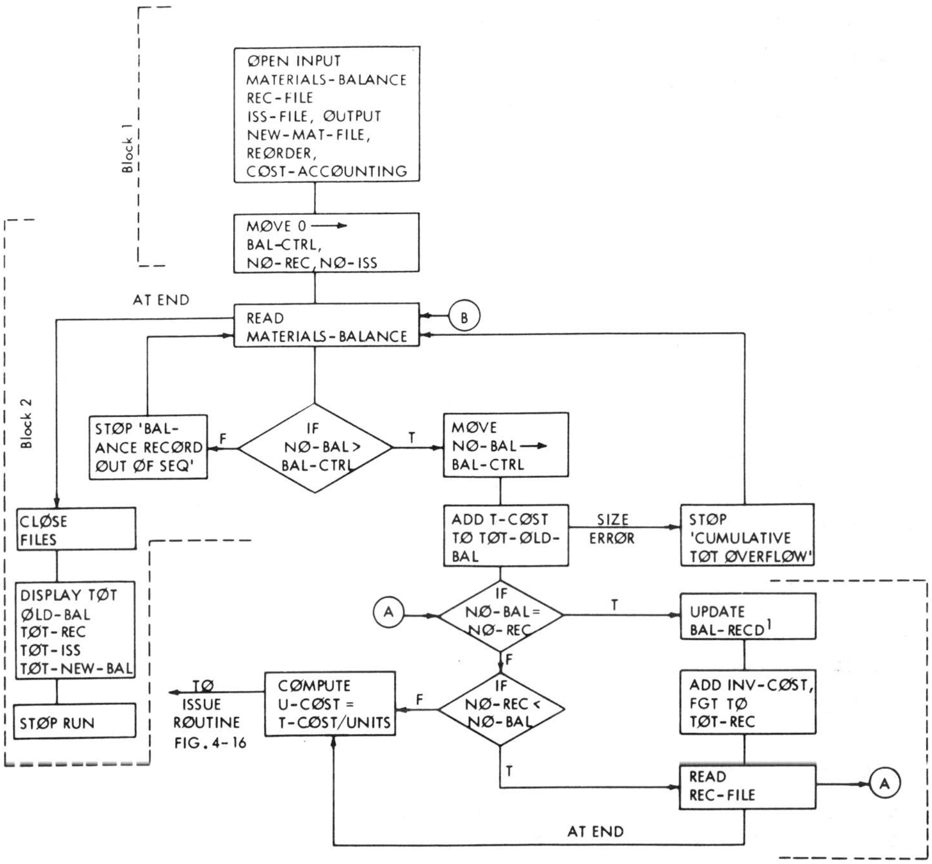

[1] Detail shown in Figure 4-17.

Note: Where flow lines would be too long or cross several others, letters in circles have been substituted. These should be considered as terminals of connectives leading from one step to another.

FIG. 4-15. Diagram of Balance and Receiving Routines

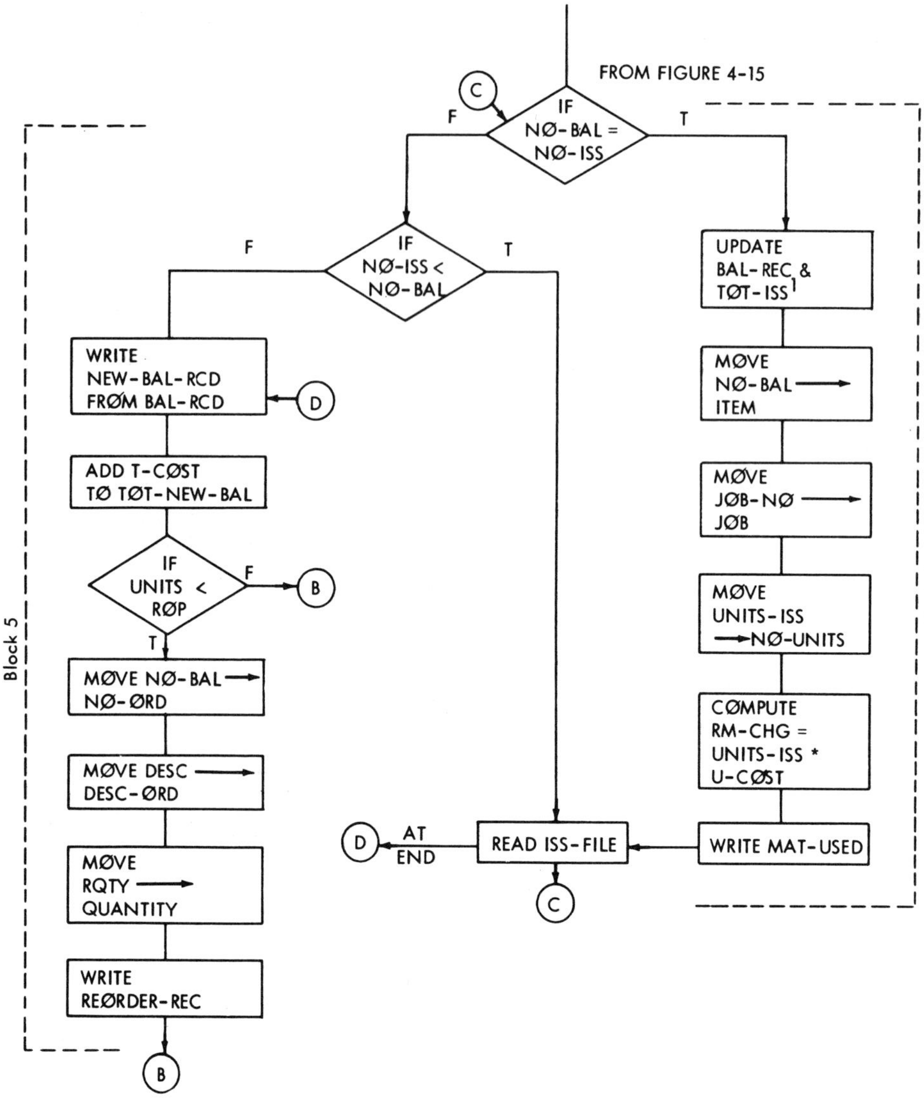

[1] Details in Figure 4-17.

FIG. 4-16. Processing Issues and Preparing Cost Records

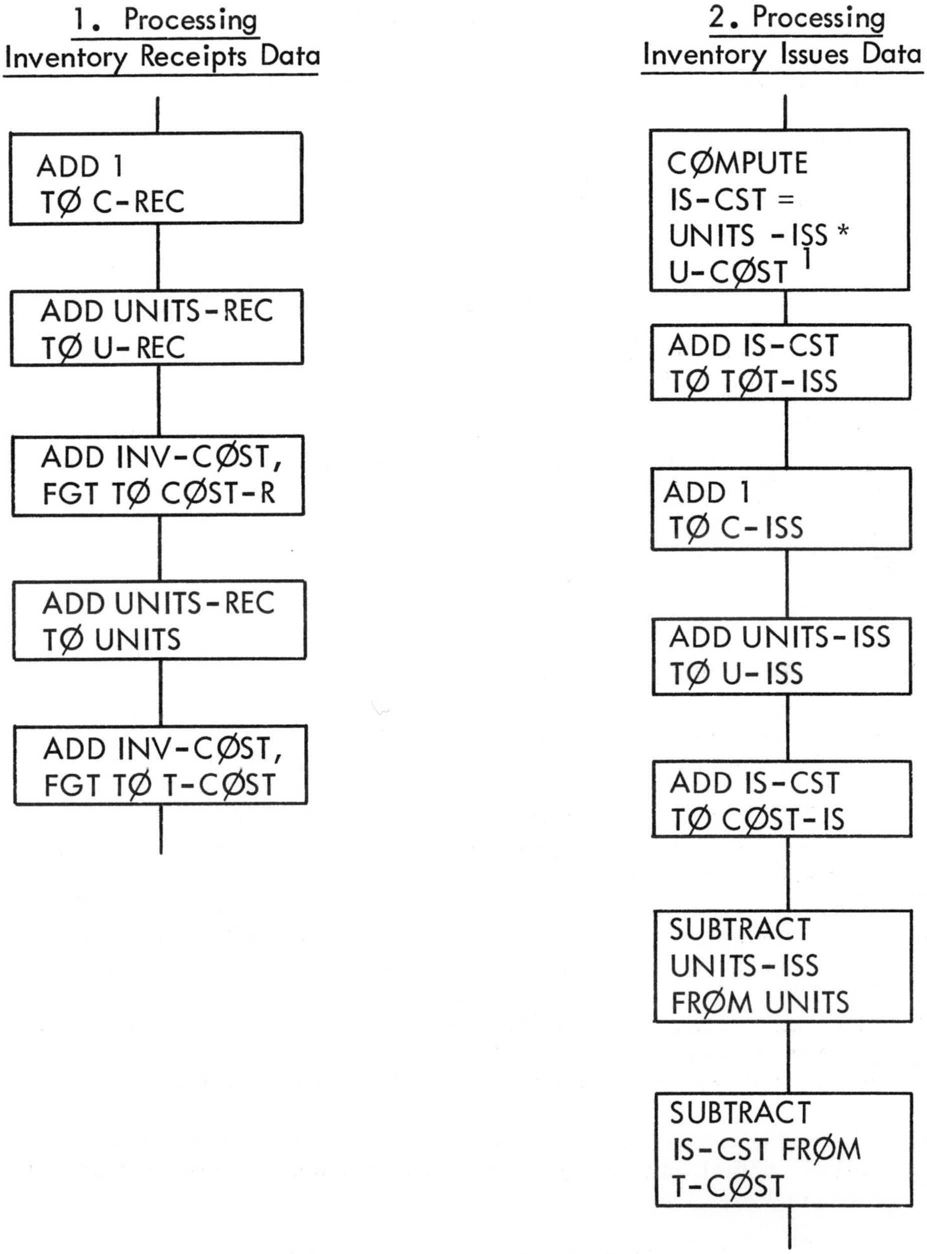

[1] IS-CST is used for the temporary storage of issue cost.

FIG. 4-17. Updating the Balance Record

QUESTIONS AND PROBLEMS

1. Distinguish between the AT END conditional and the IF conditional. When may each be used?

2. Assume that VALUE-X, a four-place data field, contains the value 7984 when the command "ADD 3402 TØ VALUE-X" is given.

   a) What will be the contents of VALUE-X after execution of the ADD command if the SIZE ERRØR conditional is not used?

   b) What will be the contents of the field if the SIZE ERRØR conditional is used?

3. The extended illustration in this chapter gives as test data the old balance and transaction records of four inventory items. Give the following for each:

   a) Ending unit cost.

   b) Ending inventory, in units.

   c) Cost of ending inventory.

   d) Is the balance of any item below its reorder point? Was an order placed?

   e) Explain how the program proceeds when all receipts or issues records have been processed. How are any inactive balance records treated?

4. Sales amounts (called SALES) are to be categorized according to their magnitude. Those for $100 or less are to be added to SMALL; those from $101 to $200, inclusive, are to be added to MØDERATE; those from $201 to $500, inclusive, are to be added to LARGE; and those exceeding $500 are to be added to VERY-LARGE. Diagram a series of conditional and add commands to execute this.

5. An input file, IN-FILE, contains records, called TRANS-RCD, which reflect actual and budgeted expense amounts. These appear as follows:

Item Description	COBOL Name
Account number	NUMBER
Actual expense	ACT-EXP
Budget allowance	BUD-EXP

   Diagram a program which will read these records, compare actual and budgeted expense amounts, and prepare the following output record, called ØUT-RCD, in the ØUT-FILE file:

Item Description	COBOL Name
Account number	ACCT-NUM
Message	MESSAGE
Percent actual over budget	ØVER
Percent budget over actual	UNDER

Explanation of output requirements:

a) The account number is the same as read in.

b) The message is to be formed as follows: Actual and budgeted expense amounts are to be compared. If actual exceeds budget, the literal ACTUAL ØVER BUDGET is to be moved here. If budgeted expense exceeds actual costs, the literal ACTUAL UNDER BUDGET is to be moved here.

c) If actual expenses exceed the budget allowance, such excess is to be divided by the budget allowance, converted into percentage by multiplying by 100, and written in the ØVER field. If budgeted expenses exceed actual costs, the excess is to be divided by the budget allowance, converted to percentage, and written in the UNDER field. The percentage is to be a positive amount. No matter which field is used, the other should be set to zero.

d) If the amount of the actual expense equals the budget allowance, space should be moved to all output records except the account number, and the record should be written.

e) The excess of actual expense over budget allowance is to be accumulated as TØT-ØVER, and the excess of budget over actual expense is to be accumulated as TØT-UNDER. Each of these is to be displayed after all records have been processed.

6. Production of a certain article is reported on PR-RCD records, which exist in the PRDCT file. The quantity of output produced is reported in the QTY field, in ounces. Diagram a program to read all such records, accumulating production in a data item called TØT-PRØ. After all production records have been read and TØT-PRØ has been calculated, convert total production into gallons, quarts, and ounces. Use data names GAL, QT, and ØZ. After reducing production to these units, display the amount of production in the following message: TØTAL PRØDUCTIØN AMØUNTED TØ ... GALLØNS, ... QUARTS, AND ... ØUNCES.

Solution hint: First reduce total production to the largest number of whole gallons (128 ounces) possible; then reduce the remainder to the largest number of whole quarts (32 ounces), leaving the number of ounces.

7. A firm calculates dividends by multiplying each stockholder's number of shares (found as data item SHARES in records called STØCK-HØLDERS in the STØCK file) by the current dividend, $0.125. However, by company policy, if a person's dividend would be less than $0.25, it is raised to $0.25.

   Diagram a program for processing these records, preparing output records called ØUT-REC which show the amount of dividend to be received, DIV, and the number of shares held, called SHARES-HELD. The total of all dividends allowed under the policy mentioned above is to be accumulated as TØT-DIV. Also, the cost of increasing dividends to the minimum is to be accumulated in a field called TØT-INCREASE. Each of these amounts is to be displayed after processing all records. The output file is named ØUT-FILE.

8. Five values, called, A, B, C, D, and E, are stored in memory. Diagram a program to find the smallest, to be named SMALL, and the largest, to be named LARGE. Display SMALL and LARGE.

9. Four values, called A, B, C, and D, are stored in memory. Diagram a program which will rearrange these values from largest to smallest as A through D, respectively, using T as a temporary storage location. Display A, B, C, and D after arranging the values.

10. A firm has inventory records as shown in Table 4-6.

Table 4-6

File name: INV-FILE

Record name: INV-RCD

Record contents:

Item Description	COBOL Name
Inventory identification number	IDENT
Kind of unit*	TYPE
Number of units sold—current month	CUR-SALES
Number of units sold—last month	LAST-MØ
Number of units sold—previous month	PREV-MØ
Number of units on hand	UNITS
Reorder point	RØP
Storage capacity	CAP

*Indicates type of unit measure used, with 1 representing pounds, 2 representing gallons, and 3 representing feet.

Instructions: You are to diagram a program for listing items requiring reorder, as follows:

a) Check the number of units on hand against the reorder point. If the inventory exceeds reorder, the item can be ignored.

b) If an order is necessary, the amount to be ordered is three quarters of a month's average sales volume (found by averaging the three months' sales reported) less the inventory on hand. However, storage capacity may not permit this much to be stored. If the computed amount to be ordered exceeds storage capacity less the current balance, only the difference between current balance and storage capacity is to be ordered.

An output record is to be prepared for each necessary order, as shown in Table 4-7.

Table 4-7

File name: ØRDER-FILE

Record name: ØRDER-RECØRD

Record contents:

Item Description	COBOL Name
Inventory identification number	ID-NØ
Kind of unit*	UNIT-DESC
Number of units to be ordered	ØRDER

*An alphabetic literal is to be written here. If the unit of measure is pounds, write POUNDS, if gallons, write GALLONS, if feet, write FEET.

11. A company pays all employees in cash. The amount owed each employee is recorded as AMØUNT in the PAY-RCD record, found in the PAY-FILE file. You are to diagram a program which will read these records and determine the number of bills—twenties, tens, fives, and ones—required to make up the pay envelopes to pay all employees. Cents may be ignored. After all records have been processed, the number of bills required is to be displayed. Use data names as follows:

Twenties	TWENTIES
Tens	TENS
Fives	FIVES
Ones	ØNES

Hint: For each employee, you should find the bills necessary for payment. This may be done by subtraction of the various denominations until a negative balance occurs, accumulating the number of successful subtractions.

12. A file contains transaction records to be posted to asset accounts in the general ledger. These appear as shown in Table 4-8.

Table 4-8

File name: LEDGER

Record name: LED-ENTRY

Record contents:

Item Description	COBOL Name
Account number	ACCT
Record type*	TYPE
Amount	AMT

*Recorded as 1 for a balance record, 2 for a debit, and 3 for a credit.

All entry records, debit and credit, have been arranged behind their proper balance record. Records containing the same account number belong to the same account. Accounts are included in ascending order by account number.

You are to process this file and prepare new ledger balance records. This should be done by reading and storing a balance record, and then by reading and processing transactions. Debit amounts should be added to the account balance; credits should be subtracted. New balance records should be prepared for each account. Use file, record, and data names in Table 4-8, prefixing each with NEW-.

Hint:

a) All records—balance and transaction—are going to be read into the same storage location. Therefore, when a balance record is read, it should be moved out of the way after writing the previous updated balance.

b) Completion of one account's processing will be signaled by reading of the next balance card. Therefore, when a balance record is read, the updated balance record just completed should be written out.

13. This problem requires the diagramming of a program to prepare depreciation schedules for assets according to the straight-line, sum-of-the-years'-digits, or declining-balance methods of depreciation. Problems at the end of Chapter 3 set out the technique of computing depreciation for the sum-of-digits method and may be referred to if necessary. Instructions on the computation of depreciation by the declining-balance method are furnished below.

A record, called the ASSET-RCD, is to be read through the ASSET-PUR file. This contains details on the purchase of a single asset, as shown in Table 4-9.

Table 4-9

Item Description	COBOL Name
Nature of asset	DESC
Estimated useful life, in years	USE-LIFE
Cost	CØST
Estimated scrap value	SCRAP
Depreciation method indicator*	IND

*This will indicate the depreciation method to be used on the particular asset, as follows: If IND = 1, the straight-line method of depreciation is to be used; if IND = 2, the sum-of-the-years'-digits method is to be used; and if IND = 3, the declining-balance method is to be used.

For this problem, the declining-balance depreciation amount may be calculated as follows: Take a depreciation rate twice that of the appropriate straight-line rate. Multiply the asset's cost less depreciation taken by this rate to arrive at the amount of current depreciation.

Your depreciation schedule will consist of a statement showing the amount of depreciation to be taken on the particular asset for each year of its estimated useful life, plus certain other information. Output will appear as shown in Table 4-10.

Table 4-10

File name: DEPREC-FILE

Record name: DEP-AMT

Item Description	COBOL Name
Nature of asset	ASSET-DESC
Depreciation method	DEPREC-METHØD
Year	YEAR
Depreciation for year	CUR-DEPREC
Accumulated depreciation	ACCUM-DEPREC
Undepreciated balance	BALANCE

The depreciation method—straight-line, sum of years, or declining balance—is to be moved into the second field as a nonnumeric literal. 'YEAR' is to be provided by the program, starting with 1966 and increasing by 1 for each line in the schedule. Depreciation for the year should represent the current year's charge, taking a full year's depreciation for the first year. Accumulated depreciation should be the sum of all depreciation taken, including the current year.

Undepreciated balance represents the asset balance after depreciation. The first output line should show the asset as of January 1, 1966, before any depreciation is taken. Thus the line should show the asset's nature, depreciation method, 1966, and its cost. The asset's nature and depreciation method should not be repeated after this line; instead, these fields should be erased by moving spaces to them.

14. Prepare a flow diagram of the following:

    Assume that $Y = 6X + 4X^2 - X^3$ is the equation of a line. Find the area beneath this line from X = 1 to X = 5, inclusive, by the following process, and store the solution at AREA:

    a) Assume the area to be a rectangle of height Y when X = 3, and length 4. Compute the area of this rectangle, and display.

    b) Assume the area under the curve to consist of 2 rectangles, each of length 2, the first of height Y when X = 2, the second of height Y when X = 4. Add the areas of these two rectangles, and display their total.

    c) Compute the areas of four rectangles of height Y at X = 1.5, 2.5, 3.5, and 4.5, respectively, each having length 1. Add the areas of these rectangles and display their total.

    In the above, you may use the following working areas, although your solution method may not require all of them:

    Y, the value of Y at any time

    X, the value of X at any time

    INC, the amount of increment in X

    CTR, a counter controlling the number of rectangles to be formed

15. The Ajax Company uses the standard cost method of cost accounting. The following procedure reflects data processing involved in the accounting for raw materials put into process.

    Standard cost records for every item of raw material, divided into separate records for each manufactured article, are maintained on magnetic tape. These records contain the data shown in Table 4-11.

Table 4-11

Item Description	COBOL Name
File name	STD-FILE
Record name	STD-CØST-RECØRD
Record contents:	
Raw material inventory number	PART-NØ
Inventory number of finished unit on which used	FIN-UNIT-NØ
Number of pieces of raw material required per finished unit	STD-PIECES
Standard cost per piece of raw material	STD-CØST-PIECE

As raw materials are issued to production, records are prepared showing the number of pieces issued and other data. These issue records, also on magnetic tape, contain the data shown in Table 4-12.

Table 4-12

Item Description	COBOL Name
File name	ACT-WIP-FILE
Record name	ACTUAL-MATERIALS-ISSUES
Record contents:	
Production job number, to which raw materials are issued	WIP-JØB-NØ
Inventory number of raw material issued	PART-NØ -ISSUED
Inventory number of finished unit on which raw material is to be used	FIN-UNIT-NUM
Number of pieces of raw material issued and used	ACT-PIECES
Number of finished units manufactured, this job	ACT-PIECES-MFG

Output records showing the standard cost of the finished units produced are to be prepared, as indicated in Table 4-13.

Table 4-13

Item Description	COBOL Name
File name	STANDARD-MAT-CØST
Record name	STD-MAT-RCD
Record contents:	
Production job number	JØB-NØ
Inventory number of finished unit	FIN-INV-NØ
Number of finished units manufactured	FINISHED-UNITS
Standard material cost per finished unit	UNIT-STD-CØST
Standard cost for all units produced on this job	STANDARD-JØB
Excess of actual cost over standard cost	VARIANCE-ØVER
Excess of standard cost over actual cost	VARIANCE-UNDER

The standard cost file contains records showing all standard material costs for all products customarily manufactured by the company. Not all of these will be active at one time. Therefore, reading from the two input files must take place as follows:

First, a record should be read from the actual issues file. Then a record from the standard file should be read. Since the latter is arranged by items of finished product, the code number of the finished unit should be checked from each record. If these do not agree and the number from the standard file is smaller, another standard record should be read. If they do not agree and the number from the standard file is larger, an error condition exists, and the program should stop, display the message ERRØR IN FINISHED UNIT NUMBER, and then return and read from the actual production file.

If the finished unit numbers agree, the program should then check the inventory number of the raw material involved. The program should prepare an output record if these agree; otherwise, tests should be made in a manner similar to those used in checking finished product numbers. The message RAW MATERIAL NUMBERS DØ NØT AGREE should be displayed if the numbers fail to agree and that from the standard file is larger, after which the program should return to read an actual production record.

Preparation of an output record involves the following steps:

a) WIP-JØB-NØ should be moved to the production job number field of the output record.

b) FIN-UNIT-NØ should be moved to FIN-INV-NØ.

c) ACT-PIECES-MFG should be moved to FINISHED-UNITS.

d) UNIT-STD-CØST should be calculated by multiplying the number of raw material pieces required per unit of finished product by the standard cost per piece of raw material.

e) STANDARD-JØB should reflect the standard unit cost for all finished units reported in the record.

f) The cost of the number of raw material pieces actually used should be calculated as ACTUAL, an independent data element. This should be compared with the standard cost of the finished units produced. If ACTUAL is greater than STANDARD-JØB, the difference should be reported as VARIANCE-ØVER, and VARIANCE-UNDER should be set to zero. If the reverse is true, the difference should be reported as VARIANCE-UNDER, and VARIANCE-ØVER should be set to zero.

g) The following should be accumulated from all processed records and displayed when processing is complete: (1) the total of all actual costs as defined in item f, above, as TØT-ACTUAL; (2) the total of all variances over standard, as TØT-VARIANCE-ØVER; (3) the total of all variances under standard, as TØT-VARIANCE-UNDER; and (4) the total of all standard costs, as TØT-JØB-STANDARDS.

CHAPTER 5

COBOL CODING: THE IDENTIFICATION, ENVIRONMENT, AND DATA DIVISIONS

Programs are ultimately readied for compilation by writing them on special forms which are then transcribed onto punched cards or some other machine-sensible form of data input. The process of writing the program is known as coding. If the program's developmental phases—determining process requirements, defining data needs, and preparing logical flow charts—have been executed properly, coding should be a matter of routine. However, a number of concise rules must be followed in the coding process. The proper procedures for coding programs are covered in this and the next chapter.

COBOL ORGANIZATION

A COBOL program is divided into four basic divisions. Three of these, the identification, environment, and data divisions, will be discussed in this chapter. The last, the procedure division, will be covered in Chapter 6.

Program Structure

The broadest segment of a COBOL program is the division. Sections are used as segments of divisions, and they may be further divided into paragraphs.

Divisions, sections, and paragraphs are named. Divisions and sections have fixed names, and these must be used by the programmer without change. Most paragraph names may be supplied by the programmer, although a few are required.

The COBOL language provides for sentences, and statements, within paragraphs. As these may be most easily seen in the procedure division, discussion of these structural levels is deferred to Chapter 6.

Using the Coding Form

Several sample COBOL programs may be found in Appendix B (page 225). These have been prepared on standard COBOL coding forms. A brief inspection of this form will indicate certain basic rules governing its use.

Each line on the form corresponds to a single punched card, and each line will be transcribed to a card as the program is readied for translation. However, not all spaces on the form (or card columns) are available for coding instructions.

The first three spaces are used for recording the page number. Spaces 4, 5, and 6 are used for line numbers.

Space 7 in the form is used for signaling a continuation of a command, indicated by a hyphen. Further consideration of the continuation is postponed to Chapter 6, inasmuch as the matter continued is usually a part of the procedure division.

Programs are actually coded in the remainder of the form. It will be noted, then, that spaces 8 through 72 are available for use in coding. A single character, whether punctuation, parenthesis, arithmetic sign, or datum, is written in a space.

Two margins may be seen in the form. The first, called the A margin, is set at space 8. The other, or B margin, is set at space 12.

Division and section names are always written at the A margin. They are followed immediately by a period, and the remainder of the line is left blank. Division and section names always contain the word DIVISIØN or SECTIØN, respectively.

Paragraph names also begin at the A margin and are followed by a period and at least one blank space, in that order, but the remainder of the line may also be used. With a few exceptions, which are noted when appropriate, paragraph names may be chosen by the programmer.

These requirements may be seen in Illustration 1 of Appendix B. Line 06, on page 1, for example, contains the name ENVIRØNMENT DIVISIØN. Line 07 contains the name CØNFIGURATIØN SECTIØN. These division and section names, respectively, occupy a line to themselves. On the other hand, line 08 contains a paragraph name SØURCE-CØMPUTER, followed by a period and the paragraph contents, IBM-7040.

Paragraph contents are written starting at the B margin. It will be seen that most of the program coding, except significant names, uses this margin.

The remainder of this chapter is devoted to the coding requirements of the first three COBOL divisions. Great attention must be given to the use of coding sheets, margin alignments, and punctuation in each entry discussed.

THE IDENTIFICATION DIVISION

The identification division is the shortest of the major COBOL program segments. It allows the programmer to assign the program a name and to set out other information serving to identify the program, its writer, and its function. Lines 01 through 05 of the first programming example in Appendix B contain the identification division for the particular program. It appears as follows:

```
A   B
IDENTIFICATIØN DIVISIØN.
PRØGRAM-ID. SALES-ACCØUNTING.
AUTHØR. F. A. MCCAMERØN.
REMARKS. EXAMPLE 1. THIS IS DRAWN FRØM THE EXTENDED
      ILLUSTRATIØN ØF CHAPTER 3.
```

The identification division is not divided into sections. Instead, it consists of one or more paragraphs. The only required paragraph is the PRØGRAM-ID, in which the program must be given a name. This may be any word meeting regular COBOL requirements. This name is associated with the program during compilation, and serves to identify the compiled program and its diagnostics, or machine-prepared comments.

The other two paragraphs shown in this illustration, AUTHØR and REMARKS, are optional. Other paragraphs which may be included are DATE-WRITTEN and DATE-CØMPILED. Each of the optional paragraphs may contain one or more sentences and must end with a period. In each instance, if an optional paragraph is to be included, it must be named just as specified here.

THE ENVIRONMENT DIVISION

This program segment has a dual purpose. First, it defines the computer equipment used to compile the program, and for which it is being translated. The second function is to relate program files with specific computer input-output units.

As may be seen on line 06 of the Illustration 1 in Appendix B, this program segment is begun by the name ENVIRØNMENT DIVISIØN, printed on a separate line and followed by a period. The division then is subdivided into two sections, each with its own heading. The first section, called the CØNFIGURATIØN SECTIØN, contains two paragraphs. The first paragraph, SØURCE-CØMPUTER, sets out the computer to be used in making the compilation. The second, ØBJECT-CØMPUTER, names the computer for which compilation is being made. The entries shown are for the IBM 7040; each computer has its particular entry, which will be described in its reference manual.

The second major section of this division is called the INPUT-OUTPUT SECTIØN. Here, a required paragraph called FILE-CØNTRØL assigns each file used in the program to a specific input or output unit of the computer. The names used to designate specific input-output units for a certain machine will be supplied by that computer's manual. When COBOL is used with the IBM 7040, for example, IN refers to the system's input unit and ØU to the system's output unit. Other units carry similar designations.

Each file used in the program is assigned to a computer unit in a separate sentence which reads "SELECT file-name ASSIGN TØ unit-name." These file names are, of course, those used in the data and procedure divisions to govern the flow of data into and from the computer. More than one file may be assigned to the same computer input-output unit, but this is not usually desirable.

The environment division of Illustration 1, Appendix B, is copied below for ease of reference. Attention should be paid to program names, margins, and punctuation, all of which are required as shown.

```
A   B
ENVIRØNMENT DIVISIØN.
CØNFIGURATIØN SECTIØN.
SØURCE-CØMPUTER. IBM-7040.
ØBJECT-CØMPUTER. IBM-7040.
INPUT-ØUTPUT SECTIØN.
FILE-CØNTRØL. SELECT SALES-FILE ASSIGN TØ IN.
    SELECT ØUT-FILE ASSIGN TØ ØU.
```

THE DATA DIVISION

The data division is usually much longer than the identification or environment divisions. This division has a number of functions. It sets out, or defines, those parts of the computer's main memory which may be used by the program and assigns data names to all these areas. It indicates the required size of each storage area, and the type of data to be stored therein. The data division also shows the relationships between file, record, group, and data names, indicating the grouping of certain data and the independence of other fields. Finally, this division is used to set up any constant values required by the program.

Naming and Ordering Data

All data names used by the program must be set out in the data division, and the nature and size of the field must be shown. This requirement, known as field definition, applies to all names related to data read in, computed, or written out. It also includes any areas used for temporary storage, subscripts, or PERFØRM indexes. It must be remembered that the program has access only to those parts of the computer's memory which are called for here, by specifying names and field sizes.

Furthermore, the order of data must be indicated. Items associated with one another must be related. Other data items must be specified as independent. This is done also in this program division.

Indicating Data Order. Data elements may exist as grouped or ungrouped items. In the process of defining fields, the proper grouping of items is also indicated. This is accomplished by the use of level numbers.

Level numbers: Grouped data. The file is the broadest category of data and is assigned the special level indicator FD to set it apart from other organizational levels. Records, the next broadest category, is always assigned the level number 01. Data groups and elements within records may be assigned any level number from 02 through 49.

Data elements independent of one another should be assigned the same level number. Elements belonging to a group should be assigned a level number larger than that assigned the group name.

For example, assume that a file called EMPLØYEE-MASTER contains records called EMPLØYEE-DATA. Each of these contains the following:

```
EMPLØYEE-NAME
SS-NUMBER
WØRK-CØDE:[1]
  WØRK-DIVISIØN
  SHØP
  WØRK-LØCATIØN
```

These items could be assigned level numbers as follows:

```
FD  EMPLØYEE-MASTER ...
01  EMPLØYEE-DATA.
    02  EMPLØYEE-NAME ...
    02  SS-NUMBER ...
    02  WØRK-CØDE.
        03  WØRK-DIVISIØN ...
        03  SHØP...
        03  WØRK-LØCATIØN ...
```

Thus the file status of EMPLØYEE-MASTER is clearly indicated by its FD level number, just as 01 clearly defines EMPLØYEE-DATA as a record name. Remaining fields consist of data elements or groups. In each instance, those fields with 02 level numbers are independent of one another, while each exists within its associated record and file. WØRK-CØDE, a group name, is subdivided into WØRK-DIVISIØN, SHØP, and WØRK-LØCATIØN. Each carries an 03 level number, indicating that it is a member of the preceding 02-level group name but is independent of its fellow group members.

The program illustrations in Appendix B provide further examples of level numbers and their use. These should be reviewed carefully.

Level numbers: Independent data elements. Some data elements do not belong to any data organization. These, called independent elements, all carry the level number 77. This level number is reserved for use in this capacity.

---

[1]The name of a data group comprising WØRK-DIVISIØN, SHØP, and WØRK-LØCATIØN.

Level numbers: Condition names. Certain conditionals may require that a value be assigned to each possible alternative and that each alternative be given a name in the data division. When this occurs, the condition names are assigned the special level number 88. This condition will be explained more fully later in this chapter and illustrated in Chapter 6, dealing with the procedure division.

Defining Data Nature and Field Size

Every data element must be defined as to nature—numeric, alphabetic, or alphameric—and size. This is another function of the data division.

Defining the Field's Nature. The symbols used to indicate the nature of data to be stored in a data element are:

Type of Data	Symbol
Alphabetic	A
Alphameric	X
Numeric	9

Of course, the symbols used to indicate field nature only show the type of character which may be stored. The character itself is a result of data read, computed, or moved into the storage area.

A field must be defined as only one type of the list above. A data element may not be partly alphabetic and partly numeric, for example. Particular field characteristics are discussed below.

1. Alphabetic data. A field described as alphabetic may contain as data only letters (A-Z) and spaces. No numerals or special characters may be included. This sometimes leads to errors, as when an attempt is made to store an address containing numbers, or data containing punctuation, in an area described as alphabetic. Generally, when a data field might contain nonalphabetic characters, it should be described as alphameric.

2. Alphameric data. A field defined as type X, or alphameric, may contain any character in the COBOL set. This includes letters, numbers, special characters, and blanks. It is certainly the safest form of data description where prediction of data type is difficult or where mixed characters may be expected.

However, data defined in this manner may not be used in computation, even though they may happen to be entirely numeric. Only certain types of numerically defined data may be used as a factor in arithmetic computations.

3. Numeric data. This type of data is further divided into two subtypes: computational and report. The first is used in computation, as the name implies. It is defined by the character 9, with optional characters S

(for sign) and V (for assumed decimal point) also used. The second type is used for output and ordinarily contains certain editing symbols which make the field unsuitable for computational use. It is also defined by the character 9, but several editing symbols may also appear. The matter of numeric computational and report fields is discussed at length as a part of the PICTURE clause, below.

Defining the Field's Size. The size of a data field is indicated by the number of times its defining character is shown. Repeating the letter A three times would indicate a three-position alphabetic field, for example. If the field is so long that repeating its definition character is undesirable, the size may be indicated by a number in parentheses immediately following the character. When this method of writing is used, the defining symbol must be followed by the left parenthesis, then the numeral and right parenthesis, without any blanks.

The PICTURE Clause

The actual assignment of nature and size to a field is executed by a statement following the field name. This is known as the PICTURE clause and consists of the word PICTURE, followed by the appropriate description.

This clause may be used only at the element level. No data group may be so defined. On the other hand, each data element must be described by a PICTURE.

Alphabetic and Alphameric Data. The definition of alphabetic and alphameric fields is quite simple. Each involves only the term PICTURE and the appropriate number of A's or X's. An example of alphabetic definition may be seen in Illustration 1 of Appendix B, where, on line 19, page 1, is found the following entry:

```
02   CUS-NAME        PICTURE   A(20).
```

The next line illustrates the definition of an alphameric item, as follows:

```
02   C-NUM        PICTURE X(5).
```

The PICTURE clause is separated from the data name by at least one space, and a space is similarly found between the word PICTURE and the defining symbols.

Numeric Data. Because numeric data may be either computational or report, and may contain either implied or editing symbols, the associated PICTURE clause is not so simple as that used with other data types. The field description of both kinds of numeric data is discussed below.

1. Computational numeric data. Numeric data items to be used in computation may contain only the numbers 0-9. Therefore the field in which they are stored may not allow any other character (including spaces) to be represented.

At the same time, values used in computation must obviously be allowed to reflect a decimal point, and they must be signed so that positive values may be distinguished from negative amounts. These requirements are met by reflecting, in the PICTURE clause, the use and location of assumed sign and decimal point.

a. The Assumed Sign. The presence of an assumed sign is indicated by the letter S shown in the first character in the PICTURE clause of a computational numeric field. There must not be a space between the S and the leading 9 which defines the field as numeric. Unless this letter (S) is present in the PICTURE clause, the data field will be considered unsigned, and negative values will not be recognized as such. For illustrative purposes, assume that the amount -123 is to be stored at a data location called FIELD-A. If FIELD-A has been defined as PICTURE 999, the value will be stored as 123, an unsigned value which will be assumed to be positive. However, if FIELD-A has been defined as PICTURE S999, the value will be properly stored as -123.

The use of the assumed sign does not affect positive numbers. For example, the value 123 stored at FIELD-A, defined as PICTURE S999, would appear as 123.

b. The Assumed Decimal Point. Data to be used in computation may not contain an actual decimal point. Instead, the proper location of the decimal point is indicated by description of the field in which the element is stored. This is done by using a V in the PICTURE clause. This may appear between or at the left of data positions.

Suppose, for example, that the value 123.45 is to be read into the computer as FIELD-A, where it is to be used for computational purposes. The value would be written in the input record as 12345, no mention being made of the decimal place. FIELD-A would be defined as PICTURE 999V99. This sets out the field as having three positions to the left of the assumed decimal point and two to the right. Thus, when the value is read in, it will be stored as 12345, but the decimal point will be considered to lie at the proper place.

c. Illustrations of Numeric Computational Items. The first five illustrations of Table 5-1 are concerned with numeric computational items. Example 1 shows that when an item is read in, an assumed decimal point is assigned according to the requirements of the PICTURE clause. The second indicates the importance of digital placement in the input field, thus controlling the magnitude actually stored. Example 3 reflects the use of the minus symbol when signed fields are used.

Examples 4 and 5 treat computed values. Example 4 reflects the truncation of low-order positions which occurs when the number of decimal places in the value exceed those in the receiving field. Example 5 shows the effect of an overflow, achieved when attempting to store a value with more significant digits to the left of the decimal point than the receiving field provides for. Truncation of the most significant positions will occur unless the SIZE ERRØR test is used.

d. Storage of numeric literals. Limitations on the presence of signs and decimals in the definition of numeric computational data items in no way restricts their use with numeric literals. In these, a negative sign may appear as the left-most character, and a decimal point may appear to the left of or between any significant digits. Example 6 in Table 5-1 illustrates this, showing that a sign and decimal point are accepted and converted to assumed symbols when a numeric literal is moved into a numeric computational data item. Example 7 shows that if no decimal point is present in the numeric literal, it is considered to be an integer and is stored accordingly.

2. Edited numeric data. Numeric data used in computation may not contain any character other than numerals. It is anticipated, however, that most COBOL programs will culminate in at least one printed report, to be used as a standard business communication. An output mode more readable than that provided by numeric computational characters is required for useful, intelligible reporting. Improved output is obtained by adding to the standard numeric characters certain editing symbols.

These symbols are never used with input fields. Instead, they are incorporated in the field description following the term PICTURE in output data elements and, when writing occurs, become a part of the written data.

The most frequently used editing symbols are:

Dollar sign[2]	$
Space	Z
Period	.
Comma	,
Sign[2]	+ or -
Account symbol	DR or CR

a. Dollar Sign. The dollar sign may be incorporated in the PICTURE clause by writing it immediately to the left of the 9 indicating the most significant numeric position of the field. When used, this character causes the dollar mark to be printed on the output record. Examples 8 and 9 of Table 5-1 show the use of the dollar mark.

The dollar mark may be "floated" in the output PICTURE clause by repeating it in several of the adjacent left numeric positions. This will cause the dollar mark nearest the most significant position of the output field to be printed, and positions to its left will be blank. The effect of the floating dollar sign may be seen in examples 10, 11, and 12. Example 10

[2] These symbols may be "floated" or moved to the position immediately to the left of the most significant digit in the output data.

shows the dollar sign floated to its right-most possible position, placing it immediately next to the first significant digit of the data element. Example 11 illustrates, on the other hand, the printing of a dollar mark unfloated. Example 12 illustrates the point that even though floating dollar signs are shown in certain numeric positions, they do not prevent the writing of numeric data when the data element is so large as to require the space. As indicated in example 13, when floating dollar signs are used, the computer must preserve the left-most one as a symbol, and this may not be used as a numeric position. This is also true of other floating symbols.

b. Space. Spaces may be introduced in numeric output fields in lieu of zeros (a process known as zero suppression) by placing the letter Z in the numeric position. These will cause zeros to the left of the first significant digit to be suppressed; they will not affect any other numeral, nor will they suppress zeros which are preceded by nonzero numerals. Examples of this character's use may be seen in a number of illustrations in Table 5-1, such as numbers 11, 14, and 15.

c. Decimal Point. A numeric output field may contain one decimal point. This may appear to the left of or between any two numeric characters, or characters used in place of numeric symbols (specifically, the dollar sign when used as a floating symbol, and the Z). Examples 8 through 24 of Table 5-1 present the decimal point as an output character. Examples 15 and 16 show that when the number of spaces in the output field do not agree with the number of spaces in the data, either decimal truncation or an overflow occurs, as appropriate.

d. Comma. The comma may be used in numeric output fields for the separation of numeric positions. It is used for this purpose in examples 8 through 24 of Table 5-1. It may be noted that where no significant digit appears in positions to the left of the comma (see examples 10 and 11, and others), that character is suppressed.

e. Plus or Minus Sign. The plus or minus sign may be used as either the first or the last character in the PICTURE description. When the minus sign is used and the data element is negative, a minus will be written in the required position; a positive data element will be unsigned. Use of a plus sign will cause that sign to be written with a positive value, while a minus value will be written with a negative sign. Note that presence of a plus sign in the PICTURE clause forces a sign to be written for each value, positive or negative, while presence of a minus sign does not write a sign for positive values. Examples 12, 14, and 15 of Table 5-1 demonstrate these points.

The plus and minus signs may also be used as floating characters. When they are so used, they must be the left-most characters in the PICTURE description. They will cause zero suppression, as does the floating dollar sign, and will be written when appropriate in the right-most suppressed position. As with regular plus and minus signs, these symbols used as floating characters will cause a minus sign, or a plus or minus sign, to be written. Examples 17 through 20 illustrate floating signs.

f. Account Symbols. The last editing characters to be introduced are the account symbols DR and CR. Each of these occupy two positions, and each must be specified as the right-most characters in the PICTURE description. The symbol specified will be printed beside a negative value, while spaces are left beside positive values. These may be seen in examples 21-24 of Table 5-1.

Determining the Number of Characters in a Field

It is sometimes necessary to determine exactly the number of characters in a field. Some computers require that input and output files state the number of characters in each record. Report spacing also makes important the ability to determine field size correctly.

Alphabetic and Alphameric Fields. Counting the exact field size of alphabetic and alphameric data items is quite simple. They always occupy one space for every character position, including blanks.

Numeric Fields. The size of a numeric field is not so directly ascertained, however. Certain symbols may be present in the field but may not require a position of storage. These are described below, as computational and report fields are discussed.

1. Computational items. Computational fields are only as large as the number of numeric positions specified. Neither the assumed decimal place nor the sign occupies a position of storage. Therefore a field defined as PICTURE S9(5)V99 occupies seven positions.

2. Report items. Numeric report fields occupy at least as many memory positions as the number of digits specified. In addition, some editing characters require additional storage space, while others do not.

Certain editing characters are referred to as insertion characters; that is, they are inserted in the numeric field. These require that storage spaces be set aside for them.

Insertion characters include the period, the comma, and the DR and CR editing symbols. The DR and CR symbols require two positions of storage; the others only one.

The dollar sign and positive and negative signs are also insertion characters when they are specified at some location other than one at which a numeral would ordinarily be written, that is, when they are not used as floating symbols.

Other editing symbols are replacement characters. These do not require extra storage spaces but replace a portion of the regular numeric field. The Z is such a symbol, specifying that spaces be used in place of leading zeros. When floated, the dollar mark and positive-negative signs are also replacement characters.

Table 5-1

The PICTURE Clause Illustrated

Data Source	Example	Value*	Entered into PICTURE	Will Be Stored as:*
		Examples of Computational Clauses		
Read in	1.	123456	999V999	123‸456
	2.	000001	999V999	000‸001
	3.	0100$\overline{0}$*	S999V999	001‸00$\overline{0}$
Computed	4.	123‸4567	999V999	123‸456†
	5.	1234‸567	999V999	‡
Moved	6.	-.123	S999V999	000‸12$\overline{3}$
	7.	125	999V999	125‸000
		Examples of Editing Symbols		
Computed	8.	1234‸56	$9,999.99	$1,234.56
	9.	0001‸23	$9,999.99	$0,001.23
	10.	0001‸23	$$,$$9.99	$1.23
	11.	0001‸23	$Z,ZZ9.99	$ 1.23
	12.	1234‸5$\overline{6}$	$$,$$9.99-	$1,234.56-
	13.	12345‸6	$$,$$9.99	‡
	14.	‸123456	$Z,ZZ9.99+	$ 0.12+
	15.	123‸456	$Z,ZZ9.99-	$ 123.45
	16.	123456‸	$Z,ZZ9.99	‡
	17.	0001‸2$\overline{3}$	-,--9.99	-1.23
	18.	0001‸23	-,--9.99	1.23
	19.	0001‸23	+,++9.99	+1.23
	20.	0001‸2$\overline{3}$	+,++9.99	-1.23
	21.	1234‸5$\overline{6}$	$Z,ZZ9.99DR	$1,234.56DR
	22.	123‸456	$Z,ZZ9.99DR	$ 123.45
	23.	123‸45$\overline{6}$	$Z,ZZ9.99CR	$ 123.45CR
	24.	1234‸56	$Z,ZZ9.99CR	$1,234.56

*Implied decimal points are indicated as carets in the proper position; implied signs as a minus sign over the low-order digit. Positive values are unsigned.

† Unless round option is used. See Chapter 6.

‡ The contents of the receiving area will depend on whether or not the SIZE ERRØR option is used. See Chapter 6.

Special Clauses

The PICTURE clause is by far the most important one used in the data division. It is used with all elementary items and is responsible for defining the field's nature and size. At the same time, two other clauses have substantial special use and merit consideration.

The VALUE Clause

This, written at the elementary level after the PICTURE statement, may be used to attach a particular value to a data name. When it is used, it must agree in size and nature with the PICTURE clause given for the same item.

The following examples show the VALUE clause used with numeric, alphabetic, and alphameric fields:

1. 02 ITEM-A PICTURE 999V99 VALUE 123.45.
2. 02 ITEM-B PICTURE A(24) VALUE 'ACCUMULATED DEPRECIATIØN'.
3. 02 ITEM-C PICTURE X(10) VALUE 'AMØUNT - $'.

Example 1 attaches the numeric literal 123.45 to data name ITEM-A. Note that while the decimal point is shown as assumed in the PICTURE clause, making the field eligible for use in computation, it is specified in the VALUE Clause. This is a numeric literal and may show the decimal point and/or the sign, as required.

A nonnumeric literal is specified as the value of ITEM-B, shown above. Note that the nonnumeric literal is enclosed in single quotations marks, as required, and contains exactly the number of characters specified in the PICTURE clause.

The third example shows the use of the nonnumeric literal in the assignment of a value to an alphameric field. In this literal, any character in the COBOL set is permitted.

As described in detail later in this chapter, the VALUE clause is used mainly in the working storage and constant sections of the data division. It can be used in the file section only when defining condition names.

The ØCCURS Clause

When data arrays, or matrices, are used, the array is given a name, and its elements are referred to by subscripting the array elements. Arrays are defined in the data division by citing the array name and its appropriate PICTURE clause and then attaching the clause "ØCCURS literal TIMES." This commands the computer to allocate sufficient memory space to store the array when the program is executed.

The ØCCURS clause is explained more fully in Chapter 7 when the nature and use of matrices are discussed.

SECTIONS OF THE DATA DIVISION

The data division is divided into three sections. These need not all be used, and any unused section is simply not cited in the program. However, the sections which are used must appear in the division in the order of their introduction below.

The following discussion sets out the exact form of entries in the data division. They must be used just as described. For convenience of discussion, certain presentation conventions are observed. These are as follows:

1. Words in capital letters are COBOL words; they are required exactly as specified.

2. Underlined COBOL words are required; others are optional.

3. Words shown in small letters indicate information to be provided by the programmer.

4. Matter included in square brackets ([ ]) is optional.

5. The presence of three dots means that the preceding clause may be repeated, if desired.

6. When matter is enclosed in shaped brackets ({ }), one of the included elements must be chosen, at the programmer's option.

7. All punctuation is required as shown.

The File Section

As has been seen previously, almost all data input and output are handled through files. This section is used to describe each file and its contents.

The File Description. The file proper is assigned the level number FD, and this must be written at the A margin of the coding paper. The level number must be followed by at least one space; then follows the name of the file. Several clauses must be included in the file description. They may be written in any order.

First, the name of the record (or records) in the file must be given. This is done by inclusion of the clause "DATA RECØRD(S) $\left\{\begin{matrix} \text{IS} \\ \text{ARE} \end{matrix}\right\}$ record-name-1 , record-name-2, ..." Ordinarily, only one record type is found within a file, and so the word RECØRD is used as a singular noun, and IS is used as the verb.

The second clause included in the file description sets out the status of file labels. This appears as follows: "LABEL RECØRD(S) $\begin{Bmatrix} \text{ARE} \\ \text{IS} \end{Bmatrix}$ $\begin{Bmatrix} \underline{\text{STANDARD}} \\ \underline{\text{ØMITTED}} \end{Bmatrix}$." The clause refers to a protective device sometimes used with magnetic tape to prevent the misuse of a reel. If labels are used, the clause should cite STANDARD; otherwise, the statement "LABEL RECØRD IS ØMITTED" should be written. This text assumes that labels are not used.

Other clauses may be required for a particular computer. For example, the IBM 7040 requires that a clause indicating the number of characters per record be included, and that this number always be some multiple of 6 and not less than 18. This clause appears as follows: "RECØRD CØNTAINS integer CHARACTERS." "Integer" should, of course, be the number of characters in the record. This is determined by counting characters, as described previously.

The description of a given file must contain the appropriate clauses without a period. A description may occupy more than one line, all lines after the first starting at the B margin. The file description must be terminated by a period. Each example in Appendix B includes several file descriptions and should be inspected.

The Record Description. Each file must contain at least one record. This is described immediately following the file description.

The record must be assigned the level number 01 written at the A margin. This must be followed by at least one space and the name of the record.

If the record is an elementary item (not further subdivided), it must contain a PICTURE clause setting out its size and nature. This is occasionally the case, and an illustration of such a description may be seen in Appendix B on page 1, line 24, of the third illustration (page 235). More frequently, however, the record name is also a group name, and so is not assigned a PICTURE clause but is instead terminated by a period. Most of the record descriptions in Appendix B are of this type.

Data Groups. Data groups are defined in much the same way as record names, except that they must be assigned some level number other than 01. The level number and group name are specified, followed by a period. The PICTURE clause is not allowed at the group level. The VALUE clause would also be inappropriate, although the ØCCURS clause may be used when arrays are defined.

Data Items. Each data element within the record, whether grouped or not, must be defined. This definition includes an appropriate level number, the data name, and the PICTURE clause. Following the PICTURE clause may appear the ØCCURS clause, when appropriate. The VALUE clause may be used in the file section also, but only when condition names are defined. This process is described in Chapter 6.

Spacing the Entries. Each entry in the file section must occupy a separate line, and each must be terminated by a period. File and record descriptions must begin at the A margin; other descriptions may begin here, or they may be indented. Indenting four spaces for each hierarchical level makes the program much easier to read than when no indention is used.

FILLER. This is a pseudo data element. Its name is provided by the COBOL language, and it is used to absorb unused space in records. Like any other element, it must be defined by a PICTURE clause.

The term may be used to spread data items by providing space between them. This is frequently done when output records which are to be printed are prepared, and makes for a more attractive and readable report.

FILLER is also used to force records to contain a proper number of characters. For example, all records processed by the IBM 7040 must contain some multiple of six characters. If a record would normally contain 40 characters, for instance, the clause "FILLER PICTURE XX" might be included to bring the record size to the required 42 (a multiple of 6). By the same token, an extremely short record might be assigned sufficient FILLER to bring it to a required minimum length.

Since it is desirable to define printed lines as containing the maximum number of characters a line may contain, FILLER is often used to absorb any unused spaces. These uses of the element may be seen in almost all record descriptions in Appendix B, as well as in the example of a file description which follows.

Example of a File Description. The output file of Illustration 1, Appendix B, has been arranged for printing. Its fields have been edited, FILLER has been interspersed between data elements, and the record length has been adjusted to 132 characters, the printer's line capacity. This file description is reproduced in Table 5-2 as an illustration. Other files may be seen in the Appendix.

The Working-Storage Section

The second major segment of the data division is the working-storage section. It is used to provide working areas when storage space is required in excess of that provided by the files. Two types of data may be found in this section.

Independent Data Items. Data elements not related to any other item are frequently needed in computations or for storage. These are known as independent items, and they are always assigned the special level number 77. These must be written first in the working storage section.

Most COBOL programs require a number of independent data elements as working areas. Arithmetic commands may use only computational numeric data as factors, meaning that many amounts computed as a part of some output file are unavailable as factors in subsequent computation. These factors must be computed as working storage amounts in unedited fields

Table 5-2

A File Description

```
FD   ØUT-FILE DATA RECØRD ØUTPUT-RECØRD LABEL RECØRD
     ØMITTED RECØRD CONTAINS 132 CHARACTERS.
01   ØUTPUT-RECØRD.
     02  FILLER                    PICTURE X(5).
     02  NAME                      PICTURE A(20).
     02  FILLER                    PICTURE X(5).
     02  T-DATE                    PICTURE 9(6).
     02  FILLER                    PICTURE X(5).
     02  UNITS-SØLD                PICTURE Z,Z99.
     02  FILLER                    PICTURE X(5).
     02  U-PRICE                   PICTURE $Z9.99.
     02  FILLER                    PICTURE X(5).
     02  SALES-PRICE               PICTURE $ZZZ,ZZ9.99.
     02  FILLER                    PICTURE X(5).
     02  SALES-TAX                 PICTURE $Z,ZZ9.99.
     02  FILLER                    PICTURE X(5).
     02  TØTAL-PRICE               PICTURE $ZZZ,ZZ9.99.
     02  FILLER                    PICTURE X(29).
```

if they are to be available later as computational elements. This problem is considered in detail in Chapter 6.

The VALUE clause may be used with independent data items. However, the ØCCURS clause may not be used. Of course, the field size and nature must be provided by a PICTURE clause.

Independent working storage areas are also used to define most subscripts, PERFØRM indexes, and areas for accumulating processing totals. There are, of course, a number of other uses to which this type of storage may be put.

Data Groups. It is sometimes necessary to design working storage areas consisting of associated data fields. Arrays are frequently constructed in this section. Furthermore, when headings are created for records which are to be printed, the records cannot be defined in the file section, and are instead described in working storage. Illustration 3 in Appendix B contains such a record description, LINE, on page 2.

Grouped data may use any level number 01 through 49. The 01 level number is used with the group name, and it may be used only once in a data group, in the same form as when it is assigned to a record name in the file section.

Items in working storage may be defined by the same clauses used in the file section. Each elementary item in a data group must have a PICTURE clause, and may have a VALUE and/or an ØCCURS clause. The VALUE clause is frequently used in defining working storage items, as this sets the original value of the data element. For example, if a data field must begin with a value of zero, it will be customarily defined as VALUE ZERØ in working storage.

The data division of Illustration 2, Appendix B, contains several independent working storage elements. Working storage entries which have their initial balance set to zero are shown in lines 24 and 25 on page 3 of this illustration.

Illustration 3 of Appendix B reflects the proper preparation of grouped working storage data. Data to be used in the output record are prepared here, on page 2. This illustration shows how columnar headings may be written when reports are prepared, a process which requires that the specified output record not contain any subdivisions, so that the heading and regular contents may be written through it. The complete process of preparing headings is described elsewhere.

The Constant Section

This program section is used to define any unchanging values and their associated data names. Each item here must have its value assigned by an attached VALUE clause; once so fixed, it may not be changed in the program. The section may be used to create independent data elements, or it may reflect the preparation of data groups.

As an example of the creation of an independent item in the constant section, assume that a number of computations are to be made, each dealing with the value of pi (3.1416). This can be done, of course, by including pi as a literal in the computational command; as, for instance, the command "CØMPUTE AREA = 3.1416 * RADIUS ** 2." It may also be done, however, by setting up the value of pi in the constant section by the following entry:

```
77 PI PICTURE 9V9999 VALUE 3.1416.
```

and then using the associated data name in the computation, as follows:

```
CØMPUTE AREA = PI * RADIUS ** 2.
```

The second form serves the same purpose as the literal. The only difference is in the fact that in the second case, pi is defined as a <u>named constant</u> in the constant section, after which its name may be used in computation in lieu of the numeric quantity. This frequently makes the computational commands easier to understand.

A "value" may also be associated with a data item defined as alphabetic or alphameric. This makes possible the creation of report headings as grouped data in the constant section. Pages 2 and 3 of Illustration 3, Appendix B, show this process. It may be seen here that the group name HEAD-1, appearing on line 18, is given the level number 01. Data items within the heading are given 02 level numbers, identifying them as part of the heading. Each item is defined by its PICTURE clause; then the VALUE clause specifies the exact wording of the caption.

Level numbers follow the same rules in this section as in working storage. Independent items must all be assigned the level number 77; grouped items follow the rules of record preparation.

SUMMARY

Three basic parts of the COBOL language have been introduced in this chapter: the identification, the environment, and the data divisions. Of these, the third is by far the most complex. Each is important, however, and its role must be understood before the language can be mastered.

The Identification Division

This, the shortest of the four divisions, has as its objective the proper identification of the program. The program's author may also be named and various facts about its creation set out. The one essential, however, is that the paragraph PRØGRAM-ID be completed properly.

The Environment Division

This program segment has two major functions. The first is to identify the computer on which the program compilation is to be made and the machine for which the object program is being prepared. The second objective is to assign all input and output files to computer input-output units. The machine-sensible names of a computer's input-output units vary and must be obtained from the particular instrument's manual.

The Data Division

This division is much more complex than those mentioned above and may be the most elaborate of the entire program. Its general purpose is to spell out all data names used in the program, indicate their relation to one another, and define their nature and size.

The relationship between data names is indicated by the use of level numbers. The PICTURE clause used with data elements serves to indicate the size of each data field and whether it is to contain numeric, alphabetic, or alphameric data. The VALUE clause may be used to associate a specific value with a data name. The ∅CCURS clause is used to create space for one- or two-dimensional data arrays.

This division is divided into three sections. The first, called the file section, is used to define all files and their contents. It shows the association between files and records, and between records and data elements.

The working-storage section sets out storage areas not required for input or output, but nonetheless necessary for proper processing. The ∅CCURS clause is used here in conjunction with the PICTURE clause to set up arrays; the VALUE clause is often used to insure the initial value of a data field to be used in computation. Data items may be independent, in which instance they are assigned a special level number, or they may be grouped. In the latter instance, they are subject to the same rules of organization which govern the construction of records in the file section.

The constant section is used to create figurative constants or to set up groups of constants such as are frequently required as headings on output to be printed. Items in this section are subject to the same rules as those in working storage, to which is added the restriction that their value may not be changed by the program itself.

QUESTIONS AND PROBLEMS

1. What is the function of the identification division? Give its required and optional segments.

2. What are the major subdivisions of the environment division? What does each do?

3. What are the three classes of data? What symbols are used to represent them in the data division?

4. What are the sections of the data division? What functions are performed by each?

5. Give the three clauses used in defining data, and indicate the function of each.

6. What is the difference between numeric computational and report data?

7. Indicate how the value shown in the left column would appear if stored at a field with the PICTURE shown in the right column (see Table 5-3).

Table 5-3

	Value	Picture
Read as:		
	1234	99V99
	$169\bar{3}$	9(4)
	$169\bar{3}$	S999V9
Computed as:		
	$12_{\wedge}34$	ZZ.99
	$12_{\wedge}3\bar{4}$	$Z,ZZ9.99-
	$12_{\wedge}34$	9.99
	$12_{\wedge}34$	++++9.99
	$_{\wedge}1234$	$$,$$$.99
	$12_{\wedge}3\bar{4}$	$Z,ZZ9.99
	$_{\wedge}1234$	9999

8. List the errors in the file description which is presented below:

```
A    B
FE   INPUT DATA RECØRD NAME IS IN-RECØRD LABEL RECØRD NØT USED
RECØRD 88
     77   IN-RECØRD                PICTURE 88.
     02   NAME                     PICTURE A(20)XXX
     02   AMT                      VALUE 14.
     02   DESC-GRØUP               PICTURE 9 (25)
     03   DESC-A.
     03   DESC-B.
     03   DESC-C.
     01   FILL                     PICTURE A(18).
```

9. Given in Table 5-4 is a list of values and their appearance in storage. You are to supply the probable PICTURE clause used for the storage field. In instances where a storage error is indicated as an overflow or invalid character, indicate the probable cause or causes of the condition.

Table 5-4

	Value	Stored as:
1.	123‸456	$ 123.45600
2.	123‸456	00123‸45
3.	1234‸5$\bar{6}$	$ 1,234.56CR
4.	0012‸34	$ 12.34
5.	12345	*
6.	123‸4$\bar{5}$	123‸45
7.	123‸45	123.45+
8.	ABCDE	AB
9.	12‸3456	0012‸34
10.	12‸345$\bar{6}$	$ 0012.34-
11.	A. N. SMITH	A. N. SMITH
12.	ØNE DØLLAR ($1)	ØNE DØLLAR ($1)
13.	J. P. JØNES	†
14.	0012‸3$\bar{4}$	$ -12.34
15.	0000‸2$\bar{5}$	$ .25DR
16.	23‸45	†
17.	HENRY ADAMS	†
18.	‸12345	0
19.	ABCDE	ABCDE--- (- stands for space)
20.	$ 123.45	†

* Results in overflow.
† Attempts to store invalid character.

Prepare the identification, environment, and data divisions on COBOL coding paper for the following problems. Each problem is drawn from a previous chapter, as cited.

The following instructions should be observed for each problem:

Identification Division

PRØGRAM-ID is to cite the problem number, as, for example, PRØBLEM-10.

AUTHØR should cite the student's name.

Environment Division

Most problems have a single input file and a single output file. Unless otherwise instructed, the input file is to be assigned to IN and the output file to ØU.

Data Division

Input Files. Use FILLER when necessary to bring the record size to a multiple of six and to a minimum of 18 characters for the record.

Output Files. All records are to contain 132 characters, and all numeric fields are to be edited, unless otherwise indicated. Dollar marks should be shown beside monetary fields. Zeros should be suppressed to the left of the decimal point, if there is one, or to the left of the units position otherwise. Commas should be used as appropriate. Use five positions of FILLER at the beginning of the output record and between each data name in the record.

Working Storage. Fields are not to be edited unless specifically stated. Data items with an asterisk beside them are to be assigned an initial value of zero.

General. Field type specifies alphabetic, alphameric, numeric computational (abbreviated Num. Comp.), and numeric report (abbreviated Num. Rpt.). Specified field sizes include all positions except those occupied by insertion editing symbols in output items.

10. Prepare the divisions mentioned above for Problem 3-6 (page 55). Field names and sizes are given in Table 5-5 (see problem notes for group names).

Table 5-5

Item Description	Name	Field Type	Field Size	Field Places to Right of Decimal
Input file	PURCHASE-FILE			
Input record	PURCHASE-RECØRD			
Record contents:				
Item name	DESC	Alphabetic	20	
Supplier code	VENDØR	Alphameric	4	
Date received	DATE	Alphameric	6	
Purchase order number	PCH-NØ	Num. Comp.	6	0
Invoice number	INVØICE	Num. Comp.	5	0
Inventory class	CLS	Num. Comp.	2	0
Inventory group	GRØUP	Num. Comp.	3	0
Inventory item	ITEM	Num. Comp.	4	0
Purpose of purchase	PURPØSE	Num. Comp.	2	0
Number of units received	UNITS	Num. Comp.	5	0
Invoice cost	INV-CØST	Num. Comp.	7	2
Freight charge	FREIGHT	Num. Comp.	6	2
Tax on purchase	TAX	Num. Comp.	5	2
Output file	ØUT-FILE			
Output record	ØUT-RCD			
Record contents:				
Item name	ITEM-DESC	Alphabetic	20	
Reference data	ØUT-REF	Alphameric	11	0
Inventory number	INVEN-NUM	Alphameric	9	0
Number of units received	NØ-UNITS	Num. Rpt.	5	0
Total cost	TØTAL CØST	Num. Rpt.	8	2
Cost per unit	UNIT-CØST	Num. Rpt.	5	3
Sales price per unit	UNIT-SALES	Num. Rpt.	5	2
Sales value of order	ØRDER-SALES	Num. Rpt.	9	2
Items of independent working storage:				
Total cost	TC	Num. Comp.	8	2
Total invoice cost*	TØT-INV	Num. Comp.	10	2
Total freight charges*	TØT-FGT	Num. Comp.	8	2
Total tax*	TØT-TAX	Num. Comp.	7	2
Display field	DIS	Num. Rpt.	10	2

11. Prepare the divisions required for Problem 3-8 (page 58). Field names and sizes are shown in Table 5-6.

Table 5-6

Item Description	Name	Field Type	Field Size	Field Places to Right of Decimal
Input file	IN-FILE			
Input record	GRØSS-RCD			
Record contents:				
Name of inventory item	NAME-IN	Alphabetic	20	
Sales price marked	SALES-PRICE	Num. Comp.	4	2
Output file	ØUT-FILE			
Output record	NET-RCD			
Record contents:				
Name of inventory item	NAME-ØUT	Alphabetic	20	
New sales price	NEW-PRICE	Num. Rpt.	4	2
Excise tax eliminated	TAX-ØFF	Num. Rpt.	3	2
Items of independent working storage:				
New price	NP	Num. Comp.	4	2
Total old sales prices	T-SALES*	Num. Comp	6	2
Excise tax eliminated	T-TAX*	Num. Comp.	4	2
Total net sales prices	NET*	Num. Comp.	6	2
Display area	DIS	Num. Rpt.	6	2

12. Prepare the divisions required for Problem 3-9 (page 59). Field names and sizes are given in Table 5-7.

Table 5-7

Item Description	Name	Field Type	Field Size	Field Places to Right of Decimal
Input file	SALES-FILE			
Input record	SALES-RCD			
Record contents:				
Salesman's number	S-NØ	Num. Comp.	5	0
Sales price, with tax	SALES-PRICE	Num. Comp.	6	2
Output file	CØM-FILE			
Output record	CØM-RCD			
Record contents:				
Salesman's number	MAN-NØ	Num. Rpt.	5	0
Sales price, less tax	NET-PRICE	Num. Rpt.	6	2
Commission earned	CØMM	Num. Rpt.	5	2
Items of independent working storage:				
Sales price, less tax	NP	Num. Comp.	6	2
Commission earned	CØM	Num. Comp.	5	2
Total commission	TØT-CØM*	Num. Comp.	8	2
Display area	DIS	Num. Rpt.	8	2

13. Prepare the divisions mentioned above for Problem 3-10 (page 60). Field names and sizes are shown in Table 5-8.

Table 5-8

Item Description	Name	Field Type	Field Size	Field Places to Right of Decimal
Input file	NØTES			
Input record	NØTE-RCD			
Record contents:				
Note identification number	NØTE-ID	Num. Comp.	8	0
Month of creation	DATE	Num. Comp.	2	0
Interest rate	RATE	Num. Comp.	2	2
Face of note	AMØUNT	Num. Comp.	6	2
Output file	AC-INT			
Output record	INT-AMT			
Record contents:				
Note identification number	NØTE-REC-NØ	Num. Rpt.	8	0
Face of note	NØTE-AMØUNT	Num. Rpt.	6	2
Amount of accrued interest	INTEREST	Num. Rpt.	5	2
Items of independent working storage:				
Amount of accrued interest	ACC-INT	Num. Comp.	5	2
Total accrued interest*	TØTAL-INTEREST	Num. Comp.	7	2
Display area	DIS	Num. Rpt.	7	2

14. Prepare the divisions mentioned above for Problem 3-15 (page 65). Field names and sizes are given in Table 5-9.

Table 5-9

Item Description	Name	Field Type	Field Size	Field Places to Right of Decimal
Input file	RAW-DATA			
Input record	ACT-BAL			
Record contents:				
Account name	ACCØUNT	Num. Comp.	5	0
Amount	AMØUNT	Num. Comp.	6	2
Index number, original	INDEX	Num. Comp.	3	0
Output file	ADJ-DATA			
Output record	ADJ-BAL			
Record contents:				
Account name	ACCT	Num. Rpt.	5	0
Amount	ØRIG-AMT	Num. Rpt.	6	2
Adjusted amount	ADJ-AMT	Num. Rpt.	6	2
Items of independent working storage:				
Current index	CUR-INDEX	Num. Comp.	3	0
Adjustment area	ADJ	Num. Comp.	6	2
Adjusted amount †	A-AMT	Num. Comp.	6	2
Total of original amounts*	TØT-CØST	Num. Comp.	8	2
Total of all adjustments* †	TØT-ADJ	Num. Comp.	7	2
Total of adjusted amounts*	TØT-NEW	Num. Comp.	8	2
Display area †	DIS	Num. Rpt.	8	2

15. Prepare the divisions mentioned above for Problem 3-18 (page 67). Field names and sizes are shown in Table 5-10.

Table 5-10

Item Description	Name	Field		
		Type	Size	Places to Right of Decimal
Input file	CØST-FILE			
Input record	CØST-RCD			
Record contents:				
Job number	JØB-NØ	Num. Comp.	5	0
Standard labor rate/hour	S-RATE	Num. Comp.	3	2
Standard hours/unit	S-HRS	Num. Comp.	2	1
Standard labor cost/unit	S-CØST	Num. Comp.	3	2
Actual labor rate/hour	A-RATE	Num. Comp.	3	2
Number of units produced	UNITS	Num. Comp.	3	0
Hours worked	HØURS	Num. Comp.	3	1
Output file	VAR-FILE			
Output record	VAR-RCD			
Record contents:				
Job number	JØB-NUM	Num. Rpt.	5	0
Standard labor cost/unit	S-UNIT-CØST	Num. Rpt.	3	2
Number of units produced	P-UNITS	Num. Rpt.	3	0
Actual unit cost	A-UNIT-CØST	Num. Rpt.	4	2
Actual job cost	ACT-CØST	Num. Rpt.	7	2
Labor rate variance †	RATE-VAR	Num. Rpt.	6	2
Labor efficiency variance †	EFF-VAR	Num. Rpt.	6	2
Standard cost	STD-CØST	Num. Rpt.	7	2
Items of independent working storage:				
Total rate variances* †	TØT-RATE	Num. Comp.	7	2
Total efficiency variance* †	TØT-EFF	Num. Comp.	7	2
Total variance* †	TØT-VAR	Num. Comp.	8	2
Standard labor cost/unit	SCT	Num. Comp.	4	2
Actual labor cost/unit	ACT	Num. Comp.	4	2
Rate variance †	R-V	Num. Comp.	4	2
Efficiency variance †	E-V	Num. Comp.	4	2
Display area †	DIS	Num. Rpt.	8	2

† Field should be signed.

16. Prepare the divisions mentioned above for Problem 4-4 (page 77). Field names and sizes are shown in Table 5-11.

Table 5-11

Item Description	Name	Field		
		Type	Size	Places to Right of Decimal
Input file	SALES-FILE			
Input record	SALES-REC			
Record contents:				
Item number	ITEM-NØ	Alphameric	5	
Item name	ITEM-NAME	Alphabetic	20	
Unit sales price	UNIT-PRICE	Num. Comp.	4	2
Number of units sold	NØ-UNITS	Num. Comp.	3	0
Output file	EXT-FILE			
Output record	EXT-RCD			
Record contents:				
Item name	I-NAME	Alphabetic	20	
Sales amount	S-AMT	Num. Rpt.	6	2
Sales tax	TAX	Num. Rpt.	4	2
Total amount	TØTAL	Num. Rpt.	8	2
Items of independent working storage:				
Sales amount	SALES	Num. Comp.	6	2
Tax amount	TAX-AMT	Num. Comp.	4	2
Record count*	RCD-CNT	Num. Comp.	5	0
Total sales*	TØT-SALES	Num. Comp.	8	2
Total tax*	TØT-TAX	Num. Comp.	6	2
Total amounts*	TØT-AMT	Num. Comp.	8	2
Display area	DIS	Num. Rpt.	8	2

17. Prepare the divisions mentioned above for Problem 4-5 (page 108). Field names and sizes are given in Table 5-12.

Table 5-12

Item Description	Name	Field Type	Field Size	Field Places to Right of Decimal
Input file	IN-FILE			
Input record	TRANS-RCD			
Record contents:				
Account number	NUMBER	Num. Comp.	4	0
Actual expense	ACT-EXP	Num. Comp.	5	2
Budget allowance	BUD-EXP	Num. Comp.	5	2
Output file	ØUT-FILE			
Output record	ØUT-RCD			
Record contents:				
Account number	ACCT-NUM	Num. Rpt.	4	0
Message	MESSAGE	Alphabetic	19	
Percent actual over budget	ØVER	Num. Rpt.	5	2
Percent budget over actual	UNDER	Num. Rpt.	5	2
Items of independent working storage:				
Excess of actual over budget*	TØT-ØVER	Num. Comp.	7	2
Excess of budget over actual*	TØT-UNDER	Num. Comp.	7	2
Display area	DIS	Num. Rpt.	7	2
Difference between actual expense and budget allowance	DIFF	Num. Comp.	7	4

18. Prepare the divisions mentioned above for Problem 4-6 (page 109). Field names and sizes are shown in Table 5-13.

Table 5-13

Item Description	Name	Field		
		Type	Size	Places to Right of Decimal
Input file	PRDCT			
Input record	PR-RCD			
Record contents:				
Quantity of output	QTY	Num. Comp.	3	0
Items of independent working storage:				
Utility area*	CTR	Num. Comp.	6	0
Number of gallons	GAL	Num. Rpt.	5	0
Number of quarts	QT	Num. Rpt.	1	0
Number of ounces	ØZ	Num. Rpt.	2	0
Total production	TØT-PRØ	Num. Comp.	6	0

19. Prepare the divisions mentioned above for Problem 4-10 (page 110). Field names and sizes are given in Table 5-14.

Table 5-14

Item Description	Name	Field		
		Type	Size	Places to Right of Decimal
Input file	INV-FILE			
Input record	INV-RCD			
Record contents:				
Inventory number	IDENT	Num. Comp.	4	0
Kind of unit	TYPE	Num. Comp.	1	0
Number of units sold—current month	CUR-SALES	Num. Comp.	5	0
Number of units sold—last month	LAST-MØ	Num. Comp.	5	0
Number of units sold—previous month	PREV-MØ	Num. Comp.	5	0
Number of units on hand	UNITS	Num. Comp.	4	0
Reorder point	RØP	Num. Comp.	3	0
Storage capacity	CAP	Num. Comp.	4	0
Output file	ØRDER-FILE			
Output record	ØRDER-RECØRD			
Record contents:				
Inventory number	ID-NØ	Num. Rpt.	4	0
Kind of unit	UNIT-DESC	Alphabetic	10	
Number of units to be ordered	ØRDER	Num. Rpt.	5	0
Items of independent working storage:				
Basic order quantity	ØRDER-AMT	Num. Comp.	5	0

20. Prepare the divisions mentioned above for Problem 4-12 (page 112). Field names and sizes are shown in Table 5-15.

Table 5-15

Item Description	Name	Field Type	Field Size	Field Places to Right of Decimal
Input file	LEDGER			
Input record	LED-ENTRY			
Record contents:				
Account number	ACCT	Num. Comp.	5	0
Record type	TYPE	Num. Comp.	1	0
Amount	AMT	Num. Comp.	7	2
Output file	NEW-LEDGER			
Output record	NEW-LED-ENTRY			
Record contents:				
Account number	NEW-ACCT	Num. Rpt.	5	0
Record type	NEW-TYPE	Num. Rpt.	1	0
Amount	NEW-AMT	Num. Rpt.	7	2
Items of independent working storage:				
Account number	ACCT-ST	Num. Comp.	5	0
Amount	AMT-ST	Num. Comp.	7	2

21. Prepare the divisions mentioned above for Problem 4-13 (page 112). Field names and sizes are given in Table 5-16.

Table 5-16

Item Description	Name	Field: Type	Field: Size	Field: Places to Right of Decimal
Input file	ASSET-PUR			
Input reord	ASSET-RCD			
Record contents:				
Nature of asset	DESC	Alphameric	20	
Estimated useful life, years	USE-LIFE	Num. Comp.	2	0
Cost of asset	CØST	Num. Comp.	8	2
Estimated scrap value	SCRAP	Num. Comp.	7	2
Depreciation method indicator	IND	Num. Comp.	1	0
Output file	DEPREC-FILE			
Output record	DEP-AMT	Alphameric	132	
Items of grouped working storage:				
Group name	ØUT-REC			
Group contents:				
Nature of asset	ASSET-DESC	Alphameric	20	
Depreciation method	DEPREC-METHØD	Alphabetic	20	
Year	YEAR	Num. Rpt.	4	0
Depreciation for year	CUR-DEPREC	Num. Rpt.	8	2
Accumulated deprecia-tion	ACCUM-DEPREC	Num. Rpt.	8	2
Undepreciated balance	BALANCE	Num. Rpt.	8	2
Items of independent working storage:				
Numerator of sum of years	NUM	Num. Comp.	15	10
Denominator of sum of years	DEN	Num. Comp.	10	5
Current depreciation charge	DEP	Num. Comp.	8	2
Accumulated depreciation*	ADEP	Num. Comp.	8	2
Undepreciated balance	BAL	Num. Comp.	8	2
Control index	I	Num. Comp.	4	0

Items of Grouped Constant Data

Prepare a heading suitable for printing over the depreciation schedule. It should contain the following captions: Asset Type, Depreciation Method, Year, Current Depreciation, Accumulated Depreciation, and Undepreciated Balance. This should be identified in this section by the group name HEAD and data names A, B, C, D, E, and F, respectively.

22. Prepare the divisions mentioned above for Problem 4-15 (page 114). Field names and sizes are shown in Table 5-17.

Table 5-17

Item Description	Name	Field Type	Field Size	Field Places to Right of Decimal
Input file No. 1[1]	STD-FILE			
Input record No. 1	STD-CØST-RECØRD			
Record contents:				
Raw material inventory number	PART-NØ	Num. Comp.	5	0
Finished unit inventory number	FIN-UNIT-NØ	Num. Comp.	7	0
Number of pieces of raw material required	STD-PIECES	Num. Comp.	2	0
Standard cost per raw material piece	STD-CØST-PIECE	Num. Comp.	4	3
Input file No. 2[2]	ACT-WIP-FILE			
Input record No. 2	ACTUAL-MATERIALS-ISSUES			
Record contents:				
Production job number	WIP-JØB-NØ	Num. Comp.	4	0
Raw material inventory number	PART-NØ-ISSUED	Num. Comp.	5	0
Finished unit inventory number	FIN-UNIT-NUM	Num. Comp.	7	0
Number of pieces of raw material used	ACT-PIECES	Num. Comp.	4	0
Number of finished units made	ACT-PIECES-MFD	Num. Comp.	4	0
Output file[3]	STANDARD-MAT-CØST			
Output record	STD-MAT-RCD			
Record contents:				
Production job number	JØB-NØ	Num. Rpt.	4	0
Finished unit inventory number	FIN-INV-NØ	Num. Rpt.	7	0
Number of finished units made	FINISHED-UNITS	Num. Rpt.	4	0
Standard material cost/finished unit	UNIT-STD-CØST	Num. Rpt.	4	3
Standard cost for job	STANDARD-JØB	Num. Rpt.	7	2
Excess actual over standard cost	VARIANCE-ØVER	Num. Rpt.	6	2
Excess standard over actual cost	VARIANCE-UNDER	Num. Rpt.	6	2
Items of independent working storage:				
Total actual costs*	TØT-ACTUAL	Num. Comp.	8	2
Total variances over standard*	TØT-VARIANCE-ØVER	Num. Comp.	7	2
Total variances under standard*	TØT-VARIANCE-UNDER	Num. Comp.	7	2
Total standard costs*	TØT-JØB-STANDARDS	Num. Comp.	8	2
Actual job cost	ACTUAL	Num. Comp.	7	2
Standard job cost	STD-JØB	Num. Comp.	7	2
Job variance over standard	VAR-ØVER	Num. Comp.	6	2
Job variance under standard	VAR-UNDER	Num. Comp.	6	2
Display area	DIS	Num. Rpt.	8	2

1. Should be assigned to U04.
2. Should be assigned to IN.
3. Should be assigned to ØU.

CHAPTER 6

COBOL CODING: THE PROCEDURE DIVISION

The procedure division is the final major segment of the COBOL program. It contains the procedural commands which activate the computer; in fact, this division may be said to be "the program," as most people think of it.

Of course, the other divisions really play a significant role in the overall program, and two of the three divisions introduced in Chapter 5 work with the procedure division in the execution of commands. The environment division provides the names of computer input and output units with which READ and WRITE commands are allied. The data division blocks out segments of the computer's memory which may be used by the program. Thus, all segments play a role in the whole of the computer's operation.

Nevertheless, it is in the procedure division that the commands introduced in this text are written. All logical diagrams have been, in fact, descriptions of the instructions stated here. The remainder of this chapter is devoted to a description of this division and to details concerning the proper coding of commands.

ORGANIZATION OF THE DIVISION

This program segment is not organized quite so inflexibly as those divisions previously discussed, and properly so, because its exact nature must reflect the commands of the particular program. However, certain definite organizational characteristics exist and must be observed.

Division Name

This program segment is introduced by its name, PRØCEDURE DIVISIØN, written at the A margin and followed immediately by a period. Nothing else may be written on this line.

Division Sections

The procedure division may be divided into sections, such as the environment and data divisions. This is not required, however, and so is not ordinarily done in short programs. If section names are used, they must be prepared by the programmer, and each must contain the word SECTIØN. Section names are written at the A margin, are followed by a period, and occupy a line by themselves.

Paragraphs

The principal subdivision of the procedure division is the paragraph. This is a program segment of at least one sentence, introduced by a name. This, the paragraph name or procedure name, is written at the A margin and followed by a period and at least one space, but the remainder of the line may be used for programming if desired. It is recommended that the remainder of the line be left blank so that the procedure name is easily found in the program, but this is a convention, not a requirement.

Procedure names may be any word meeting the requirements of a data name set out on page 155. However, they are not required to contain an alphabetic character and may be completely numeric if desired.

All of the procedure division must be written in the framework of paragraphs. Thus the division must contain at least one paragraph. Just how many paragraphs the program should be divided into is partly a matter of programming requirements, partly a matter of form.

Every transfer command references a procedure name. This includes the unconditional transfer, "GØ TØ ...," as well as the PERFØRM instructions covered in the next chapter. Therefore a minimum number of paragraphs will be demanded by the construction of these transfers. Beyond this minimum, it is a good idea to use a new paragraph to begin each major segment of the division, making later reading of the program easier than if various activities were combined without dividing headings.

Sentences

Sentences exist within paragraphs. A sentence, in COBOL, is one or more commands terminated by a period. Every paragraph must end in a complete sentence; that is, the final character in a paragraph must be a period. Sentences must be written at or to the right of the B margin.

Sentences are considered simple if they contain a single COBOL command; as, for example, "ADD 10 TØ ITEM-A." They are compound if they contain more than one command; as, for example, "ADD 10 TØ ITEM-A GØ TØ PRØCEDURE-3."

It is generally a sound programming practice to use simple sentences whenever possible, thus improving the value of computer-prepared diagnostics. As programs are compiled, a copy is prepared by the computer which numbers the sentences. Error messages then reference the incorrect command through these numbers. A sentence containing many commands will have only one reference number, and any error is thus much more difficult to find than in a program where shorter sentences are used.

The most rigorous sentence requirements are imposed by the fact that each paragraph must end in a completed sentence, and the fact that sentences play a major role in the operation of conditionals. In several conditional commands, including the AT END, the SIZE ERRØR, and one version of the IF statement, the TRUE branch is written in the same sentence with the conditional, while the FALSE branch occupies the sentence following. Thus the minimum sentence requirements are set by these two terms, the paragraph terminal and conditional construction.

Punctuation of COBOL Sentences. The rules for punctuation of sentences and their contents must be observed. Careful adherence to these rules is absolutely necessary. Punctuation rules are as follows:

1. At least one space must always appear between two successive words and/or parenthetical expressions. Two or more successive spaces are treated as a single space except in nonnumeric literals.

2. If a period or comma follows a word or parenthetical expression, it must appear immediately after the word or expression and then be followed by a space.

3. Each sentence must be terminated by a period and a space, in that order.

4. When an arithmetic operator or an equal sign is used, it must be preceded by a space and followed by another space.

5. When a series of operands occurs within a statement, the items may be separated by series separators, which are the comma, the word AND, and the comma followed by AND.

6. Subscripts must be enclosed in parentheses. If two or more subscripts are present within the parentheses, they must be separated by a space and can be separated by commas as well. Other subscript characteristics are covered in the next chapter.

7. Parentheses may be used whenever needed in arithmetic expressions and conditional expressions. Where ambiguity would result from their omission, they must be used.

8. The rules of punctuation do not apply to constants defined in the data division or to nonnumeric literals, which may contain any character except the quotation mark.

9. The statement separator THEN may be placed before or after any imperative statement but should not be used at the beginning or end of a sentence.

Examples of all these punctuation rules may be found in the illustrative programs in Appendix B (pages 224-241). These should be reviewed and mastered before any attempt is made to code a program, since a simple punctuation error often prevents a program's compilation.

Division of Sentence Components. Of course, sentences may occupy more than one line on the coding form. A space is considered to exist between coding position 72 on a given line and position 12 on the next line. Thus a character may be written in position 72 and another in position 12 of the next line, and the statement will be treated as if these characters are parts of two different words.

It may be the programmer's intent that these characters form part of the same item, however. COBOL words and data names may be continued from one line to the next by writing through column 72, placing a hyphen in column 7 of the next line, and beginning the divided element in column 12 of that line. An example of such a continuation may be found in lines 24 and 25 on page 4 of the Illustration 2 in Appendix B.

Continuing nonnumeric literals from one line to the next is slightly more difficult than the continuation of other items. In addition to a hyphen in column 7, a quotation mark must also be written in column 12 of the line onto which the item is continued. An example of this continuation may be found in lines 12 and 13 on page 4 of the Illustration 2 in Appendix B.

Generally speaking, to continue COBOL words or literals from one line to another is simply to introduce one more error possibility to a program. A far better practice is to terminate writing on a given line with a complete item and then begin the next line with the next sentence component.

Statements

A statement is a basic COBOL command. The statement may be conditional, like the IF, or it may be imperative. A list of principal types of statements follows:

1. Input-output
2. Data transfer
3. Arithmetic
4. Control

The major part of this chapter is devoted to a detailed consideration of these statements.

Data Names

While not a part of the language hierarchy, data names are of great importance because they serve to refer to most of the data being processed. Data names are of course used within statements. The basic requirements of data names are:

1. They are formed by combining any of the following characters: the letters A-Z, the numerals 0-9, and the hyphen.

2. They must not contain blanks.

3. They may contain from 1 to 30 characters.

4. They may neither begin nor end with a hyphen.

5. Data names and condition names must contain at least one alphabetic character. Procedure names may consist entirely of numerals, if desired.

6. Names must not be the same as restricted COBOL words.

7. Names must be unique, or they must be capable of becoming so through qualification.

Qualification of Data Names. Data names which are not otherwise unique may be made so by referencing the name of some group to which the name belongs. This is done by using the preposition ØF or IN; thus a data name may be made unique by writing "data-name ØF group-name" or "data-name IN group-name." Of course, this process of qualifying must in fact differentiate one data item from another.

To demonstrate this process, assume that the following files, records, and data names are present in a program:

File 1		File 2	
FD	FILE-1	FD	FILE-2
01	RECØRD-1	01	RECØRD-2
02	ACCØUNT	02	ACCØUNT

The data name ACCØUNT may be seen to exist in both records. These data names could be differentiated by qualification; as, for instance, citing ACCØUNT ØF RECØRD-1, or ACCØUNT ØF FILE-2. Obviously, the names of independent data elements must be unique because, belonging to no data group, they are not amenable to qualification.

If a data name is not unique, it must be qualified each time it is used. Any group name superior in the hierarchy of the item may be used to qualify it, so long as another item of the same name does not exist within the group.

TECHNICAL NATURE OF COBOL COMMANDS

The remainder of the chapter is devoted to a consideration of the technical nature of COBOL statements. In this, certain writing conventions are used which serve to set out required words, optional phrases, and the like. These, the same as used in Chapter 5, should be reviewed before turning to the commands themselves.

1. In all COBOL statements, capitalized words are COBOL words. If used at all, they must appear exactly as in the illustrative command.

2. Underlined COBOL words are required words. They must appear in the statement. On the other hand, COBOL words not underlined may be included for readability but are not required.

3. Phrases enclosed in square brackets [ ] are optional. If they are used, they must be employed as shown, and any underlined COBOL words must be present.

4. Enclosure in shaped brackets { } indicates that one of the enclosed items or phrases must be specified. The choice is the programmer's, of course, but one of the alternatives must be included in the command.

5. Three dots (...) indicate that the previous phrase may be repeated any number of times.

Input-Output Commands

ØPEN. The ØPEN instruction serves to open files and check labels if they are used. It is of the nature:

ØPEN [INPUT file-name-1 [, file-name-2, ...]] [ØUTPUT file-name 3 [, file-name-4, ...]].

All input and output files may be mentioned in the same ØPEN command. This must be given prior to a READ or WRITE instruction.

CLØSE. This instruction closes the named file or files. It is of the nature:

CLØSE file-name-1 WITH [{LØCK / NØ REWIND}] [, file-name-2 ...] .

If neither the LØCK nor the NØ REWIND option is specified, the reel of the file will be rewound. If LØCK is specified, the reel will be rewound in such a way as to prevent its reuse without operator intervention. Using the NØ REWIND option causes the file to be closed and to be ineligible to accept a READ or WRITE command, but the reel will stay in its present position.

READ. This command appears as follows:

READ file-name [INTØ area-name] AT END {any imperative statement / NEXT SENTENCE}.

Ordinarily, this instruction causes the contents of a record from the specified file to be read into memory in the space provided therefor. However, use of the INTØ option may be used to cause reading into some other area—perhaps another input file area, working storage, or an output file area. When this option is used, the receiving area must of course be of the proper size and nature to accept the read-in material. Use of this option causes the results of the reading to be stored at the designated location.

The AT END conditional is optional in some versions of COBOL and required in others. Here, it is treated as required, consistent with the specifications of the IBM 7040.

The conditional must specify some alternative activity to be performed should the file be exhausted. The programmer may specify any appropriate imperative command or, if the nature of the program permits, simply assign NEXT SENTENCE. This will cause the program to proceed to the next sentence in the event of an AT END condition and has the effect of canceling the AT END conditional.

Any steps to be taken if the READ file is exhausted must be written as a part of the READ sentence; then a period should appear. Statements following the AT END conditional will be executed as the TRUE side of the conditional branch; statements in the next sentence will be executed as the FALSE side. If the routine to be executed after completing reading is long, it is a sound practice to use a "GØ TØ" to jump to a new paragraph, and write the routine there. This practice may be seen in the Appendix B illustrations.

WRITE. The WRITE command is as follows:

WRITE record-name [FRØM area-name] .

The FRØM option may be used in much the same way as the INTØ option associated with the READ command. Ordinarily, writing occurs from the record name area. However, use of the FRØM option causes this command to work as a MØVE and WRITE instruction. First, data are moved from the memory location designated as area-name to the output area; then, they are written. The area name location may be a part of the input, working storage, or constant area.

The "WRITE record-name FRØM area-name" option is used when writing headings above statement contents. In this instance the output record is simply defined as PICTURE X(132), and the output line is defined as grouped data in working storage. The heading, properly spaced with FILLER, is defined in the constant section of the data division. Then, to write the heading, a command such as "WRITE ØUTPUT-LINE FRØM HEAD-1" is given (record and group names are assumed). To write the line contents of the statement, the command "WRITE ØUTPUT-LINE FRØM DATA-LINE" is given, assuming DATA-LINE to be the name assigned the data group in working storage.

Illustration 3 of Appendix B (page 234) presents the proper method of creating statement headings. First, in the data division may be seen the construction of the output record as a single data item, generally defined. The regular data line is set up in working storage and the heading in the constant section. Then, on line 07 of page 3, the heading is written by the command "WRITE DEP-LINE FRØM HEAD-1." On line 08, it may be seen that the output line is then cleared to spaces and written, thus placing one empty line between the heading and the first body line.

Line 22 of page 3 presents the writing command used to transmit the report content line, writing the output line from the working storage section.

As in the MØVE command (see below), data will assume any editing symbols specified by the output area. Therefore, care should be taken to see that data moved in and written conform to any PICTURE clauses specified for the output area. Ordinarily, when the FRØM option is used, the output area is designated in a general fashion as PICTURE X(--). This avoids any conflict of data types or field sizes.

DISPLAY. This instruction is of the form:

$$\underline{\text{DISPLAY}} \begin{Bmatrix} \text{literal-1} \\ \text{data-name-1} \end{Bmatrix} \left[, \begin{Bmatrix} \text{literal-2} \\ \text{data-name-2} \end{Bmatrix} \ldots \right] .$$

This command, as discussed in Chapter 3, is used to display literals and/or the contents of data names on the computer's low-volume output unit. Literals and data name contents may be displayed in the same command, mixed in any desired fashion. For example, if a data field called TØT-SALES has been used to accumulate sales amounts from input records, this control total could be written out with a caption by the command "DISPLAY 'AMØUNT ØF TØTAL SALES ' TØT-SALES." If the value stored at TØT-SALES is $1,584.60, the displayed message will appear as follows:

AMØUNT ØF TØTAL SALES $1,584.60.

In setting up captions, it must be noted that the literals and data items displayed will be written out in adjacent positions unless spacing is provided for. The simplest way to insure the proper spacing between the literal and data name contents is to include the space requirement in the literal itself. It may be observed that this was done in the previous example.

When setting up literals in the DISPLAY command, one should be careful about continuations from one line to another. These are perfectly acceptable when properly coded, but mistakes in the use of quotation marks or hyphens are easily made. The rules for proper continuation from one line to the next have already been covered in this chapter; they should be uppermost in the programmer's mind when displaying literals.

Data Transfer Instructions

The transfer command is available in two versions.

SIMPLE MØVE. The first, used extensively in previous chapters, is of the nature:

$$\underline{\text{MØVE}} \begin{Bmatrix} \text{data-name-1} \\ \text{literal} \end{Bmatrix} \quad \underline{\text{TØ}} \text{ data-name-2 } [, \text{ data-name-3, } \ldots] .$$

Upon execution, the literal or data name contents specified will be copied into data-name-2 and as many subsequent locations as are specified.

This command is executed in a way which makes the nature of data involved in the move very important. The following points should be noted:

1. Moving data to a numeric field. (a) Only numeric data may be moved. (b) Data will be aligned by decimal point in the receiving area and either end filled in with zeros or truncated, as required. (c) Data may be moved from a numeric computational to a numeric report field. When this is done, any editing symbols specified in the latter field will be filled in. Transfers from a numeric report to a computational field are not permitted.

2. Moving data to an alphameric field. This is permitted for all kinds of data, of course, because the alphameric field is capable of containing all forms of data. Data are placed in the receiving field, from left to right. Unfilled positions to the right are filled with spaces. Should the source be larger than the receiving area, the right-most characters of the data being moved are lost.

3. Moving data to an alphabetic field. Generally, only an alphabetic field should be moved to another alphabetic area. Data are loaded into the receiving area as in item 2 above.

MØVE CØRRESPØNDING. The second MØVE option is of the following nature:

> MØVE CØRRESPØNDING group-name-1 TØ group-name-2 [, group-name-3, ...].

In the execution of this command, the contents of any data groups or data elements having the same names in the source and receiving areas will be moved from the former to the latter. Any fields in the source area not matched by the same names in the receiving area are ignored. All moves take place in accordance with the characteristics mentioned when describing the basic MØVE version above.

As an example of this command, assume that certain data areas are as shown in Table 6-1, and contain the indicated data before and after executing the MØVE CØRRESPØNDING command.

Table 6-1

Data Area	Contents	
	Before MØVE	After MØVE
01 RECØRD-1.		
02 AREA-1 PICTURE A(5).	ABCDE	Unchanged
02 AREA-2 PICTURE 9(5).	12345	Unchanged
02 AREA-3.		
03 GRØUP-1 PICTURE X(5).	$1.00	Unchanged
03 GRØUP-2 PICTURE A(10).	JØHN ADAMS	Unchanged
03 GRØUP-3 PICTURE 9(5)V9(5).	1234598765	Unchanged

A second data group and its contents appear as shown in Table 6-2. After execution of the command "MØVE CØRRESPØNDING RECØRD-1 TØ AREA-X," the receiving area appears as shown in the right column. Data areas which do not have names the same as an area in the source group are unchanged, as in AREA-4. All receiving areas having a name in common with a source area are changed, data from the source area being moved into them. Note that these fields need not appear in the same order in the two groups, nor must they have the same PICTURE clauses. However, any move which would be invalid (as, for example, the movement of numeric data to an alphabetic field) in version 1 of this command will also be invalid here.

Table 6-2

Data Area	Contents	
	Before MØVE	After MØVE
01 AREA-X.		
02 AREA-4 PICTURE $9,999.99.	$1,000.00	Unchanged
02 AREA-3.		
03 GRØUP-1 PICTURE X(5).	AAAAA	$1.00
03 GRØUP-2 PICTURE X(6).	BBBBBB	JØHN A
03 GRØUP-3 PICTURE $999.999.	$123.456	$345.987
02 AREA-1 PICTURE X(7).	$$$$$$$	ABCDE--

Arithmetic Instructions

Simple Commands. A summary of the basic simple arithmetic commands is given below:

$$\underline{\text{ADD}} \begin{Bmatrix} \text{data-name-1} \\ \text{literal-1} \end{Bmatrix} \left[, \begin{Bmatrix} \text{data-name-2} \\ \text{literal-2} \end{Bmatrix} \right] \underline{\text{TØ}} \text{ data-name-n.}$$

$$\underline{\text{SUBTRACT}} \begin{Bmatrix} \text{data-name-1} \\ \text{literal-1} \end{Bmatrix} \left[, \begin{Bmatrix} \text{data-name-2} \\ \text{literal-2} \end{Bmatrix} \right] \underline{\text{FRØM}} \text{ data-name-n.}$$

$$\underline{\text{MULTIPLY}} \begin{Bmatrix} \text{data-name-1} \\ \text{literal} \end{Bmatrix} \underline{\text{BY}} \text{ data-name-2.}$$

$$\underline{\text{DIVIDE}} \begin{Bmatrix} \text{data-name-1} \\ \text{literal} \end{Bmatrix} \underline{\text{INTØ}} \text{ data-name-2.}$$

Several optional phrases may be used with each of these. These options are described below.

1. The GIVING option. As mentioned previously, the basic command shown above stores its result at the location specified by the last-named data name (data-name-n for the ADD and SUBTRACT commands, data-name-2 for the MULTIPLY and DIVIDE instructions). This can be changed,

and the result stored in another location, by use of the GIVING option. In the ADD command, this is effected by deleting TØ, or changing it to AND. The optional phrase "GIVING data-name-n" is simply written after the other arithmetic commands. In each instance the factor formerly used as a receiving area for the result can be either a data name or a literal when this option is used.

2. The RØUNDED option. If, when the result of an arithmetic command is obtained, it contains more decimal positions than called for by the PICTURE of the receiving area, the right-most unwanted decimal positions are lost. However, the answer may be rounded in the least significant saved decimal position by specifying the term RØUNDED after naming the receiving area. This causes the answer to be rounded up by one if the value in the most significant truncated position is a 5 or greater.

To illustrate this option, assume that two memory positions have been defined as shown below and contain the indicated data:

		Contents
FIELD-A	PICTURE 999V999	472 386
FIELD-B	PICTURE 99999V99	00246 03

The command "ADD FIELD-A TØ FIELD-B RØUNDED" is given. Since FIELD-B, the receiving area, only calls for two positions to the right of the decimal point, one decimal position from FIELD-A is to be lost. Use of the RØUNDED option causes this truncated position to round up, however, and the solution is stored as 00718 42 rather than 00718 41.

3. The SIZE ERROR Option. As pointed out previously, this option serves to guard against the loss of significant digits through an attempt to store a value in a space with too few places to the left of the decimal point. The phrase may be attached to any arithmetic command and is always written as the last part of the instruction. It is of the general nature:

ØN SIZE ERRØR { any imperative statement / NEXT SENTENCE }.

If an overflow (a "size error") occurs, the remainder of the arithmetic sentence is executed as the TRUE side of the conditional. The remainder of the sentence is ignored if an overflow has not occurred, and the program proceeds to the next command appearing after the period. Thus again may be seen the importance of punctuation when conditionals are used.

The CØMPUTE Command. This, a complex form of arithmetic instruction, also permits use of the RØUNDED and SIZE ERRØR options. It appears as follows:

CØMPUTE data-name-1 [RØUNDED] = { data-name-2 / formula / literal } [ØN SIZE ERRØR { any imperative statement / NEXT SENTENCE }].

Forming arithmetic statements. Certain significant rules pertaining to arithmetic are set out below. All of these apply to the CØMPUTE command; items 1 and 2 apply to the simpler arithmetic instructions also.

1. Data items used in computation are called arithmetic operands. These must refer to items which have been defined as numeric computational, or to be figurative constants or literals whose value is numeric.

2. The maximum size of any operand (literal or data name) is eighteen decimal digits. Intermediate results (those encountered during the evaluation of an expression) will be carried to one more place to the right and to the left of the decimal point than is specified for the largest operand involved in the operation.

3. In the CØMPUTE command the normal precedence for execution, arranged from highest to lowest order, is:

   Inner to outer parentheses
   Exponentiation
   Multiplication and Division
   Addition and Subtraction

   Within the hierarchy specified above, arithmetic commands are evaluated from left to right.

4. Two operational signs may not appear in adjacent positions in the CØMPUTE command. Parentheses must be used to avoid this when necessary.

Control Commands

This group of instructions includes those as simple as the GØ TØ and those as complex as the PERFØRM. It also includes the IF statement, the major conditional. These are discussed in turn.

GØ TØ. This transfer instruction is found in two forms. The first, or unconditional transfer, is of the nature:

GØ TØ procedure-name.

"Procedure-name" may be the name of any paragraph in the procedure division. This form of the command is covered on page 68.

Another form, not before introduced, provides a multiple branch. It is of the nature:

GØ TØ procedure-name-1, procedure-name-2
[, procedure-name-3 ...] DEPENDING ØN data-name.

This, when executed, causes a transfer to the procedure name specified by the value of the data name. For example, the instruction might be written as follows:

GØ TØ PAR-A, PAR-B, PAR-C, PAR-D DEPENDING ØN CØDE-NØ.

Then, if CØDE-NØ were 2, the program would transfer to PAR-B. If it were 4, the program would transfer to PAR-D. Of course, CØDE-NØ must not assume a value greater than the number of specified addresses to which transfer may be made.

The STØP Instruction. This instruction, of the form STØP {literal / RUN}, may be used either to effect a pause or to signal the logical end of the program. The command's logical characteristics may be found on page 69.

The Conditional. This, the IF statement, is available in two forms. Version 1, a simple form, is of the nature:

IF conditional expression statement-1.

The conditional expression specified in this command may be one of those discussed at length in Chapter 4, the relational test or the sign condition test; or it may be a condition name test such as described below. Statement-1 (which may actually be a series of statements) will be executed if the expression is found to be true. If the expression is false, the program will automatically transfer to the next sentence for its next instruction.

Proper punctuation is most important when this form of the conditional is set up. Care must be taken to see that all parts of the program unique to a true condition are written as a part of the conditional sentence. This may include imperative and/or conditional statements. Unless that program portion designated as the false branch is also to be executed when a true result is found, an unconditional branch must be used as the last command in the true side to transfer control away from the false branch.

Version 2 of the IF statement provides a means for automatically avoiding any possibility of confusing true and false branches. It is of the nature:

If conditional expression {statement-1 / NEXT SENTENCE} {ELSE / ØTHERWISE} {statement-2 / NEXT SENTENCE}

In this version the true branch is found at the statement-1 area and the false branch at the statement-2 area. Either statement-1 or statement-2, or both, may be a series of statements, including conditionals. In either instance, use of the NEXT SENTENCE option converts this form to one quite similar to version 1.

The routines to be executed after making a conditional test in the IF statement may be quite complex, of course. Should the true routines become complicated, it is well not to try to write them as a part of the conditional sentence, because to do so makes the sentence much too long. Instead, the true branch should contain an unconditional transfer, or GØ TØ command, which designates another paragraph as the program segment to be executed. When version 2 of the conditional is used, this is true of the false branch also.

Compound Conditionals. Either version of the IF statement may be used to make compound tests, in which the conditionals are connected by AND or ØR, as appropriate. If the conditionals have a common first operand, it may be implied in tests after the first. If the operand is implied and the relational operator does not change, it too may be implied. For example, assume the following to be a proper IF statement:

```
IF FIELD-A GREATER THAN FIELD-B AND FIELD-A GREATER
THAN FIELD-C GØ TØ PRØC-1 ELSE GØ TØ PRØC-2.
```

In this statement, FIELD-A is the first operand, and GREATER the relational operator. Inasmuch as neither changes in the second conditional, the above could be written as follows:

```
IF FIELD-A GREATER THAN FIELD-B AND FIELD-C
GØ TØ PROC-1 ELSE GØ TØ PRØC-2.
```

In this version, both the operand and the relational operator of the second conditional are implied.

Operands and relational operators may be implied only in certain instances. The operand may be implied only so long as it does not change. The relational operator may be implied only when the operand is also implied. Furthermore, the "object" of a conditional—the second operand—may never be implied, although in some instances the temptation to do so is great. For example, suppose that A is to be compared with B, and if greater than or equal to the latter, the program should proceed to PRØC-A. A tendency exists to write this conditional as follows:

```
IF A GREATER THAN ØR EQUAL TØ B GØ TØ PRØC-A.
```

However, this implies the object in the second conditional, an implication which is not permitted. The command must be written:

```
IF A GREATER THAN B ØR EQUAL B GØ TØ PRØC-A.
```

Thus, while the first operand in a conditional may be implied, the second may not.

Testing Condition Names. In this form of the IF statement, a name (called a condition name) is associated with every alternative of a particular condition. Then the status of the item is queried by citing the condition-name, as follows:

```
IF condition-name .... .
```

This conditional may be used in either form of the IF statement, may be used in a simple or compound structure, and may form part of a nested conditional complex.

Setting up and using condition names requires close interplay between the data and procedure divisions. First, the item to be tested is established in the data division, probably in the file section, inasmuch as it is most likely a part of a read-in record. Then, every possible condition associated with the item is assigned a name by use of a special level number, 88. When the item is tested in the procedure division, only the condition name need be specified.

To illustrate this command and its use, assume that a certain firm uses three means of employee compensation for various types of employees—salaries, hourly wages, or commissions. Each employee's method of compensation is included in his master employment record, where in the compensation field a 1 is the code designation for salary, a 2 is the code for wages, and a 3 is the code for commission.

This data item could be set up in the data division as a part of its record and a condition name assigned to each possible code symbol, as follows:

```
A   B
    02   CØMPENSATIØN PICTURE 9.
         88 SALARIES VALUE 1.
         88 WAGE-EARNER VALUE 2.
         88 CØMMISSIØN VALUE 3.
```

Then, in the procedure division, the compensation field could be tested by use of the condition names assigned above. Thus the following conditional and transfer commands might be appropriate for determining the mode of compensation and sending the program to the proper computational routines:

```
A   B
    IF SALARIES GØ TØ SALARY-PRØC ELSE IF WAGE-EARNER
    GØ TØ WAGE-PRØC ELSE GØ TØ CØMMISSIØN-PRØC.
```

This would be equivalent to a conditional reading as follows:

```
IF CØMPENSATION = 1 GØ TØ SALARY-PRØC ELSE
IF CØMPENSATION = 2 GØ TØ WAGE-PRØC ELSE
GØ TØ CØMMISSIØN-PRØC.
```

While the latter form of the conditional is perfectly acceptable, the first makes later reading of the procedure division much easier and the program easier to follow.

Nested Conditionals. A conditional statement may be written as part of the true branch of another conditional. In this case the first is said to be "nested" in the second. There is no particular limit to the number of conditionals which may be nested, but the logical structure very quickly becomes quite confusing.

A situation which might give rise to the programming of nested conditionals is cited below:

Assume that data input records pertaining to collections of accounts receivable contain the following fields, among others:

TIME, the time elapsed between the date of sale and collection
C-TYPE, a code designating the customer type
INV-CLASS, a code designating the inventory class
QTY, the number of units of inventory sold

Assume further that the following statement governs the granting of customer discounts: "Accounts collected in less than ten days after sale are allowed a discount, while those collected after a longer period are not. Customers of C-TYPE 1 are extended a discount depending on the inventory class and quantity sold; other customers are extended a discount of 2 percent. C-TYPE 1 customers are granted a 3 percent discount if the sale is of Y-class items; if the sale is of inventory class X, a 5 percent discount is allowed for sales of fewer than 1,000 units or 6 percent for sales of 1,000 units or more."

This complex statement may be more clearly understood if diagrammed in the form of a "decision tree." Such a diagram appears in Figure 6-1. Here, each applicable test is shown as a fork in the tree. The

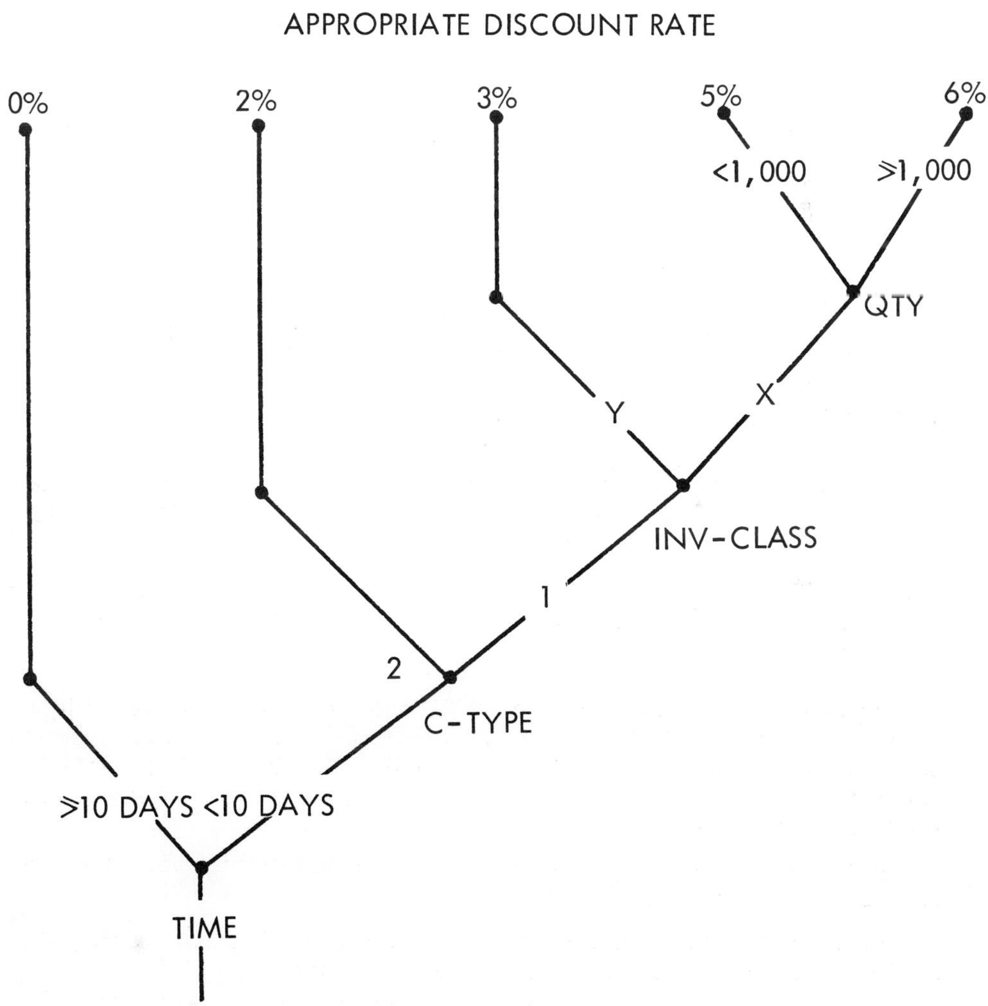

FIG. 6-1. Decision Tree of Discount Policy

condition tested is presented as the fork label, and the situation applicable to each branch is shown beside that branch. Each branch, or route, is shown as leading to a discount rate.

Using nested IF statements, this might be programmed as follows:

```
IF TIME LESS THAN 10 IF C-TYPE = 1 IF INV-CLASS = X IF QTY EQUAL
1000 ØR GREATER 1000 MØVE .06 TØ DIS-RATE ELSE MØVE .05 TØ DIS-RATE
ELSE MØVE .03 TØ DIS-RATE ELSE MØVE .02 TØ DIS-RATE ELSE MØVE 0 TØ
DIS-RATE.
```

In the above sentence the conditionals must be considered in much the same fashion as equation segments which are enclosed in parentheses. The innermost IF establishes a conditional for which the first ELSE separates true and false branches. Then, IF may be paired with ELSE until the outermost conditional is evaluated.

This may be more clearly understood if the above COBOL sentence is reexamined, and conditionals and their related true and false branches are pointed out. In Figure 6-2, C refers to condition, T to true, and F to false. Thus, it may be seen that the innermost set of true-false branches

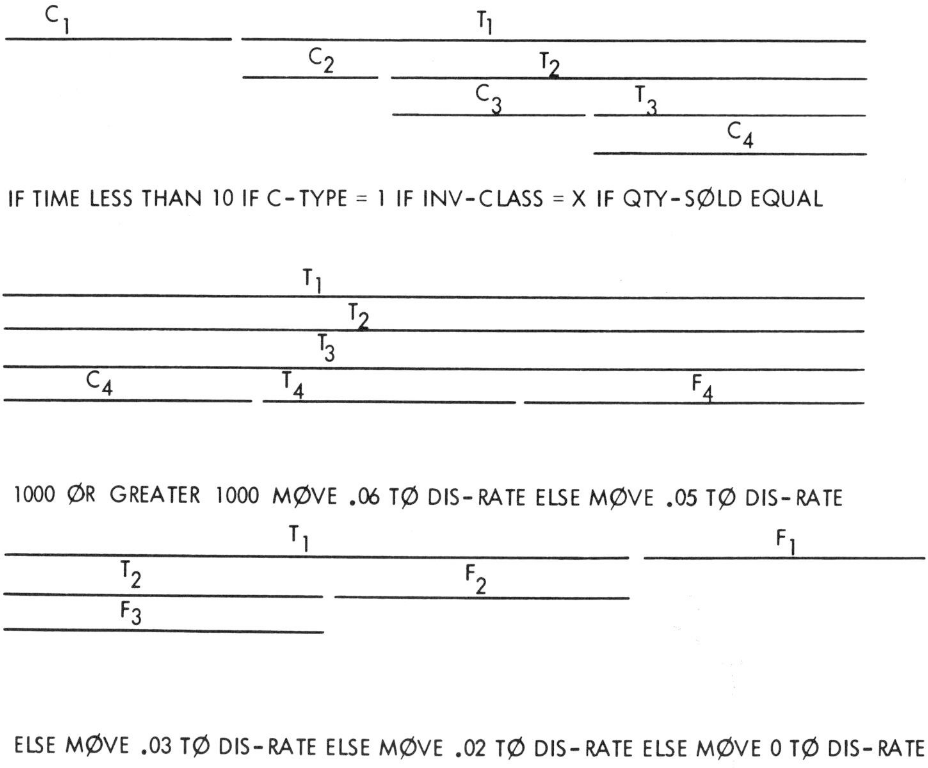

FIG. 6-2

belongs to the innermost conditional, and so on, until the outer conditional is evaluated. It may also be seen that the nesting of conditionals is somewhat confusing and should be used only when shorter conditionals are for some reason inappropriate.

CONCLUSION

The technical nature of all the commands introduced in Chapters 3 and 4 has now been covered. In Chapter 7 will be introduced the group of PERFØRM commands available in COBOL, and their logical and technical nature will be explored simultaneously. These commands perform computer operations also controlled by other instructions and so have been separated from the basic parts of the language considered to this point.

It is quite possible to construct very elaborate programs of the instructions already covered. To summarize many of the rules introduced at various points throughout the text, and to provide the programmer with a series of points which should be verified before attempting to compile a program, the following check list is included here.

ERROR CHECK LIST

No program should be considered ready for compilation until all the following questions are answered affirmatively. The following list, while by no means covering all technical and logical errors which may be committed, does cover the ones most commonly found.

I. General

1. Are division and section heads:
   a) Spelled properly?
   b) Written at the A margin?
   c) Followed by a period?
   d) On a line by themselves?

2. Are paragraph names:
   a) Spelled properly, where specified?
   b) Single words?
   c) Not COBOL words?
   d) Written at the A margin?
   e) Followed by a period?

3. Are paragraph contents written at (or to the right of) the B margin?

II. Identification division

1. Is the program name a single word?

2. Are other paragraphs properly named, and do they terminate with a period?

III. Environment division

1. Do source computer and object computer paragraphs contain single words?

2. Are file names properly assigned to Input-Output units?

IV. Data division

1. Are the sections in proper sequence?

2. Is the PICTURE clause used only at the element level?

3. Does each element have a PICTURE clause?

4. Is each entry terminated by a period?

5. In the file section:
   a) Is the file name fully defined by the proper level number and clauses?
   b) Does the number of characters claimed in the file description agree with the sum of PICTURE clause characters?
   c) Are record names assigned their proper level number?
   d) Is the VALUE clause used only with condition names?

6. In the working storage section:
   a) Is the VALUE clause used to initialize values when appropriate?
   b) Are all working areas included and described in sufficient size?

7. In the constant section:
   a) Is each element assigned a value?
   b) Do field size, nature, and value agree?

8. In the working storage and constant sections:
   a) Are independent items written before data groups?
   b) Are the names of independent items unique?

V. Procedure division

1. General
   a) Does every program branch lead logically to STØP RUN?
   b) Do all paragraph names agree with the names specified in transfer statements?
   c) Are all paragraphs terminated by a period?
   d) Are all data names unique or properly qualified?
   e) Are data names spelled consistently in the data and procedure divisions?

2. Related to specific commands:
   a) Are files opened before READ commands are given?
   b) Do all READ commands contain an AT END clause?

c) Does the READ command specify a file name?
d) Is the nature of source and destination fields compatible in MØVE commands?
e) Do arithmetic commands use only numeric computational operands?
f) Have the RØUNDED and SIZE ERRØR conditionals been used when appropriate?
g) Are commands (especially conditional and computational) punctuated properly?
h) Are continued conditionals and other terms puncuated properly?
i) Does the WRITE command specify a record name?
j) Are all files closed?

QUESTIONS AND PROBLEMS

1. What is the difference between a statement and a sentence, as these appear in the procedure division?

2. How may data names be qualified? Why must the names of independent data elements be unique?

3. Contrast the MØVE and MØVE CØRRESPØNDING commands.

4. Contrast the two types of IF statements. What is the difference between the two following commands?

```
IF FIELD-A GREATER THAN FIELD-B CØMPUTE X = Y + Z.
GØ TØ PRØC-2.

IF FIELD-A GREATER THAN FIELD-B CØMPUTE X = Y + Z
ELSE GØ TØ PRØC-2.
```

5. ITEM-1 has been defined as PICTURE 9(5)V999 and contains 1473‸211. ITEM-2 has been defined as PICTURE 999V99 and contains 884‸63. What will each data element contain of the command "MØVE ITEM-1 TØ ITEM-2" is executed?

6. ITEM-X has been defined as PICTURE $Z,ZZ9.99 and contains $1,476.40. ITEM-Y has been defined as PICTURE 999V999 and contains 873‸559. What will each data element contain if the command "ADD ITEM-Y AND 454.117 GIVING ITEM-X RØUNDED" is executed?

7. Indicate the logical and technical errors in the following procedure segment. Assume that all file and data items have been properly defined.

```
START-1. READ IN-FILE.AT END CLØSE IN-FILE, ØUT-FILE STØP RUN.

    IF ITEM-A GREATER THAN 1111 GØ TØ PAR-B.

PAR-B. ADD VAL-X TØ VAL-Y. WRITE ØUT-RCD. GØ TØ START-1.
```

8. List all technical errors in the following program. You may assume that the logic is proper.

```
A       B
IDENTIFICATIØN DIVISIØN
PROGRAM-NAME.  THIS IS EXERCISE  8.
ENVIRØNMENT-DIVISIØN.
     SØURCE-CØMPUTØR.  IBM  7040.
     ØBJECT-CØMPUTØR.  IBM  7040.
INPUT-ØUTPUT. ASSIGN IN-FILE TØ IN.ASSIGNØUT-FILE TØ ØU.
DATA DIVISIØN.
FD  IN-FILE RECØRD IS IN-RCD LABELS ØMITTED.
01  IN-REC.
02  ACCØUNT                    PICTURE 20A
02  KEY
    77 RETAIL PICTURE 1.
    77 WHØLESALE PICTURE 2.
02  UNITS                      PICTURE 999 VALUE 0.
02  AMT                        PICTURE 9.99.
FD  ØUTFILE.
01  RECØRD
    02  ACCØUNT                PICTURE 9(5).
    02  SALE-AMT               PICTURE $Z,ZZZ.99.
    02  DIS-AMT.               PICTURE $ZZZ.99
    02  TØT-AMT                PICTURE $Z,ZZZ.99.
WØRKING STØRAGE.
77  GRAND-TØTAL                PICTURE $ZZZ,ZZZ.99.
PRØCEDURE DIVISIØN
PAR-1. ØPEN IN-FILE, ØUT-FILE.
NEXT PAR. READ IN-FILE. AT END DISPLAY GRAND-TØTAL.
    CLØSE IN-FILE, ØUT-FILE. STØP RUN. MØVE ACCØUNT
    FRØM IN-REC TØ ACCØUNT IN ØUT-FILE.
IF KEY IS RETAIL GØ TØ RØUTINE-1 THØUGH IF KEY IS WHØLE-
    SALE GØ TØ RØUTINE-2. GØ TØ NEXT-PAR.
    RØUTINE-A. CALCULATE SALE-AMT RØUNDING =UNITS*
    AMT, THEN MØVE TØ TØT-AMT. SET DIS-AMT = 0. ADD
    TØT-AMT TØ GRAND-TØTAL. WRITE RECØRD GØ TØ NEXT-
    PAR.
    RØUTINE-B. MULTIPLY AMT TIMES UNITS GIVING SALE-
    AMT. IF SALE-AMT BETWEEN 500 and 1000 CØMPUTE
    DIS=.02*SALE-AMT THØUGH IF SALE-AMT EQUAL TØ ØR
    GREATER THAN 1000 CØMPUTE DIS AS .03 ØF SALE-AMT.
    ELSE MØVE 0 TØ DIS. SUBSTRACT DIS FRØM SALE-AMT
    TØ GET TØT-AMT. ADD TØT-AMT TØ GRAND-TØTAL.
    WRITE RECØRD. GØ TØ NEXT-PAR.
```

9. The cost-or-market rule of inventory valuation states that "market" means the cost of replacing the inventory item in question, provided that this amount shall not exceed net realizable value (sales price less cost to complete and sell) nor be less than the net realizable value reduced by a normal profit. Where the market value would lie outside these limits, the nearer limit is used to represent market instead. The selected market figure is compared with the item's cost, and the lower is used in valuing the inventory.

Instructions: Draw a flow diagram, and prepare the procedure division segment, for a routine for selecting the proper inventory valuation under the cost-or-market rule. The correct value should be stored at a data location called CØMWIL.

The following data items are available; all may be assumed to be numeric computational elements:

Item	COBOL Name
Replacement Cost	REPL-CØST
Sales price	SALES-PRICE
Cost to complete and sell	CØMP-CØST
Normal profit	NØRMAL-PRØFIT
Actual cost	CØST

Hint: First, find the value to be used as market; then, compare this with cost, and select the smaller amount as the inventory value to be stored at CØMWIL. MARKET may be used as a temporary storage area.

Program Notes

Each of the following problems requires coding of the procedure division only. In each instance the other three divisions are required by the same-numbered problem in Chapter 5, and details pertaining to the data division may be found there.

The flow diagram originally prepared for each problem provides the logical structure now required for coding the data division. These should be referred to in preparing the COBOL coding for the procedure division. However, certain coding requirements are not represented in the flow charts. These, mentioned below, are very important if proper coding is to be achieved.

Each procedure division coding should comply with the following:

1. The first command in each procedure division after opening files should be "MØVE SPACE TØ output-record-name." This blanks out all FILLER items in the output record and provides improved readability.

2. Only data items which are defined as numeric computational may be used as operands in arithmetic instructions. This means that an edited receiving area should not be used to accept the result of arithmetic commands if the amount is to be used in subsequent computation. To avoid this, all working storage required has been provided in each problem's data division description in Chapter 5. The working storage provisions set out in Chapter 5 should be observed as each problem is coded, and only those data items provided should be used in the procedure division.

3. When TRUE branches of conditionals are long, an unconditional transfer should be used to branch to a new paragraph. There, the TRUE commands may be written, and the program may proceed to the proper address. This recommendation applies also to the FALSE side of a version 2 IF statement.

Problems 10-15 below, refer to situations described in Chapter 3. These descriptions do not contain any reference to the AT END clause or end routines. In preparing the procedure division, however, the AT END clause should be used with each READ command. It should transfer the program to a new paragraph, where control totals should be displayed after moving them to the edited display area, DIS. Then, files should be closed and the STØP RUN command given.

10. Prepare the procedure division for Problem 3-6 (page 55). Details of the first three divisions may be found in Problem 5-10 (page 140).

11. Prepare the procedure division for Problem 3-8 (page 58). Details of the first three divisions may be found in Problem 5-11. (page 142).

12. Prepare the procedure division for Problem 3-9 (page 59). Details of the first three divisions may be found in Problem 5-12 (page 142).

13. Prepare the procedure division for Problem 3-10 (page 60). Details of the first three divisions may be found in Problem 5-13 (page 143).

14. Prepare the procedure division for Problem 3-15 (page 65). Details of the first three divisions may be found in Problem 5-14 (page 144).

15. Prepare the procedure division for Problem 3-18 (page 67). Details of the first three divisions may be found in Problem 5-15 (page 145).

16. Prepare the procedure division for Problem 4-4 (page 77). The AT END conditional should transfer the program to a paragraph named FINISH. Details of the first three divisions may be found in Problem 5-16 (page 146).

17. Prepare the procedure division for Problem 4-5 (page 108). If actual cost exceeds the budget allowance, the program should transfer to a paragraph called ØVER-BUDGET. Details of the first three divisions may be found in Problem 5-17 (page 147).

18. Prepare the procedure division for Problem 4-6 (page 109). Details of the first three divisions may be found in Problem 5-18 (page 148). Use CTR as a working area to avoid the misuse of edited fields.

19. Prepare the procedure division for Problem 4-10 (page 110). Details of the first three divisions may be found in Problem 5-19 (page 148).

20. Prepare the procedure division for Problem 4-12 (page 112). Details of the first three divisions may be found in Problem 5-20 (page 149).

21. Prepare the procedure division for Problem 4-13 (page 112). In programming the sum-of-the-years'-digits method, the denominator of the years fraction may be computed as DEN before entering the program loop in which depreciation for each year is calculated. The "WRITE ... FRØM" option should be used to write headings from the constant section and report contents from the working storage section. Details of the first three divisions may be found in Problem 5-21 (page 150).

22. Prepare the procedure division for Problem 4-15 (page 114). Each READ command should occupy a separate paragraph. The first READ instruction should specify NEXT SENTENCE as the true branch of its AT END conditional. Details of the first three divisions may be found in Problem 5-22 (page 150). Use the working storage provided to avoid comparing or computing with edited fields.

CHAPTER 7

ADVANCED CONTROL LOGIC: THE "PERFORM" COMMAND AND DATA ARRAYS

All of the basic COBOL commands have been introduced, and their technical nature has been discussed. This chapter treats an advanced control instruction, known as the PERFØRM command. It is a principal member of the logic control group. There are four main versions of this instruction and one significant modified version. A major purpose of this chapter is to describe the logic and coding requirements of these PERFØRM versions and to set out their general areas of use.

Methods of processing grouped data are discussed as the second major chapter topic. This involves the construction of data arrays, or matrices, as well as the routines devised for the manipulation of their contents. The PERFØRM command is frequently used in array processing, and it is for this reason that these topics are covered in a single chapter.

THE "PERFØRM" COMMAND

The PERFØRM command is a form of conditional branch. Like the IF statement, it processes no data, but instead governs the flow of the program according to certain criteria in the command itself. All versions of the PERFØRM instruction permit the program to follow one instructional path for one or more iterations and then to shift to another when requirements governing the first are satisfied.

General Structure

The basic versions of the PERFØRM instruction are introduced below. Examples of use are furnished with each. These should be taken as suggestive of the range of applications to which this, the most powerful instruction in the language, may be put.

Form 1: The Basic PERFØRM

The fundamental PERFØRM command is of the following form:

PERFØRM procedure-name-1 [THRU procedure-name-2] .

When the PERFØRM command is encountered, control is shifted from the regular program path to that paragraph designated by procedure-name-1. The section of the program starting with this procedure name and extending through procedure-name-2, if designated, is executed once. Then the computer returns automatically to the statement following the PERFØRM command for its next instruction.

The program segment controlled by the PERFØRM command is known as its "range." Thus, if the command specifies "PERFØRM PRØC-A," its range includes those instructions comprising the paragraph called PRØC-A. Should the command specify "PERFØRM PRØC-A THRU PRØC-C," all instructions in program segment PRØC-A through those in segment PRØC-C will be executed.

An example of the simple PERFØRM's coding and use may be found in the Illustration 2 of Appendix B (page 228). Here, on line 16 of page 4, the command "PERFØRM REC-PRØCESS" is given. This will cause the computer to jump to the paragraph named REC-PRØCESS on page 5, execute it, and return to the statement following the PERFØRM instruction. Thus the command "ADD INV-CØST, FGT TØ TØT-REC" will be the instruction executed after the PERFØRM command is satisfied.

This version of the PERFØRM is very useful when relatively small program subdivisions must be written but the programmer does not want to set them up at the required logical point. He may instead insert a PERFØRM statement to serve as a bridge to the subprogram and then continue writing the central program portion. Subprograms may then be grouped at the end of the main routine.

This situation might arise as in the Illustration above, or when error routines are written. It is frequently inconvenient to write all phases of error routines at the point where data are tested; instead, the PERFØRM may be used to reference another program segment where the routine is set up.

Of course, the command's usefulness is not limited to treating error or other special routines. In large programs where certain major branches exist, it may be possible to fragmentize the program and prepare it section by section, using the PERFØRM command as a connective for each part.

Illustrations of Form. The following illustrations are intended to suggest how this command might be applied in a program. The first example demonstrates the use of the PERFØRM as a means of handling special routines. The second shows the command as it might be employed in governing the segments of a fairly large program.

1. Use in controlling special short routines. Assume that data necessary to compute weekly gross pay for employees are stored in two files. One, called MASTER, contains certain basic information such as pay rate. The other, called HØURS, contains the hours worked this week.

Gross pay (GRØSS) is to be calculated as follows: A record (containing data on one employee) is to be read from each file. Employee numbers, stored as EMP and NØ in the MASTER and HØUR files, respectively, are to be compared. If they agree, GRØSS should be calculated by multiplying hourly rate (RATE) by hours worked (HRS). GRØSS should be checked for overflow; and if one occurs, a suitable message should be written and control returned to read the MASTER file. The output record PAY-REC should be written if there is no overflow.

If EMP is less than NØ, the employee has no weekly hours record. This indicates that he did not work this week. A message to this effect should be displayed, and the program should read another record from the master file. The number of absences is to be accumulated as ABS.

If EMP is greater than NØ, a record exists in the current file not matched by a master record. The program should stop after printing a message when this occurs and then return to read the HØURS file upon operator intervention.

A suitable flow diagram for this program is shown in Figure 7-1. It may be seen in this diagram that the PERFØRM command is symbolized by a rectangle with a broken line leading from it, as follows:

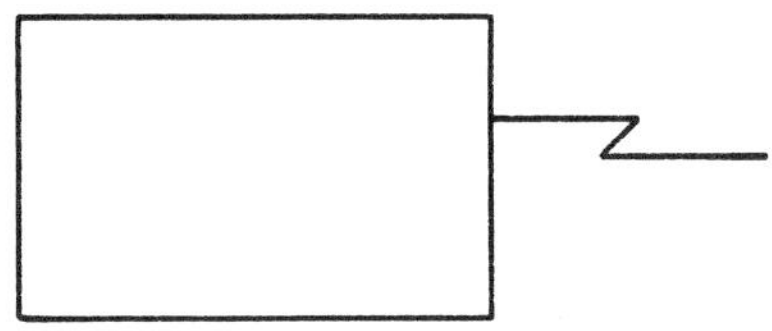

The procedure name in the PERFØRM command leads to a program segment shown elsewhere in the diagram. The broken line indicates the path to be followed after execution of the PERFØRM instruction. For example, the program segment END-RØUTINE, shown at the bottom of Figure 7-1. will be executed when the AT END conditional is true in the READ HØURS command. Control will then return to the command following the PERFØRM, and the program will stop. The other PERFØRM commands also lead from the main program to a subroutine; in each instance, control returns to the statement following the PERFØRM command after executing the appropriate segment.

<u>Coding the simple PERFØRM.</u> The coded procedure division for this illustration is shown in Figure 7-2. Here, it may be seen that the PERFØRM command cites a paragraph name appearing elsewhere in the program. Control is shifted by the PERFØRM command to this named paragraph, it is executed, and the program returns to the command following the PERFØRM.

In Figure 7-2, for example, if a SIZE ERRØR condition occurs in the command on line 09, the paragraph named ØVER-RØUTINE will be executed. Then the program will return to line 10 and execute the command which states "GØ TØ READ-1." While the PERFØRM commands in this illustration are not really essential, they do serve to show the nature of the instruction.

2. Use in controlling large program segments. Assume that a company uses several different pay plans—straight salary, hourly rate, or piece rate. An indicator, called PAY-TYPE, in each employee's record indicates his method of pay, where 1 signifies straight salary, 2 hourly rate, and 3 piece rate.

In processing the payroll records, the PAY-TYPE is tested after reading an employee's record. The program is then transferred to one of three routines for pay computation, according to type of compensation, after which the pay record, PAY-RCD, is written.

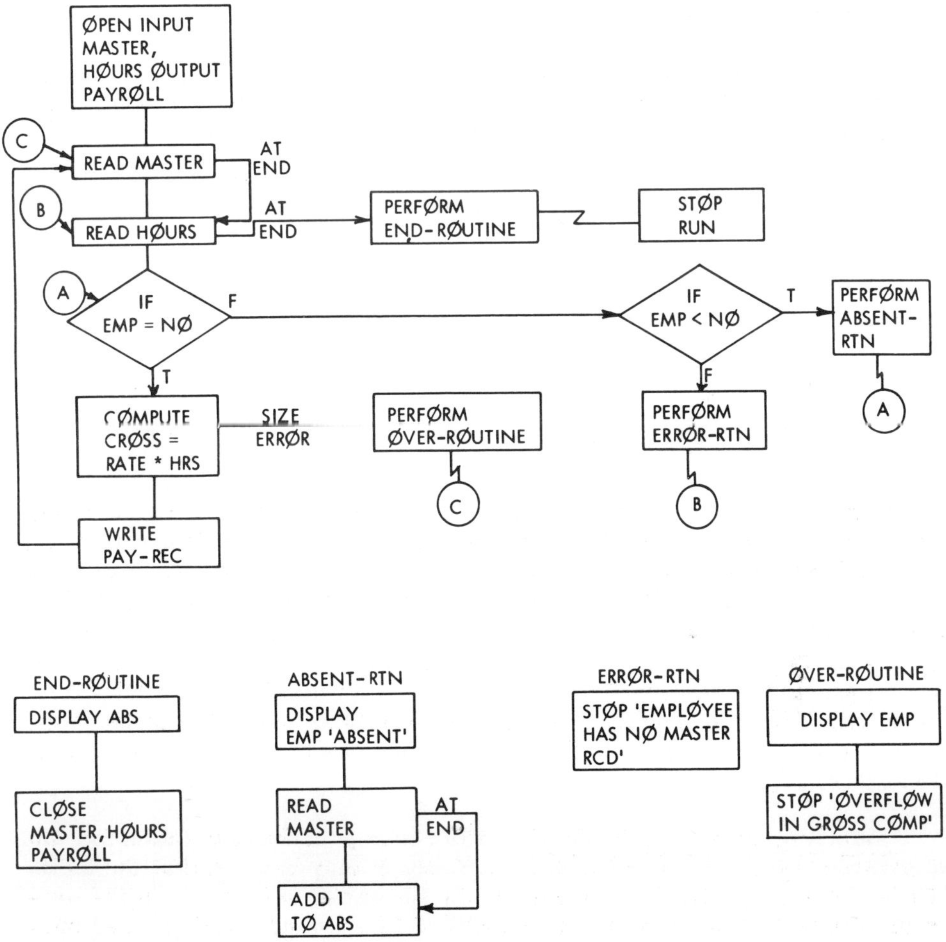

FIG. 7-1. Controlling Short Routines with the PERFØRM Command

223010A

COBOL PROGRAM SHEET

PAGE 1 3	PROGRAM: FIGURE 7-2	SYSTEM	SHEET 1 OF 1
	PROGRAMMER: MC CAMERON	DATE	IDENT. 73 80

```
PROCEDURE DIVISIØN.
START. ØPEN INPUT MASTER, HØURS, ØUTPUT PAYRØLL.
    MØVE SPACE TØ PAY-REC.
READ-1. READ MASTER AT END NEXT SENTENCE.
READ-2. READ HØURS AT END PERFORM END-RØUTINE, STØP RUN.
TEST-PAR. IF EMP = NØ GØ TØ PRØC-PAR, ELSE IF EMP LESS THAN
    NØ PERFØRM ABSENT-RTN, GØ TØ TEST-PAR. PERFØRM ERRØR-RTN.
    GØ TØ READ-2.
PRØC-PAR. CØMPUTE GRØSS RØUNDED = RATE * HRS, ØN SIZE ERRØR
    PERFØRM ØVER-RØUTINE GØ TØ READ-1. WRITE PAY-REC.
    GØ TØ READ-1.

END-RØUTINE. DISPLAY 'NUMBER ØF EMPLØYEES ABSENT, ' ABS.
    CLØSE MASTER, HØURS, PAYRØLL.

ABSENT-RTN. DISPLAY 'EMPLØYEE NØ. ' EMP ' IS ABSENT'.
    READ MASTER AT END NEXT SENTENCE. ADD 1 TØ ABS.

ERRØR-RTN. DISPLAY 'EMPLØYEE NØ. ' NØ.
    STØP ' HAS NØ MASTER RECØRD'.

ØVER-RØUTINE. DISPLAY 'EMPLØYEE NØ. ' EMP.
    STØP ' ØVERFLØW IN GRØSS CØMPUTATIØN'.
```

FIG. 7-2

The use of the PERFØRM command in this situation may be seen in Figure 7-3. Input and output file names are assumed. Details of computational procedures are omitted, inasmuch as they have nothing to do with the basic application of the PERFØRM command.

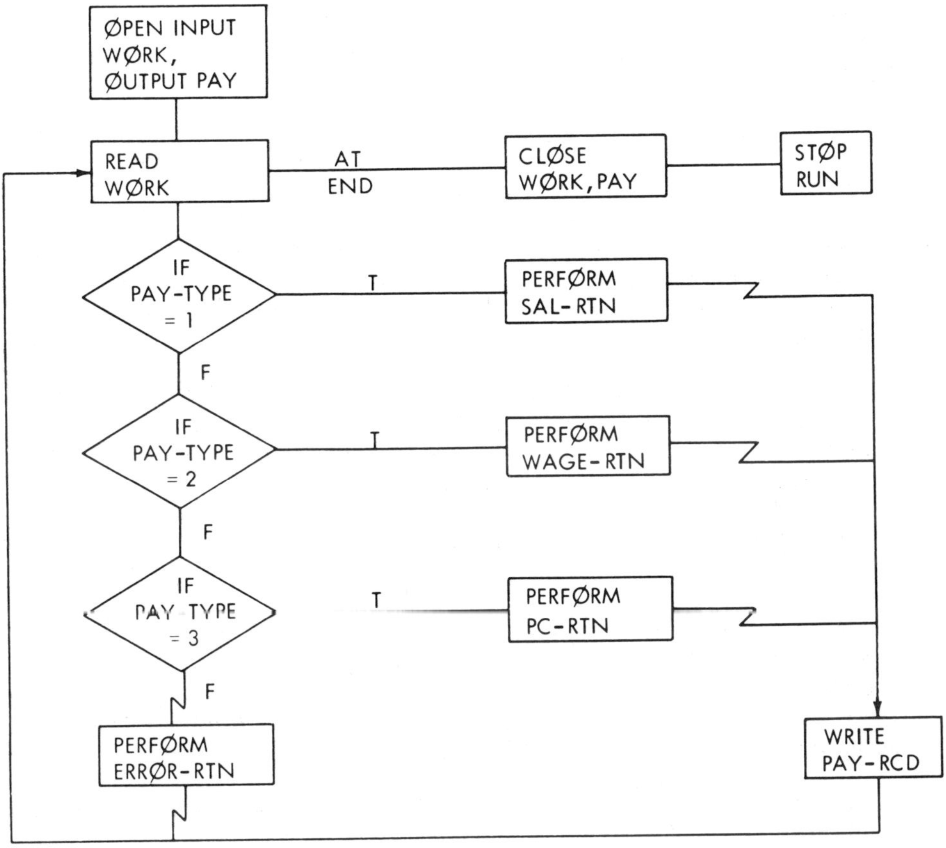

FIG. 7-3.
Controlling Major Program Segments with the PERFØRM Command

Basic Characteristics. The basic PERFØRM indicates the general nature of all the command's versions. The instruction cites the procedure name of a paragraph existing somewhere in the procedure division—above or below the PERFØRM command itself. This transfers operations to the paragraph; its contents are executed, and the program returns automatically to the statement following the PERFØRM command for its next instruction. This statement may be in the same sentence as the PERFØRM, but this is not required.

Form 2: PERFØRM n TIMES

This version of the PERFØRM command differs from the first in that it causes a routine to be repeated any number of times, while the first type always causes the routine to be executed only once. The general form of the command is:

PERFØRM procedure-name-1 [THRU procedure-name-2]n TIMES

where n may be either a numeric literal or a data name. If n is a literal, the specified routine will be executed exactly as many times as called for. If a data name is specified, the routine will be executed the number of times specified by the value stored at the data name. In either instance the controlling value must be a positive whole number. After executing the procedure name paragraph(s) as many times as specified, the computer returns to the statement following the PERFØRM command for its next instruction.

It is most important that n, if a data name, be defined in the data division as a <u>numeric computational</u> item and that its contents be an unsigned integer. The data name may be identified in either the file or the working storage section, as appropriate.

By the same token, if a numeric literal is specified, it too must be an unsigned integer.

To illustrate the use of this PERFØRM instruction, assume that a series of sum-of-the-years'-digits depreciation schedules are to be prepared for assets having various costs and scrap values, each asset having a use life of 25 years. Asset cost (CØST) and scrap value (SCRAP) will be read as ASSET-RCD records, in the ASSET-PCH file.

Output, as DEP-LINE records in the DEP-SCH file, will contain the following:

Data Description	COBOL Name
Year	YEAR
Current depreciation	CUR-DEP
Accumulated depreciation	ACC-DEP
Undepreciated balance	BALANCE

All the data items in the output record are assumed to be of numeric report mode except YEAR, which is assumed to be numeric computational. Additional computational areas required, assumed to exist in working storage, are:

NUM, used to contain the numerator of the use-life fraction
DEN, used to contain the denominator of the use-life fraction
DEP, used to store the amount of current depreciation
ACCUM, used to store the amount of accumulated depreciation
BAL, used to store the original cost of the asset

After preparing each depreciation schedule, the computer is to pause, displaying a statement indicating completion, and then return to read another asset purchase record and prepare another depreciation schedule.

The flow chart for this program is shown in Figure 7-4. Note here that after computing the required denominator of the year's fraction and reading cost and scrap value information, the program moves into the range of the PERFØRM command. This instructs the computer to execute the DEP-CØMP routine 25 times. This routine is diagrammed immediately beneath the PERFØRM instruction, varying slightly the flow-charting process used with simple PERFØRM commands. This is advantageous because now the flow chart shows just what the DEP-CØMP routine includes near the statement which causes execution of the program segment.

After completing one iteration, during which depreciation amounts are computed, certain fields are updated, and an output record is written, the computer automatically returns to the first command in the DEP-CØMP routine and repeats the process. No GØ TØ command is required; the return is automatically effected under the control of the PERFØRM command. Finally, when the DEP-CØMP routine has been executed 25 times, the program transfers out of this segment to the alternative branch where the STØP instruction is written.

The PERFØRM command restarts each time it is entered. Thus, if more than one input record is processed, the second is processed in exactly the same manner as the first.

The IF statement has also been illustrated as a device for controlling iterations. However, where use of the IF statement in this context requires that a counter be set up, incremented, and then tested, none of these steps are necessary when the PERFØRM command is used. The PERFØRM instruction simply specifies the routine to be executed and the number of times it is to be followed; built-in features of the command do the rest.

The usefulness of the illustrated depreciation schedule routine is severely limited by the fact that it can only process assets having a use life of 25 years. However, the program can very easily be changed to prepare schedules for any useful life. This is done by reading in the asset's use life along with its cost and scrap value, and then using this data item to control the PERFØRM command.

A diagram showing this more general form of the program may be seen in Figure 7-5. The following procedural changes may be noted when programs in Figures 7-4 and 7-5 are compared:

1. The input record is expanded to include USE-LIFE, the anticipated useful life of the asset.
2. DEN is computed as (USE-LIFE * (USE-LIFE + 1))/2, yielding the appropriate denominator for any useful life.
3. NUM is initialized by moving USE-LIFE to it.
4. The PERFØRM command is changed to read as follows:

   PERFØRM DEP-CØMP USE-LIFE TIMES.

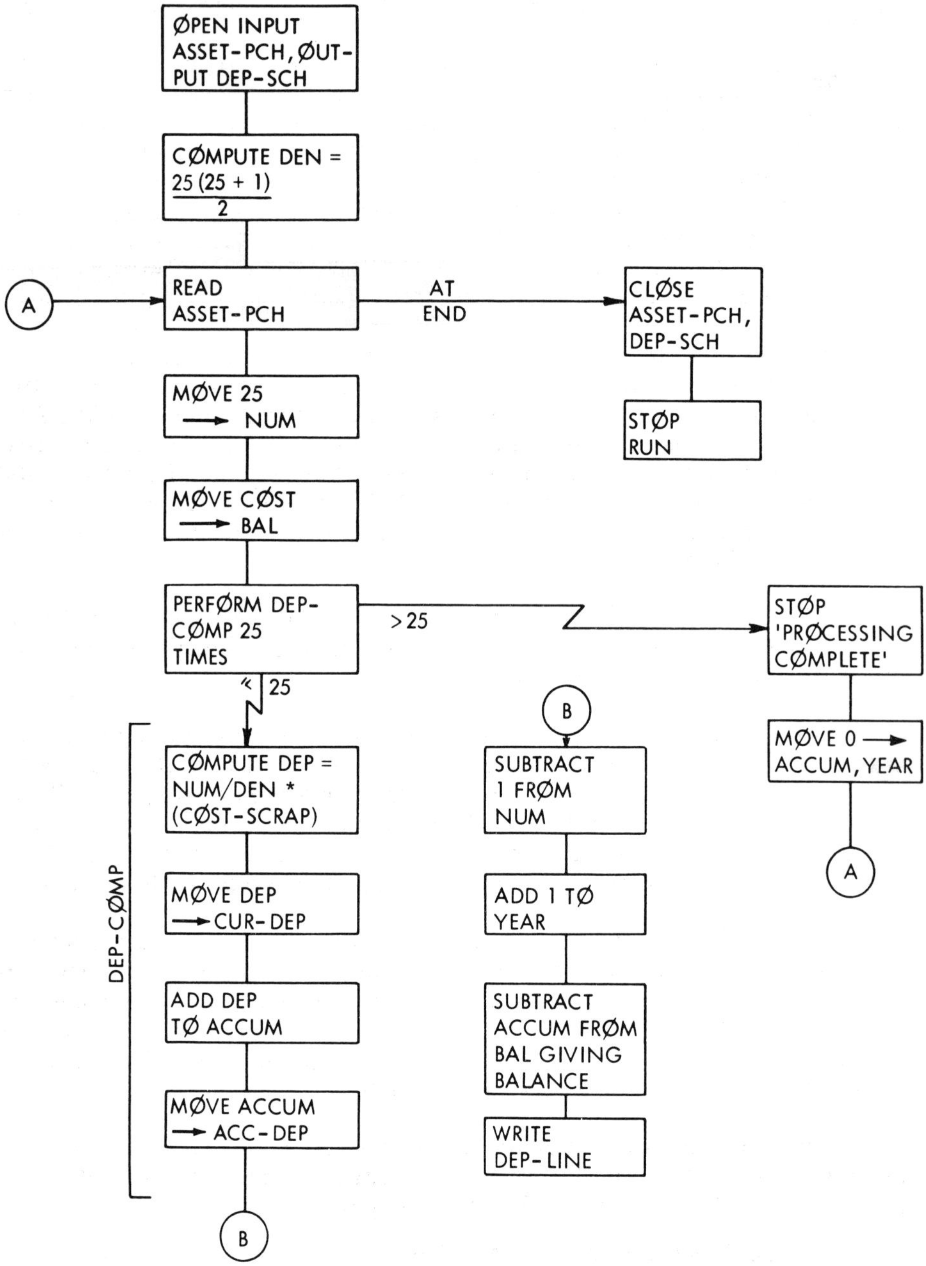

FIG. 7-4. Illustrating the PERFØRM n TIMES Command

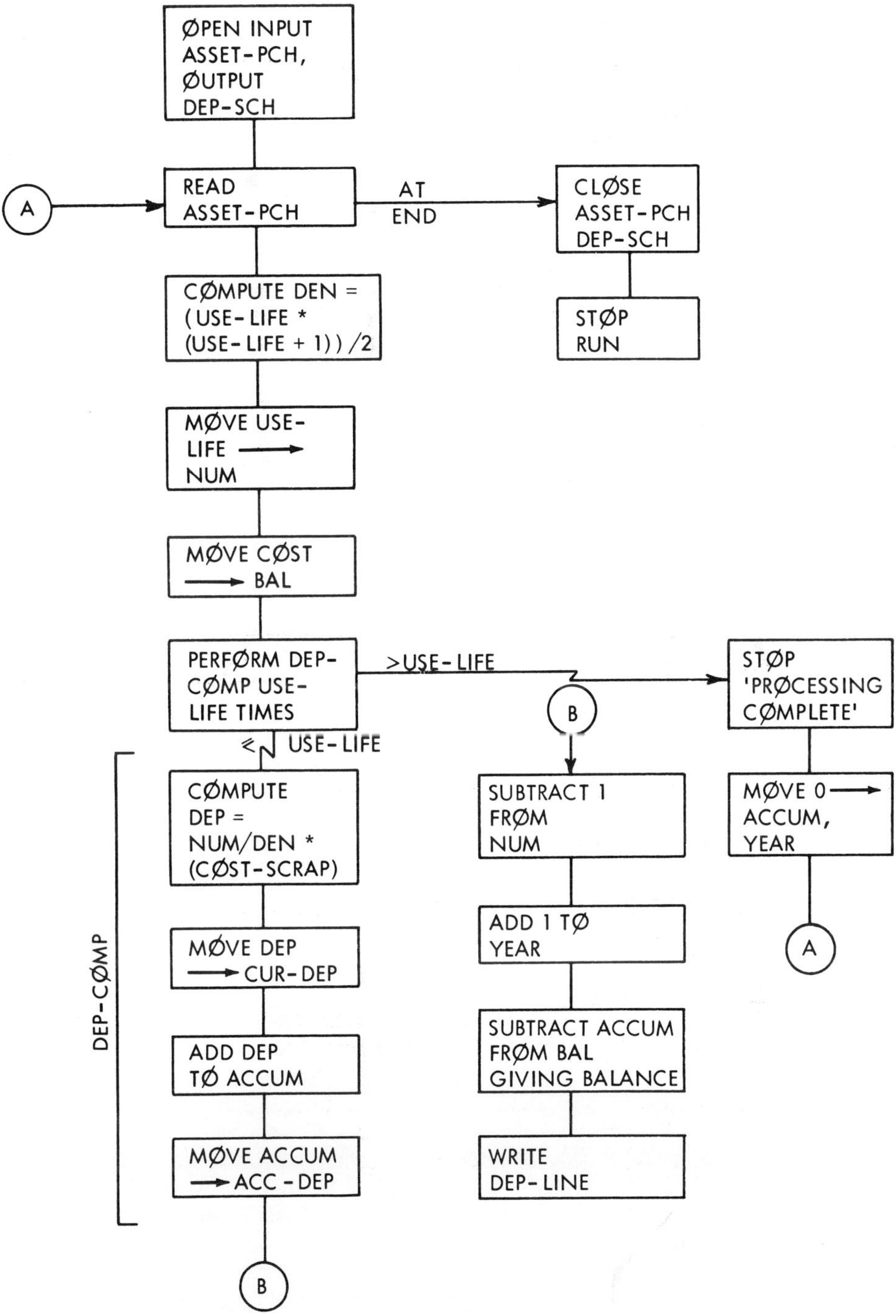

FIG. 7-5. A Generalized Form of the PERFØRM n TIMES Command

Thus the DEP-CØMP routine will be executed as many times as called for by the life of the particular asset being processed. With these minor changes, the highly inflexible program shown in Figure 7-4 is modified to represent one capable of preparing depreciation schedules predicated on the sum-of-the-years basis for assets with any useful life.

When a general program is sought, the value of the limit may be read in, as in the example above, or it may be computed. The only requirements are that it be nonnegative and an integer.

Coding the PERFØRM n TIMES Command. Figure 7-6 contains the coded procedure division for this version of the program. Line 09 contains the PERFØRM command. When executing this program, the computer will jump from here to the paragraph called DEP-CØMP and execute it the number of times dictated by the value of USE-LIFE. This will cause the preparation of output lines consistent with the cost and useful life of the asset. After preparing the entire depreciation table, the program transfers back to the command following the PERFØRM instruction. After displaying a message to indicate the completion of the table, certain work areas are reset to zero, and the program returns to read another asset record.

Form 3: PERFØRM UNTIL

The complete structure of the third PERFØRM version is as follows:

PERFØRM procedure-name-1 [THRU procedure-name-2] UNTIL condition-1.

This permits the programmer to specify some condition, chosen from among those discussed in Chapter 4, to be fulfilled. The PERFØRM command interrogates the specified conditional and, if false, causes the program segment in the PERFØRM range to be executed. Then, interrogation is again made. The process is repeated if the conditional is still not satisfied. When a true result is finally obtained, the program leaves the range of the PERFØRM command and transfers to the instruction following the PERFØRM. Thus the range of the PERFØRM command is in reality the false branch of a conditional, with the regular program constituting the true side.

This command form may be used as a substitute for form 2, if desired. To achieve the desired number of iterations, a counter would be created and incremented, and its status would be checked as condition-1 in the controlling PERFØRM command.

When the PERFØRM UNTIL instruction is used to control iterations, care must be taken to see that the desired number of passes through the range are made. It should be remembered that the range of the PERFØRM is followed only so long as the conditional is false; as quickly as a true result is found, the program transfers out of the PERFØRM loop. It must also be remembered that the condition is tested before making an iteration.

PAGE	PROGRAM	FIGURE 7-6	SYSTEM		SHEET 1 OF 1
	PROGRAMMER	MC CAMERØN	DATE		IDENT. 73 80

```
SERIAL CONT. A   B
 4  6      8   12

01     PRØCEDURE DIVISIØN.
02     ØPEN-FILES. ØPEN INPUT ASSET-PCH, ØUTPUT DEP-SCH.
03         MØVE SPACE TØ DEP-LINE.
04     START. READ ASSET-PCH, AT END CLØSE ASSET-PCH, DEP-SCH,
05         STØP RUN.
06         CØMPUTE DEN = (USE-LIFE * (USE-LIFE + 1)) / 2.
07         MØVE USE-LIFE TØ NUM.
08         MØVE CØST TØ BAL.
09         PERFØRM DEP-CØMP USE-LIFE TIMES. STØP 'PRØCESSING CØMPLETE'.
10         MØVE 0 TØ ACCUM, YEAR. GØ TØ START.
11     DEP-CØMP. CØMPUTE DEP RØUNDED = NUM / DEN * (CØST - SCRAP).
12         MØVE DEP TØ CUR-DEP. ADD DEP TØ ACCUM.
13         MØVE ACCUM TØ ACC-DEP. SUBTRACT 1 FRØM NUM.
14         ADD 1 TØ YEAR. SUBTRACT ACCUM FRØM BAL GIVING BALANCE.
15         WRITE DEP-LINE.
```

FIG. 7-6

To illustrate the kind of error which may easily be made in counting iterations, assume that this PERFØRM version is to be used in control and that a loop is to be executed exactly once. The program is written as follows:

```
MØVE 1 TØ N.

PERFØRM PRØC-A UNTIL N = 1.
```

In this instance, N = 1 the first time the PERFØRM command is encountered. The condition thus met, control does not pass to the PERFØRM range but to the statement following the PERFØRM command. Thus, PRØC-A will not be executed at all. To avoid this, the PERFØRM command should have read "PERFØRM PRØC-A UNTIL N GREATER 1" (or N should have been set to zero), thus insuring a single iteration.

The condition specified by the PERFØRM command need not be predicated on a test of an increasing value. Any form of condition test may be used. For example, the illustration used with PERFØRM version 2, requiring the preparation of depreciation schedules, contains several data elements which could be used to end computation. One, the data element NUM, is decreasing in value. The PERFØRM command could have used this in developing its limit, by specifying "PERFØRM DEP-CØMP UNTIL NUM = 0" or "PERFØRM DEP-CØMP UNTIL NUM LESS THAN 1." Control might also be effected in this instance by specifying "PERFØRM DEP-CØMP UNTIL BAL LESS THAN SCRAP" or "PERFØRM DEP-CØMP UNTIL ACC-DEP + SCRAP GREATER THAN CØST." Any number of values, moving to an upper or lower limit, could have been employed as a control in this situation. This is typical of many repetitive programs.

In all likelihood, however, the form 2 PERFØRM command will prove easier to use when a certain program loop is to be executed a known or determinable number of times. The PERFØRM UNTIL version is most valuable when a loop must be performed repeatedly but the number of iterations required to satisfy some condition is not predictable.

One of the illustrations pertaining to the IF statement may be restructured as an example of this PERFØRM application. In example 3 (page 87) a record search is undertaken wherein one record, called the "finder record," is read; then a file of data records is scanned in search of a record bearing the same number as the finder. This can be programmed with the use of the IF statement, but it is more concisely stated if the PERFØRM command is used. With the PERFØRM, the routine would appear as shown in Figure 7-7. Note that the specification of a test comparing FINDER-NØ and ACCT-NØ, required when the IF statement is used, is now unnecessary. This test is executed by the PERFØRM command itself; if the two values are equal, the program branches from the PERFØRM loop, writes the proper record, and stops. The search continues, however, so long as the values are not equal.

Coding the PERFØRM ... UNTIL ... Command. Figure 7-8 contains the coded procedure division prepared from the flow chart in Figure 7-7. It may be seen here that the coded routine is quite short. The PERFØRM routine controls the reading of records from the ACCT-FILE, the file being searched. The PERFØRM command itself governs the testing of FINDER-NØ and ACCT-NØ, account numbers in the FINDER-FILE and ACCT-FILE files, respectively. If a matching account number is found, the program leaves the range of the PERFØRM and writes out the discovered record. If no match is found, an error is assumed to exist; the program writes out an error message and then returns for the reentry of the corrected number being sought.

A glance at the routine coded in Figure 7-8 will show that the first test is really a sham. The finder record has been read at this point, but the first account record has not. Therefore a "not equal" result is certain to be obtained, causing the program to enter the range of the PERFØRM and read the first record from the ACCT-FILE.

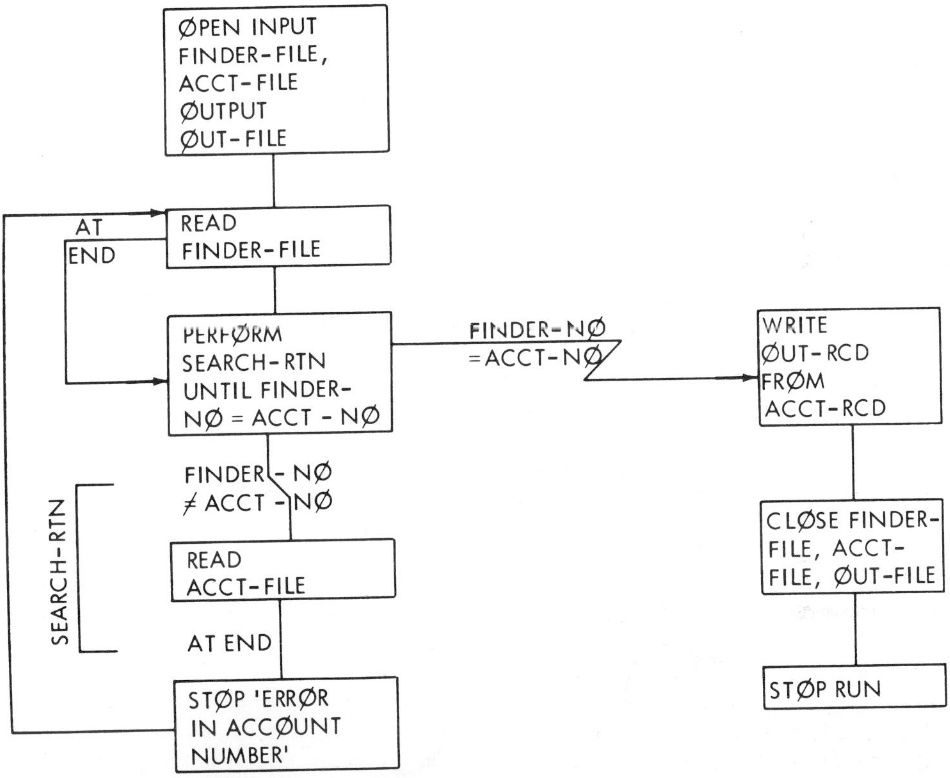

FIG. 7-7. Illustration of the PERFØRM ... UNTIL ... Command

COBOL PROGRAM SHEET

223010A

PAGE 1 3	PROGRAM: FIGURE 7-8	SYSTEM	SHEET 1 OF 1
	PROGRAMMER: MC CAMERØN.	DATE	IDENT 73 80

```
SERIAL CONT. A   B
4    6       8   12
01       PRØCEDURE DIVISIØN.
02       ØPEN-FILES. ØPEN INPUT FINDER-FILE, ACCT-FILE, ØUTPUT ØUT-FILE.
03       START. READ FINDER-FILE, AT END NEXT SENTENCE.
04           PERFØRM SEARCH-RTN UNTIL FINDER-NØ = ACCT-NØ.
05           WRITE ØUT-RCD FRØM ACCT-RCD.
06           CLØSE FINDER-FILE, ACCT-FILE, ØUT-FILE.
07           STØP RUN.
08       SEARCH-RTN. READ ACCT-FILE, AT END
09           STØP 'ERRØR IN ACCØUNT NUMBER', GØ TØ START.
```

FIG. 7-8

Form 4: PERFØRM VARYING

This last version of the PERFØRM command is the most powerful of all. It incorporates the testing abilities of version 3 with the ability to vary the value of a data name. Its general form is as follows:

```
PERFØRM procedure-name-1 [THRU procedure-name-2]
VARYING data-name FRØM value-1 BY value-2
UNTIL condition-1.
```

In this command a data item, specified as "data-name" in the general statement form above, is varied by the PERFØRM statement from the initial designated value (value-1) in the specified increments (value-2). Either value-1, value-2, or both, may be a numeric literal or a data name. They may be integers, but it is not required. Either or both may be negative; thus the instruction segment "VARYING DATA-A FRØM 50 BY-.1" would cause data element DATA-A to assume an initial value of 50, and this would be decreased by .1 with each iteration.

"Data-name" must be defined in the data division, as must value-1 and value-2 unless they are literals. Only numeric computational items should be used for the index "data-name," the initial value "value-1," and the increment "value-2."

The terminal of the PERFØRM loop is specified by the UNTIL clause, as in version 3. This clause may test data controlled by the VARYING clause, or it may deal with other values.

The data item controlled by the VARYING clause may be used in the program in any desired way, so long as its value is not changed. This may be illustrated by once more considering the preparation of a depreciation schedule by the sum-of-the-year's-digits method, as described in the treatment of PERFØRM version 2 above. For purposes of the present example, assume that use-life is a variable and is included in input data as the element USE-LIFE. Figure 7-9 contains an example of this use of the PERFØRM command, using YEAR as a control element.

The data element used to control the PERFØRM loop, YEAR, is a part of the output record, DEP-LINE. Its use in output does not detract from its usefulness as a control field in the PERFØRM command. In fact, the PERFØRM instruction causes YEAR to vary from one through the maximum set by USE-LIFE in increments of one and makes it useful as output data.

Illustration 3 in Appendix B (page 234) represents the COBOL coding for this problem. All divisions of the program are coded, thus permitting the necessary relationships between the data and procedure divisions to be noted.

Here, it may be seen that the data item YEAR is a part of the output record, defined as a numeric computational element. Its value will be supplied by the PERFØRM command; therefore, there is no need for any command setting up an amount in this area.

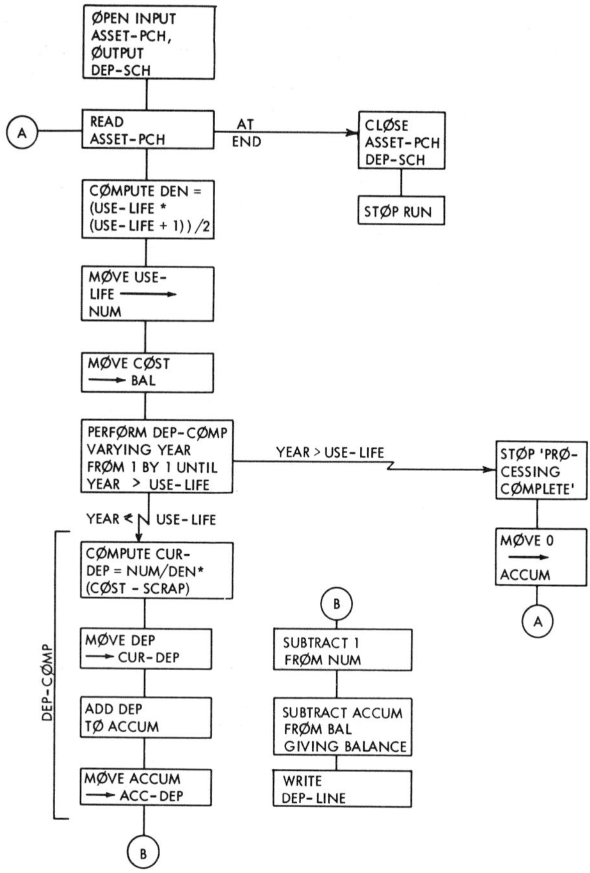

FIG. 7-9
Using the VARYING ... UNTIL Version of the PERFØRM Command

The proper clause for terminating the PERFØRM may be seen on line 12, page 3, of the coded problem solution. It may be seen that the clause "UNTIL YEAR GREATER USE-LIFE" must be used, not "UNTIL YEAR = USE-LIFE," as might be expected. If the clause is true when it is evaluated, the program does not go to the paragraph named in the PERFØRM command, but to the statement following the PERFØRM. Thus, if the "UNTIL YEAR = USE-LIFE" clause were used, the last iteration desired would not be executed.

Characteristics of the PERFØRM

All versions of the PERFØRM command have certain characteristics quite different from any other instructions studied. The main ones are considered below.

Premature Termination. PERFØRM routines may be interrupted by transfers outside their range. For example, it is permissible to construct

IF statements testing certain data as a part of the PERFØRM range, with either the true or the false branch leading to commands outside the PERFØRM loop. If this is done, reentry to the PERFØRM loop should probably not be attempted by the beginner, because it is possible only under certain circumstances.

The value of any index maintained by the PERFØRM command is available for use by the program after leaving the instruction's range, either by satisfying the PERFØRM or by branching. Thus, if a program is written to seek a certain condition within a PERFØRM loop, an index indicating the iteration on which the condition is met may be kept by the control command.

End of the PERFØRM Range. The range of the PERFØRM command ends with the last sentence in the program segment specified as procedure-name-1 (or procedure-name-2, if used). This last sentence may not contain a GØ TØ command, because this would interfere with the regular ending of the range. It would attempt to transfer control, a function which at this point must be exercised by the PERFØRM command if that instruction is to be completed.

If the range of the PERFØRM command contains two or more branches, these must be rejoined before the end of the range is encountered. All branches must eventually arrive at the same place—the last sentence in the command's range. Where program logic prevents a recombining of branches—as, for example, when the program proceeds along two mutually exclusive paths—the rule is satisfied by creating a separate paragraph containing the single command EXIT, and each branch is transferred to this. This paragraph, mentioned as procedure-name-2 in the PERFØRM, contains the last sentence in the command's range.

Execution by "Dropping Through." All PERFØRM commands call for the execution of some program segment, identified by one or more procedure names. This program segment may be separate from the main program and accessible only through the PERFØRM command. On the other hand, it may be an integral part of the main program. These conditions are diagrammed in Figure 7-10 for clarity.

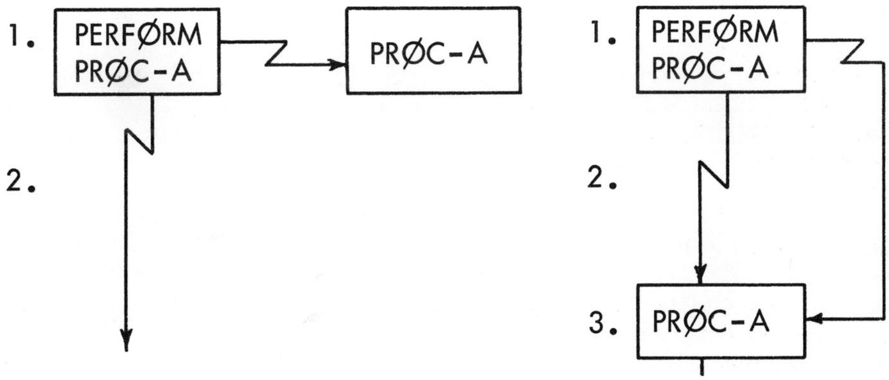

a) PRØC-A outside the regular program

b) PRØC-A as an integral part of the regular program

FIG. 7-10

In the first instance, PRØC-A is accessible only through the PERFØRM command. In the second, however, PRØC-A is accessible through the PERFØRM and as a part of the regular program. It will be executed first under control of the PERFØRM command, the program returning to step 2 immediately after execution. In the normal sequence of the program, PRØC-A will again be executed, after which the program proceeds to step 3. The second execution is termed execution by "dropping through."

Programs using the PERFØRM command must be carefully constructed to cause execution of the required number of iterations whenever there is a chance of execution by dropping through the procedure. Assume, for instance, that program requirements call for the execution of PRØC-A 25 times. This may be written as shown in Figure 7-11. This design of the program will cause PROC-A to be executed once more than required: 25 times under control of the PERFØRM and once by dropping through.

This mistake is easily avoided by placing all routines controlled by the PERFØRM command at the end of the program, where there is no chance of their execution by dropping through. Of course, an exception must be made when the routine is a necessary part of regular processing.

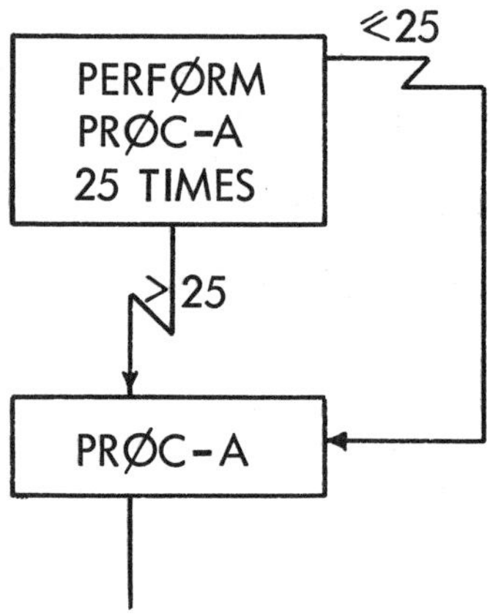

FIG. 7-11

Multiple Access to the PERFØRM Range. The same procedure segment may be referred to by more than one PERFØRM command. It will be executed when required, and control will return to the statement following the appropriate PERFØRM when execution is completed. This may be seen in the diagram in Figure 7-12. In this instance, PRØC-A is first performed under the control of the PERFØRM command, shown as step 1. Afterwards, control transfers to the statement following step 1. Then, at step 3, PRØC-A is again called for and again executed. This time, however, control transfers to the statement to be found at step 4 after PRØC-A has been completed.

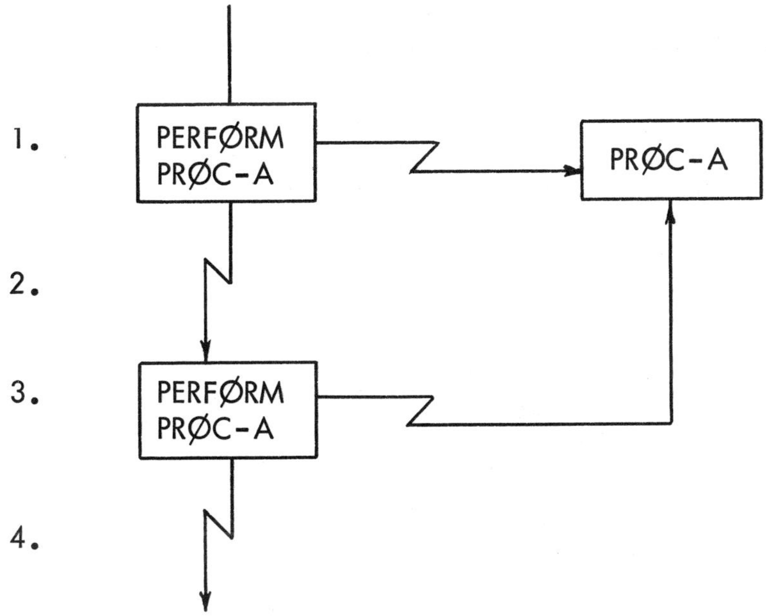

FIG. 7-12

Using More than One PERFØRM. It is possible to use more than one PERFØRM command, of the same or different types, in a program. These may be used sequentially, as suggested by the diagram in Figure 7-13.

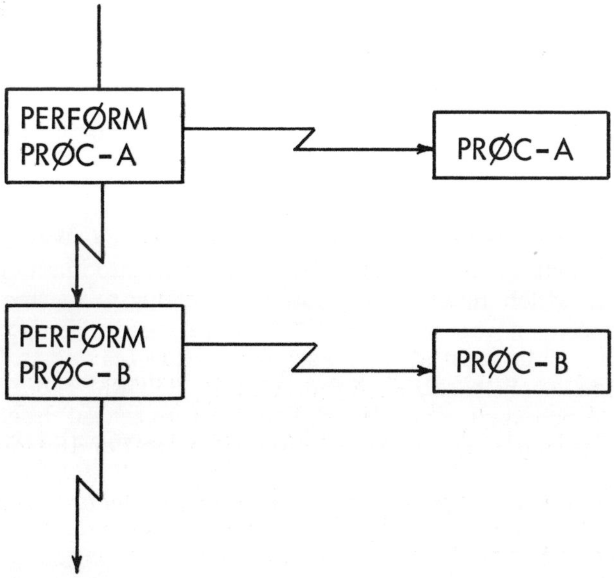

FIG. 7-13

Nested PERFØRM Commands. Multiple PERFØRM commands may be written, one inside another. For example, the diagram in Figure 14 might represent a part of a program: Here, the first PERFØRM includes another PERFØRM command in its range. Thus the second is said to be "nested" in the first.

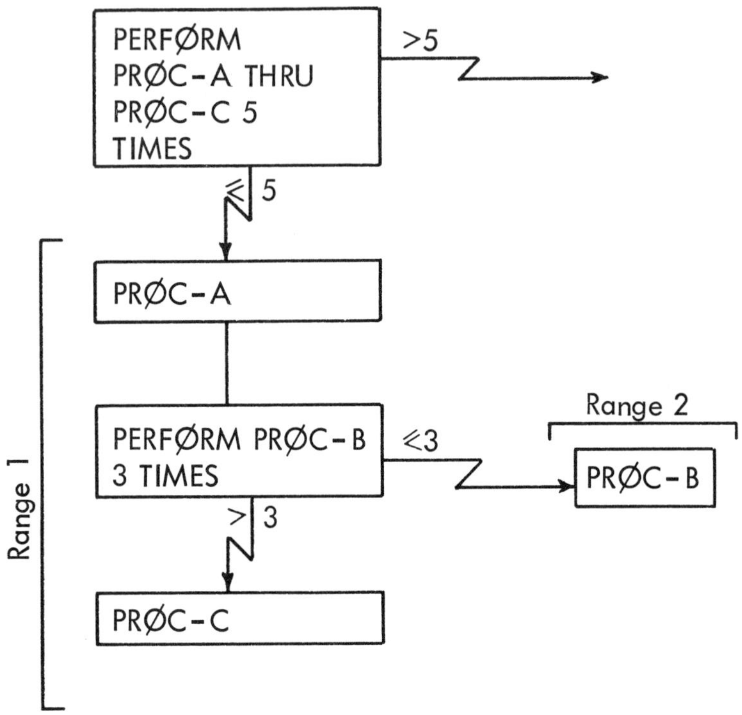

FIG. 7-14

In this illustration, PRØC-B will be executed 15 times. When PERFØRM commands are nested, the program moves first into the control of the outer statement, which must be executed according to its requirements. Then, as execution of the outer PERFØRM proceeds, it encounters the inner PERFØRM. This must also be satisfied before leaving it. Therefore, in the illustration, each iteration of the outer PERFØRM requires that the inner PERFØRM be executed 3 times. PRØC-B, executed three times for each pass through range 1, will be carried out a total of 15 times.

Several rules governing the use of nested PERFØRM commands are given below.

1. The range of each PERFØRM command must terminate with a different procedure name. Where more than one PERFØRM command would logically terminate with the same procedure name,

a dummy procedure paragraph containing only the procedure name and the command EXIT may be used.

2. Procedures controlled by the inner PERFØRM of a nested set must lie entirely inside or entirely outside the range of the outer PERFØRM. This requirement, followed properly and improperly, may be illustrated as shown in Figure 7-15.

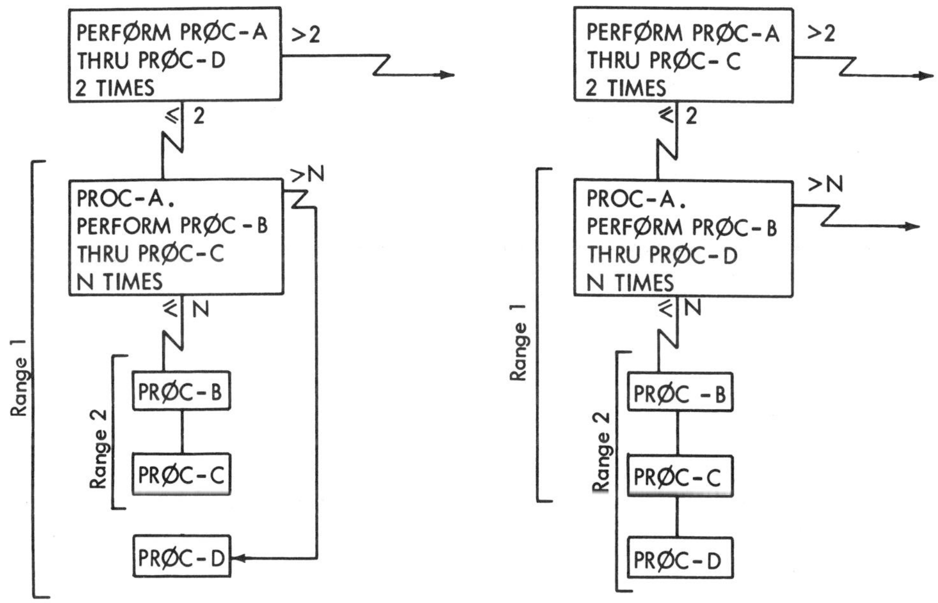

a) Acceptable—range 2 nested entirely in range 1

b) Unacceptable—range 2 not nested entirely in range 1

FIG. 7-15

3. PERFØRM ranges may overlap, provided the second PERFØRM command is not nested in the first. This may be illustrated by proper and improper procedures, as shown in Figure 7-16.

Much of COBOL's power is drawn from the ability to nest PERFØRM commands, thus achieving quite lengthy iterations with a minimum of programming. To avoid all nesting would severely limit the computer's use in certain types of programs. Nested PERFØRM commands can become rather complicated, however, and they should be used with care.

EXIT. It must be remembered that while a series of procedures specified by a PERFØRM command may contain a conditional, the series must also have a single end point. Where this would not otherwise be the case, because a conditional creates two or more branches which do not naturally rejoin in the PERFØRM loop, the EXIT command is used to provide an artificial end point. It is also used to provide each of a series of nested PERFØRM loops with a unique end point, as required by the language.

The command must occupy a paragraph by itself. This will always appear as follows:

Paragraph-name. EXIT.

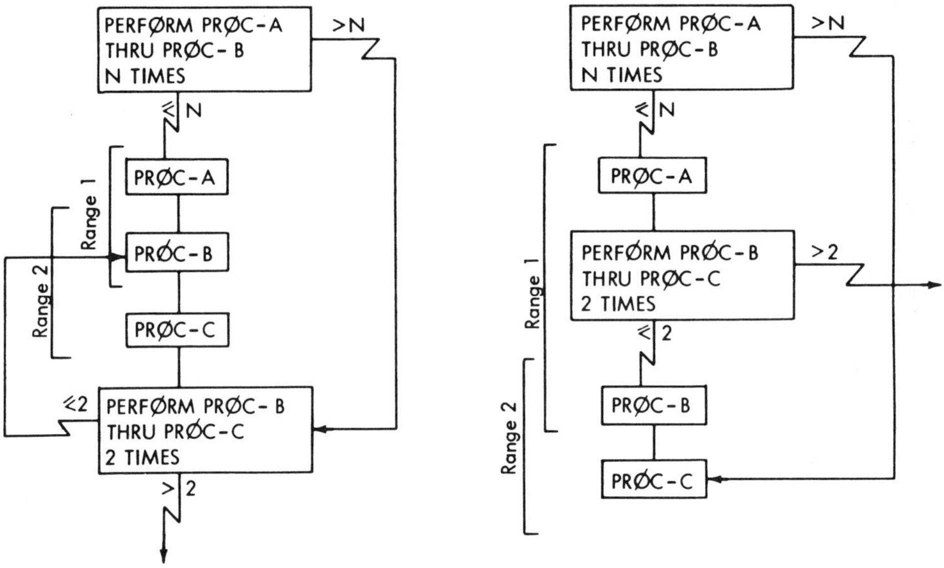

a) Acceptable—range 1 not nested in range 2; second PERFØRM not in range of first

b) Unacceptable—range 1 not nested in range 2; second PERFØRM nested in range of first

FIG. 7-16

DATA ARRAYS

Certain computer uses require that masses of similar data be stored in memory. In many such instances the same basic processing routines are to be used in treating each data element; when this is the case, the same program steps could be used for all items if the data name of the stored data did not change.

This problem—the necessity of maintaining the unique nature of data elements, yet subjecting each element to the same basic processing routine—has given rise to the use of data arrays.

The Nature of an Array

Any group of data elements arranged in a logical grouping by some common characteristic may be called a data array. Thus a file is a data array in its broadest sense. In electronic data processing, however, the term is not used in a context of this scope but is restricted to items stored in the computer's main memory.

An array may be thought of as a list of values which is given a name. Arrays may be single columns. For example, a list of account balances at the end of a certain month might be grouped into an array called ACCØUNTS, as follows:

Item	
1	100
2	150
3	75
4	200
5	750

This is also called a matrix; having but one column, it would be considered a single-dimensional matrix or array.

Each item in the list is an array element and is referenced by subscripting the item name. Thus, if items are assigned the name BALANCE, the fourth account balance in the list above might be referred to as BALANCE (4), where the number enclosed in parentheses is the subscript as used in COBOL.

Subscripts may be in the form of unsigned literals, as shown above, or they may be in the form of data names, taking on as a value whatever amount is stored at the data name location. For example, a reference such as BALANCE (N) might be made. Which of the BALANCE elements of the ACCØUNTS array is selected depends on the value assumed by N at the time.

Defining an Array: The ØCCURS Clause

Before they may be used, arrays must be defined in the data division, just like other data items. However, the name is to be attached to several data elements rather than just one item. This is done by using the ØCCURS clause. This is written following a data name and is of the nature "ØCCURS literal TIMES." For example, the entry "ITEM-X ØCCURS 40 TIMES" indicates that 40 items are to be associated with the data name. The size of each element depends, as always, on the related PICTURE clause.

The number of times an item is to occur must be set out explicitly. Therefore, in the ØCCURS clause, "literal" must be an unsigned numeric integer literal.

The ØCCURS clause must not be given at the 01, 77, or 88 level, these level numbers being reserved for special use. However, any other level number 02 through 49 may be used with an item to which the clause is attached.

Arrays may be set up in the file, working storage, or constant section of the data division. In all cases, because of the level number limitations cited above, the array must exist as a part of some larger data group; it may not be given independent status.

Single-Dimension Arrays. The set of five account balances mentioned above might be defined in working storage in the following way:

```
01  ACCØUNTS.
    02  BALANCE PICTURE 999 ØCCURS 5 TIMES.
```

This assigns the group name ACCØUNTS to the array. The name BALANCE is associated with each array element. The ØCCURS clause indicates that the data item BALANCE exists five times. The PICTURE clause specifies that each BALANCE item will be a three-place numeric field.

To refer to a particular element, the subscripted element name will be used. Thus, BALANCE (4) is the fourth element in the array. The entire array may be referenced by citing the array name. Therefore a command such as "MØVE TABLE-X TØ ACCØUNTS" would fill all elements of the ACCØUNTS array, assuming the appropriate existence of data in TABLE-X.

Data items in arrays are frequently subjected to systematic processing, where each item in turn is used in the same processing routine. When this is to be done, array elements are cited by variable subscripts rather than by literals. Thus, whichever element is specified by the variable value of the subscript at a given time will be subjected to the processing sequence.

To illustrate the processing of arrayed data and the use of variable subscripts, assume that the list of account balances shown above is stored in the computer's memory and that each element is to be displayed with its element number. This could be done quite simply by using the PERFØRM command, as shown in Figure 7-17. The exact value assumed by the subscript at any given time is controlled by the PERFØRM command. Thus, on the first iteration, when N = 1, the first element will be displayed. Then, as N becomes 2, the second element will be displayed, and so on, until the entire BALANCE array has been written out.

Two-Dimensional Arrays. An array, or matrix, may have more than one column, in which case it is called two-dimensional.[1] If the previous example were expanded to include the account balances of several months, for example, the array might appear as shown in Table 7-1. Each account is shown in a separate row, and each month's balances occupy a separate column.

Data Division Specification. The area for storage of a two-dimensional array is set out in the working storage section of the data division by a double specification, the second subordinate in level number to the first.

---

[1]As a matter of fact, 3-dimensional matrices may be constructed in COBOL. However, these will not be shown in this text.

Elements in the array are then referred to by citing the subordinate data name and using a double subscript.

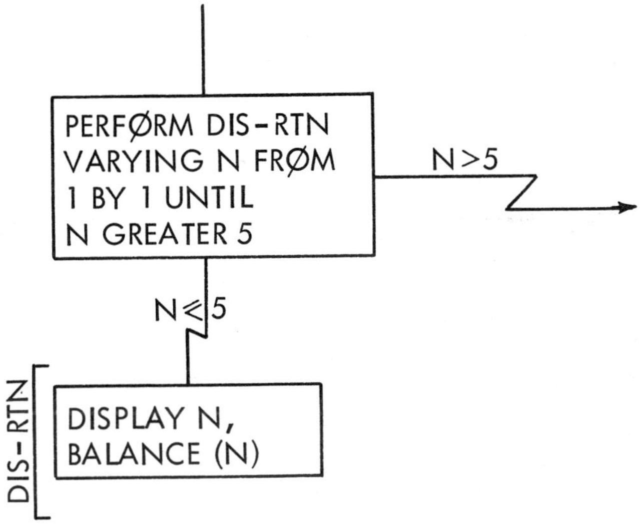

FIG. 7-17

Table 7-1

		Months					
		1	2	3	4	5	6
Accounts	1	100	175	300	450	500	750
	2	150	150	100	75	100	150
	3	75	100	125	150	175	200
	4	200	250	300	500	750	900
	5	750	700	650	400	500	450

To set up the storage area for the two-dimensional array shown in Table 7-1, for example, the following description would be required:

```
01 ACCØUNTS.
   02 EXPENSE ØCCURS 5 TIMES.
      03 BALANCE PICTURE 999 ØCCURS 6 TIMES.
```

The array name, ACCØUNTS, is mentioned at the most significant hierarchical level. Then, at the 02 level the number of rows is specified. No PICTURE clause is given here because EXPENSE is not an element but a group, as indicated by the subordinate 03 level item which follows. The existence of EXPENSE at the 02 level indicates the number of rows to be found in the matrix.

The BALANCE entry at the 03 level indicates the number of elements that are to exist in each row, which is the same as saying that it indicates the number of columns in the matrix. Thus the ACCØUNTS array is to consist of 5 rows and 6 columns. This may be referred to as a 5 x 6 matrix. Each element in the array will have a PICTURE 999, assumed to be appropriate for this situation. Of course, the PICTURE clause could specify any field size and type.

Referencing Entries. Reference to any particular entry in a two-dimensional array requires that the element name be cited, followed by a double subscript. The first subscript refers to the row in which the element is to be found; the second, to its column number. These subscripts must be enclosed in parentheses following the element name after at least one space, and they must be separated from one another by a comma and/or a space. The subscripts may be unsigned integer literals or data names which refer to such unsigned numeric computational integers. If data names are used as subscripts, these must be defined in some part of the data division.

Thus, in referring to an element in the array above, BALANCE (2, 3) would cite the item in the second row, third column. A reference such as BALANCE (I, J) would refer to whichever item is in the row specified by the value of I and the column specified by the value of J.

The contents of an entire row in the matrix may be referenced by citing the row name and a single subscript. Thus, EXPENSE (2) refers to the contents of the second row in the ACCØUNTS array.

Such a reference might be incorporated in a MØVE command, such as "MØVE EXPENSE (2) TØ FIELD-A." Assuming that FIELD-A is of the proper shape and size for use as a receiving area, the entire contents of the second row would be moved to that address.

By the same token, the entire two-dimensional array may be referred to by simply citing the array name, ACCØUNTS.

Processing Arrayed Data

Arrayed data are ordinarily entered in the matrix by reading from some external record or records, or by computing their element amounts. Assuming the elements to be defined as numeric computational items, they may be used in arithmetic in exactly the same manner as any other data item. Finally, the array contents may be written out.

The commands used in reading, manipulating, and writing an array may best be seen in an illustration. For this purpose, the illustration involving the two-dimensional array ACCØUNTS is continued.

Assume that the firm has two operating departments, each using the same set of five account numbers. Account balances for the past six months appear as shown in Table 7-1 for the first department, and the account balances for department 2 appear as indicated in Table 7-2.

Table 7-2

		Months					
		1	2	3	4	5	6
Accounts	1	250	325	400	650	400	250
	2	325	250	175	100	150	200
	3	100	150	200	250	175	250
	4	225	400	350	575	700	850
	5	800	700	750	500	650	600

Each set of expense balances is contained in a different record for each department; thus, there are 10 input records which will be read and stored. The balances of department 1 are to be stored in an array called ACCT-1, having rows named EXP-1 and columns called BAL-1. The balances of department 2 are to be stored in an array called ACCT-2, having rows named EXP-2 and columns called BAL-2.

After reading these balance records and storing their contents in the required manner, a new array called TØT is to be created by adding the elements of the old matrices. This array will have rows named T-EXP and columns called T-BAL.

After all the elements of the input arrays have been added, the elements of the TØT array are to be written out. Finally, the elements of the TØT array are themselves to be summed in three ways—by account, by month, and in grand total. The first two accumulations will themselves result in the creation of one-dimensional arrays. The first, to be called ACCT-BAL with elements named ACT, will represent the balances of the five accounts. The second, called MØNTH, will represent the total expenses for each of the six months. Its elements will be called MØ.

Inasmuch as the grand total (GRAND) is a single amount, no array is needed for it.

The one-dimensional arrays ACCT-BAL and MØNTH are to be written out, using the same file employed in the output of TØT. The single amount GRAND is to be displayed.

The Version 5 PERFØRM. Because data are frequently processed in array form, a special version of the PERFØRM command is available to simplify programming. This, which may be termed version 5, is of the following form:

PERFØRM procedure-name-1 [THRU procedure-name-2]
VARYING s-name-1 FRØM initial-value-1 BY increment-1
UNTIL condition-1 AFTER s-name-2 FRØM initial-value-2
BY increment-2 UNTIL condition-2.

In this form, "s-name" stands for subscript name.

In this, all parts of the command dealing with s-name-1 may be thought of as comprising the outer range of a nested PERFØRM; portions dealing with s-name-2 represent the controls necessary for the inner range. Thus the complete range of the inner PERFØRM is satisfied for each iteration of the outer loop.

Reading and Storing Arrays. Data to be stored in arrays may be read in as separate items or as data groups. Data read as separate items must be moved into the proper array, one element at a time. For example, if three data items called ITEM-A, ITEM-B, and ITEM-C have been read as parts of a record and are to be stored as elements in an array, the commands

```
MØVE ITEM-A TØ X (1)
MØVE ITEM-B TØ X (2)
MØVE ITEM-C TØ X (3)
```

might be used assuming X to be the proper name of the array element.

Data, if read in properly, may be moved to the receiving array in groups. In storing expense amounts in the example introduced above, this technique is used. All of one department's expense balances for a given month are recorded in one input record. In each record the expense balances are not divided according to months, but are recorded in adjacent positions, and the record is treated as a single data unit containing 18 characters. Five input records are used to contain the expense balances for each department.

Under the control of a PERFØRM command, the five records of department 1 are read and their contents transferred to successive rows of the ACCT-1 array. Then the records of department 2 are read and their contents transferred to successive rows of the ACCT-2 array.

The flow diagram for reading and processing these expenses is shown in Figure 7-18. Here, in the first two commands after files are opened, PERFØRM commands may be seen to control the reading of expense amounts and their transfer, one row at a time, to the receiving array. The actual coding of the commands may be seen in Illustration 4 of Appendix B (page 238). Here, on the seventh and eighth lines of page 2, may be seen the PERFØRM commands. They control the READ and STØRE routines coded at the bottom of page 2 and the top of page 3.

Array Arithmetic. Once the data from the two departments are stored in array form, they may easily be manipulated arithmetically. Using the PERFØRM command which controls two subscripts—called version 5 in this text—the elements of the ACT-1 and ACCT-2 arrays are added (in the step called ADD-MATRIX) to form a new array, called TØT.

This process may be seen symbolically in the flow diagram in Figure 7-18, and in coded form in Illustration 4, Appendix B.

In the program segment called ALL-CØMP, the elements of the TØT array are summed by rows to yield expense totals by expense accounts. These are stored as elements of the one-dimensional array, ACCT-BAL. Then the same elements are summed by columns to yield expense totals by months, which are stored as elements of the one-dimensional array, MØNTH. Finally, elements of the TØT array are added to yield GRAND, the total of all expense for the six-month period.

The arithmetic shown in this example—matrix addition, and the accumulation by rows and columns—is but a sample of the kinds of manipulation which are possible. The value of array processing is limited only by the type of data involved and the imagination and ingenuity of the system designer.

Writing Arrayed Data. The output record may be set up in such a way that complete rows of matrices may be written in a single command, by using the "WRITE output-record-name FRØM row-name" option. For example, given an appropriately described output record, it would be possible to write out the TØT array by the following:

```
PERFØRM WRITE-ØUT VARYING I FRØM 1 BY 1 UNTIL I GREATER 5. ...
WRITE-ØUT. WRITE ØUT-RCD FRØM T-EXP (I).
```

It may be recalled that T-EXP is the name used for rows in the TØT matrix. Thus, as I is set at 1 by the PERFØRM command, the first array row would be written. Then, as I proceeds to 5, subsequent rows would be written in turn. Each row would be written in a separate output record.

This output method has the disadvantage of writing out matrix entries in adjacent positions, without editing or spacing. Therefore, it is not useful when the matrix is to be printed. Instead, routines designed to move array elements to positions in the output record are used, after which the record is written.

Figure 7-18 contains a routine called MV-AR which serves to move a row of the TØT array to the output area, element by element. When a row is thus set up, it is written out, and the next row is moved to the output record.

The movement of data elements to the output record and their subsequent writing involves a set of nested PERFØRM commands in actual coding. This may be seen in Illustration 4, Appendix B. Here, on lines 11 and 12 of page 2, may be seen the outer PERFØRM command. This controls the number of output records to be written—one for each of the matrix rows. Then, on line 04, page 3, may be seen the inner PERFØRM command—controlling the movement of data elements from the row controlled by the outer PERFØRM. Line 06 contains the paragraph in which data movement occurs.

The outer PERFØRM range includes the inner—controlling the movement of data to output—and a WRITE command as well. Thus, execution of the nested statements proceeds as follows: The range of the outer PERFØRM is entered. This controls the selection of data from a particular matrix row. The inner PERFØRM is then entered, and this causes the systematic movement of the six row elements to the output area, after which the inner PERFØRM is satisfied. Completion of an iteration of the outer loop causes WR-AR, the paragraph containing the WRITE command, to be executed, and control returns to the outer PERFØRM for the next iteration. When the fifth outer loop is executed, the outer PERFØRM is satisfied, and control passes to the next statement, to be found on line 13, page 2.

The ACCT-BAL array and the MØNTH array, containing combined expense accounts and months, respectively, are moved to the write-out area in diagram sections called WRITE-MØ and WRITE-AC. Inasmuch as they are one-dimensional arrays, their movement and writing are simpler than in the case of the TØT array and so will not be traced through the coding in Appendix B.

After the two input arrays illustrated above are added, and expenses by accounts and months are computed, the program's output would appear as shown in Table 7-3. The total of all expenses incurred by both departments, displayed as GRAND, would be $21,875.

Table 7-3

Combined Expenses of Departments 1 and 2
COBOL Array Name: TØT

Accounts	Months					
	1	2	3	4	5	6
1	$ 350	$ 500	$ 700	$1,100	$ 900	$1,000
2	475	400	275	175	250	350
3	175	250	325	400	350	450
4	425	650	650	1,075	1,450	1,750
5	1,550	1,400	1,400	900	1,150	1,050

Total Expenses, by Accounts (COBOL Array Name: ACCT-BAL)		Total Expenses, by Months (COBOL Array Name: MØNTH)	
1	$4,550	1	$2,975
2	1,925	2	3,200
3	1,950	3	3,350
4	6,000	4	3,650
5	7,450	5	4,100
		6	4,600

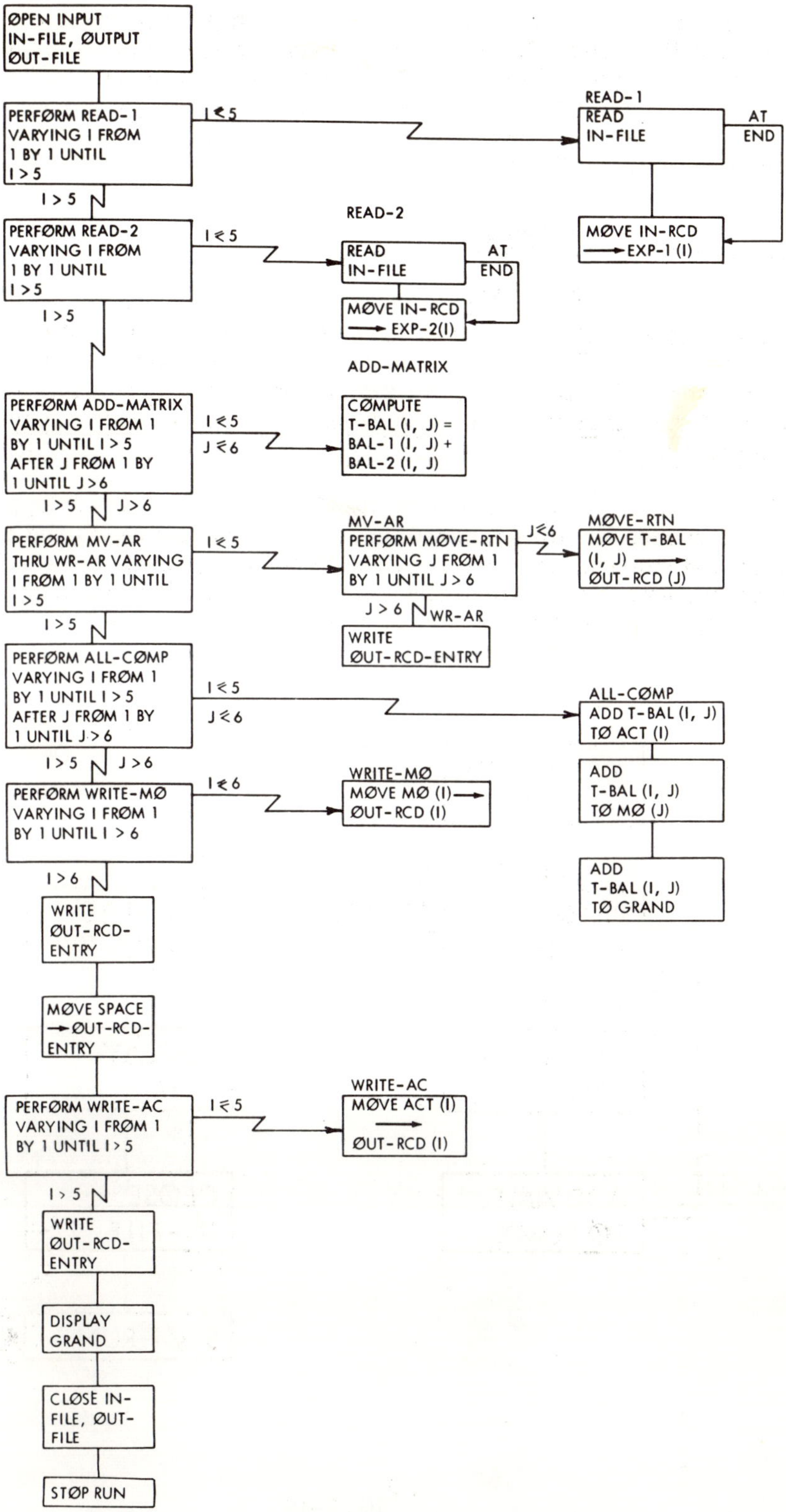

FIG. 7-18. Diagram of Array Manipulation

The data and procedure divisions for this problem are included in Appendix B as Illustration 4 (page 238) and have been referred to in parts as certain characteristics of array processing were discussed. This should be reviewed carefully in its entirety, as it shows proper array coding techniques and offers one more example of the way in which the PERFØRM statement functions.

When Should Data Be Arrayed?

Once the possibility of constructing data arrays has been introduced, some confusion always arises as to the need for establishing an array. Actually, the rule for setting up arrays, as opposed to data summaries in the form of totals, is quite simple. If the detailed quantities are required for further processing, they should be arrayed. If not, they should be summarized.

This may be illustrated by the following situations. Suppose that a list of values is to be added and their mean computed and displayed. Individual amounts are here required to be summed, and the exact quantity of each element is unimportant once the summation has occured. Thus, this program could be constructed as shown in Figure 7-19.

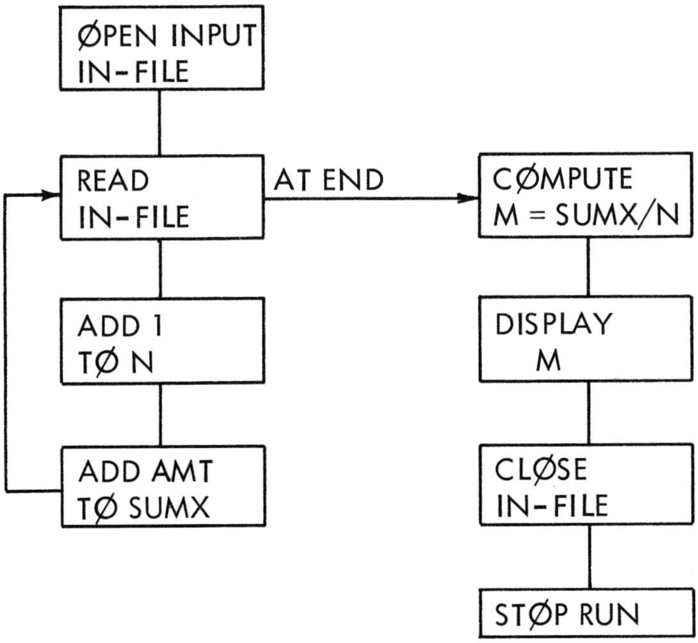

FIG. 7-19

On the other hand, suppose the problem requires that values are to be read and summed and the mean is to be taken, after which all values exceeding the mean are to be displayed. Here, obviously, the exact value of each element must be maintained for comparison with the mean. This will be done by storing each amount as an element of the VAL array. A suitable flow chart is shown in Figure 7-20.

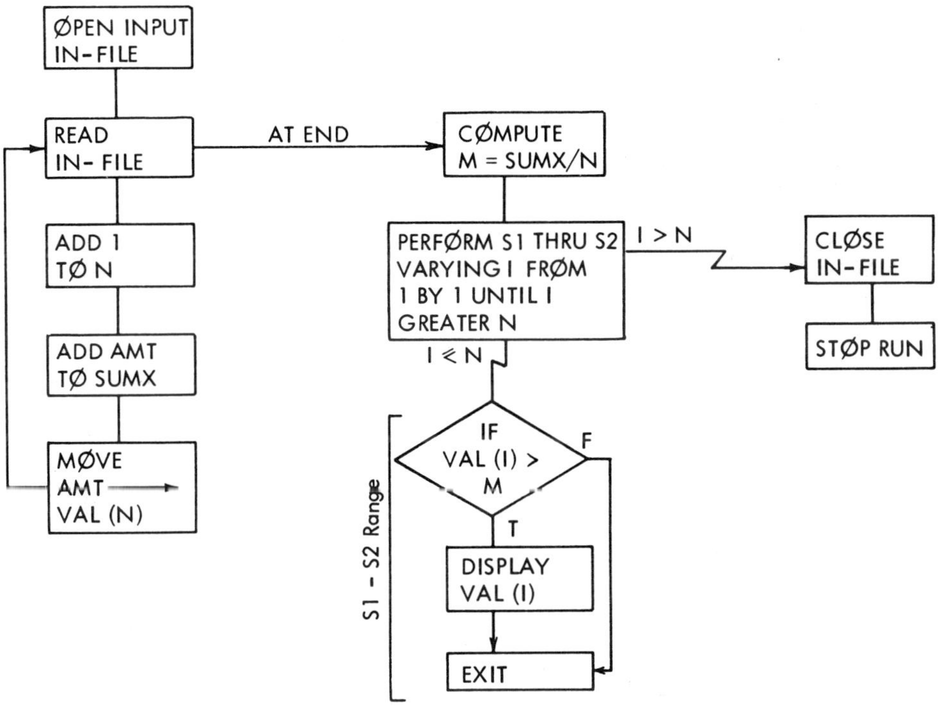

FIG. 7-20

Amounts are summed as read, and a count is made of the number of of values processed. Each value is also moved to a position in the VAL array, as determined by N, the counter. The mean is computed after all values are read. Then the amounts are scanned, and each is compared with the mean. All values exceeding the mean are displayed; others are ignored. It may be seen that the PERFØRM command is quite useful in governing the program during the search routine.

SUMMARY

This chapter introduces the last control commands in the COBOL instruction set and a new way of storing data in the computer's memory. The instruction is the PERFØRM command and is available in five basic forms.

The PERFØRM Command

All versions of this command require that a portion of the program be executed under its control. The portion need not appear directly after the PERFØRM command; in fact, it probably does not. After the program portion has been executed the proper number of times, control is returned to the statement following the PERFØRM command. It is possible to create a program in which control does not return naturally but is transferred elsewhere. In this case the PERFØRM command is never satisfied.

Summary of the PERFØRM Command Forms

Each of the five versions of this command are available for particular purposes, although each will serve in more than one role. The basic commands are listed below.

1. The Basic PERFØRM. Nature:

   PERFØRM procedure-name-1 [THRU procedure-name-2].

This causes the named routine to be executed once. It is quite useful when writing special routines or for steering the program along general lines.

2. PERFØRM n TIMES. Nature:

   PERFØRM procedure-name-1 [THRU procedure-name-2] {data-name | literal} TIME [S].

This command causes the named program segment to be executed a set or determinable number of times.

3. PERFØRM UNTIL. Nature:

   PERFØRM procedure-name-1 [THRU procedure-name-2] UNTIL condition-1.

This version of the PERFØRM causes the command's range to be repeated until a condition, named in the instruction, is satisfied.

4. PERFØRM VARYING. Nature:

   PERFØRM procedure-name-1 [THRU procedure-name-2]

   VARYING data-name-1 FRØM {literal-1 | data-name-2} BY {literal-2 | data-name-3}

   UNTIL condition-1.

This incorporates a variable and allows the command to set its beginning value and its increment. The program leaves the PERFØRM's range when a condition specified in the command is satisfied.

5. PERFØRM VARYING S-Name. Nature:

```
PERFØRM procedure-name-1 [THRU procedure-name-2]
VARYING data-name-1 FRØM {literal-1     } BY {literal-2     }
                         {data-name-2   }    {data-name-3   }
UNTIL condition-1 [AFTER data-name-4 FRØM {literal-3     }
                                          {data-name-5   }
BY {literal-4    } UNTIL condition-2 [AFTER data-name-7
   {data-name-6  }
FRØM {literal-5    } BY {literal-6    } UNTIL condition-3]] .
     {data-name-8  }    {data-name-9  }
```

Version 5 is really nothing more than a modification of version 4, in which a nest of as many as three PERFØRM commands may be constructed. This is the only nesting form where more than one PERFØRM loop may end at the same statement. Version 5 is often used for controlling programs dealing with 1-, 2-, or 3-dimensional matrices, in which case the control command may be used to set up and modify subscripts. However, the command is by no means limited to this use.

Data Arrays

The COBOL language permits one-, two-, or even three-dimensional arrays to be constructed in the computer's memory. These arrays should consist of data having some common characteristic. Each array element maintains its unique value and may be referred to by citing the array name, followed by appropriate subscripts. Processing of arrayed data is simplified by the fact that variable subscripts may be used and put in the control of PERFØRM commands.

QUESTIONS AND PROBLEMS

1. Name and describe the five forms of the PERFØRM command.
2. In what ways are the PERFØRM and GØ TØ commands similar? In what ways do they differ?
3. In what ways are the PERFØRM and IF commands similar? In what ways do they differ?
4. Can you describe any situation where the IF statement would serve properly but the PERFØRM command would not? Where the PERFØRM serves but the IF does not?
5. What is the difference between a data element and a data array?

6. Ten input records contain four values each. The records are in the IN-FILE. The values are in the IN-GROUP group. Diagram a program segment which will read and store these values as elements of the 2-dimensional ST array, where each record contains a different row of data. Rows are called ST-RØW. Use I for the subscript name.

7. Ten input records contain four values each. The records are in the IN-FILE. The values are in the IN-GROUP group and are arrayed as IN-ARRAY elements. Diagram a program segment which will read and store these values as elements of the 2-dimensional ST array where each input record contains a different column of data. Columns are called COL. Use I and J for the subscript names.

8. Assuming that it is intended to process a number of records, indicate the logical error or errors in the following procedure segment.

   Assume that all file and data items have been properly defined.

```
START-1. READ X-FILE AT END GØ TØ FINISH
    IF X GREATER THAN 25 PERFØRM PAR-2 ELSE GØ TØ
      START-1.
PAR-2. ADD A TØ B. WRITE ØUT-RCD.
FINISH. CLØSE X-FILE, ØUT-FILE. STØP RUN.
```

The problems below contain complete situation descriptions and may be programmed for computer execution if desired. The following should be prepared for each problem:

1. A flow diagram

2. Such of the following divisions as are assigned by the instructor:

   a) Identification division. PRØGRAM-ID is to cite the problem number. AUTHØR should cite the student's name.
   b) Environment division. Most problems have a single input file and a single output file. Unless otherwise instructed, the input file is to be assigned to IN and the output file to ØU.
   c) Data division. Please observe the following:

      Input files: Use FILLER when necessary to bring the record size to a multiple of six and to a minimum of eighteen characters for the record.

      Output files: All records are to contain 132 characters, and all numeric fields are to be edited, unless otherwise indicated. Dollar marks should be shown beside monetary fields. Zeros should be suppressed to the left of the decimal if there is one, or to the left of the units position otherwise. Commas should be used as appropriate. Use five positions of FILLER at the beginning of the output record and between each data name.

      Working storage: Fields are not to be edited unless specifically stated. Data items with an asterisk beside them are to be assigned an initial value of zero.

d) Procedure division. After opening files, space should be moved to the output record. Other instructions on page 173 should also be observed.

9. This problem involves the processing of cost accounting records containing data on actual and standard costs. Details on files and their contents are provided in Table 7-4.

Table 7-4

Item Description	Name	Field Type	Field Size	Field Places to Right of Decimal
Input file:				
File name	CØST-FILE			
Assigned to input unit	IN			
Record name	CØST-REC			
Record contents:				
Account number	ACCT	Num. Comp.	5	0
Number of units produced	UNITS	Num. Comp.	4	0
Standard cost per unit	STD	Num. Comp.	6	3
Actual cost per unit	ACT	Num. Comp.	6	3
Output files:				
File-name-1	ØVER-FILE			
Assigned to output unit	ØU			
Record-name-1	ØVER-RCD			
Record contents:				
Account number	ACCØUNT	Num. Rpt.	5	0
Variance amount	ØVER-VAR	Num. Rpt.	6	2
File-name-2	UNDER-FILE			
Assigned to output unit	U04			
Record-name-2	UNDER-RCD			
Record contents:				
Account number	ACCT-NØ	Num. Rpt.	5	0
Variance amount	UNDER-VAR	Num. Rpt.	6	2
Working storage:				
Variances over standard*	LARGE-ØVER	Num. Comp.	7	2
Variances under standard*	LARGE-UNDER	Num. Comp.	7	2
Variances within range* †	SMALL-VAR	Num. Comp.	7	2
Working area †	VNCE	Num. Comp.	6	2
Display area †	DIS	Num. Rpt.	7	2

† Field should be signed.

Processing is to achieve the following:

a) Actual and standard costs are to be compared. If actual exceeds standard by more than 10 percent of the latter, a routine called ØVER-LIMIT is to be performed. This requires that the variance for all units in the record is to be accumulated as LARGE-ØVER, at the same time writing out the ØVER-RCD, showing the account number and the amount by which actual costs exceed standard for all units.

b) If standard cost exceeds actual by more than 10 percent of the former, a routine called UNDER-LIMIT is to be performed. This requires that the variance for all units in the record is to be accumulated as LARGE-UNDER, at the same time filling and writing out the UNDER-RCD.

c) Any variances within the limits set above are to be accumulated as SMALL-VAR, and no output record is to be written.

d) LARGE-ØVER, LARGE-UNDER, and SMALL-VAR are to be displayed after all records have been processed.

10. The present value of one can be found by the formula

$$P = \frac{1}{(1 + r)^n}$$

where r represents the discount rate and n the number of periods. You are to prepare a table showing the present value of one at discount rates of 1 percent through 6 percent, using whole percents only, for one through 25 years. Your table should show the different rates as columns, the different years as rows.

<u>Data division requirements</u>: No input file is used. The output file should be named ØUT-FILE and should be cited as containing records called ØUT-RCD, each of which contains the following: "YEAR, PICTURE Z9," representing the period number; and "PRES-VAL, PICTURE Z(5).9(4) ØCCURS 6 TIMES." This item, an array, is to be used in the output of present values at discount rates 1 through 6 for the particular period.

<u>Working storage</u>: The following elements of working storage are required: "I PICTURE 9" (this may be used as a subscript); "R PICTURE 99" (this may be used as the discount rate); and "N PICTURE 99" (this may be used as a subscript and as the period indicator).

<u>Hint</u>: This program may be organized as a nest of two PERFØRMs. The outer loop may be used to control the 25 iterations required as time periods. The inner loop may be used to control the computation of discount amounts at the six required rates.

11. Robert Jones purchases a house for $25,000, paying $5,000 down and assuming a mortgage payable for the remainder. Each month, he must pay $175; this first covers interest (at .5 percent on the unpaid balance) and then reduces principal.

Instructions: Prepare a schedule showing the retirement of Mr. Jones's loan, assuming that in the last month the necessary payment will be limited to the amount of unpaid principal. The contents of the output file and available working storage are shown in Table 7-5.

Table 7-5

Item Description	Name	Field Type	Field Size	Field Places to Right of Decimal
Output file name	AMØRT-FILE			
Output record name	AMØRT-RECØRD			
Record contents:				
Month number	MØ	Num. Rpt.	3	0
Payment amount	PMT	Num. Rpt.	5	2
Interest charge	INT	Num. Rpt.	5	2
Principal reduction	RED	Num. Rpt.	5	2
Unpaid balance	BALANCE	Num. Rpt.	7	2
Elements of independent working storage				
Unpaid balance†	BAL	Num. Comp.	7	2
Current interest amount	I	Num. Comp.	5	2
Principal reduction	PRIN-RED	Num. Comp.	5	2
Index	K	Num. Comp.	3	0

† Should be assigned an initial balance of $20,000.

In output: MØ should begin at one and continue without regard to years until the loan is repaid. PMT should be $175, except in the final period. INT should reflect the amount of interest on the unpaid balance at .5 percent, and RED should be the difference between the payment amount and the interest amount. BALANCE should show the unpaid balance after each month's payment.

12. The X Company maintains its inventory accounting records in a file called INV. Periodically, these records are read and stored in the computer's memory as array components. Then, transaction records—receipts and issues—are processed against the old balances, the results being stored back in the arrays. After all transaction records have been processed, the updated balances are written out of the arrays and stored pending the next updating.

Data on file and working storage are shown in Table 7-6.

Table 7-6

Item Description	Name	Field: Type	Size	Places to Right of Decimal
Input file name	INV-FILE			
Assigned to input unit	U04			
Input record name	INV-BAL			
Record contents:				
Filler	FILLER	Alphameric	4	
Inventory number	INØ	Num. Comp.	5	0
Total cost of all receipts	REC	Num. Comp.	9	2
Total cost of all issues	ISS	Num. Comp.	9	2
Cost of balance on hand	BAL	Num. Comp.	9	2
Input file name	TRANS			
Assigned to input unit	IN			
Input record name	TRAN-RCD			
Record contents:				
Inventory account number	A-NØ	Num. Comp.	5	0
Transaction indicator	KEY	Num. Comp.	1	0
Amount	AMT	Num. Comp.	6	2
Output file name	NEW-BALANCE			
Output record †	NEW-INV-BAL			
Record contents:				
Inventory number	NEW-INØ	Num. Comp.	5	0
Total cost of all receipts	NEW-REC	Num. Comp.	9	2
Total cost of all issues	NEW-ISS	Num. Comp.	9	2
Cost of balance on hand	NEW-BAL	Num. Comp.	9	2
Working storage:				
Independent items:				
Array subscript	I	Num. Comp.	3	0
Number of balance records*	CØUNT	Num. Comp.	3	0
Total receipts processed	TØT-REC	Num. Comp.	9	2
Total issues processed	TØT-ISS	Num. Comp.	9	2
Display area	DIS	Num. Rpt.	9	2
Grouped items: ‡				
Group name	INV-DATA			
Inventory account number	IN-NØ	Num. Comp.	5	0
Total cost of all receipts	C-REC	Num. Comp.	9	2
Total cost of all issues	C-ISS	Num. Comp.	9	2
Cost of balance on hand	C-BAL	Num. Comp.	9	2

† This record should not contain FILLER, (except in the first 4 spaces) but should look just like INV-BAL.

‡ Each of the items in this group is the name of an array item. Each should be assigned the clause "ØCCURS 200 TIMES."

Instructions: Processing is to proceed as follows:

a) Records containing inventory balances and associated data are to be read and their contents stored in the four arrays—INØ in IN-NØ, REC in C-REC, ISS in C-ISS, and BAL in C-BAL. Storage should proceed in such a way that the data pertaining to a particular inventory record may be found in the same position in each array. There are never more than 200 balance records, and there may be fewer.

b) When all inventory balance records have been read and their contents stored, as evidenced by the emptying of the balance file input unit, the processing of transaction records should begin.

   A record should be read from the TRANS file and its account number matched against those in the IN-NØ ARRAY. When the account numbers equal, the proper balance record has been found.

   Balance records should be updated. The nature of the transaction record should be determined by testing KEY, where a 1 represents an inventory receipt and a 2 an inventory issuance. Receipts costs should be added to the proper element of C-REC and C-BAL. Issues costs should be added to C-ISS and subtracted from C-BAL.

   The sum of all receipts and issues processed should be accumulated as TØT-REC and TØT-ISS, respectively.

c) After all transaction records have been processed, new balance records should be written by moving array elements to the proper field in the output record and then writing the record. A count of the number of balance records read in originally should be made, so that the proper number of updated balances may be written out.

d) Cumulative totals of receipts and issues transactions should be displayed after writing the updated balance records.

13. Data input and working storage areas for this problem appear as shown in Table 7-7.

Table 7-7

		Field		
Item Description	Name	Type	Size	Places to Right of Decimal
Input file name	IN-FILE			
Input record name	IN-RCD			
Record contents:				
Amount field	AMØUNT	Num. Comp.	5	0
Working storage:				
Independent elements:				
Number of array components*	N	Num. Comp.	3	0
Subscript-1	I	Num. Comp.	3	0
Storage location	SMALL	Num. Comp.	5	0
Storage location	LARGE	Num. Comp.	5	0
Grouped data:				
Group name	AMT-TABLE			
Element names†	AMT	Num. Comp.	5	0

†Provisions should be made for 200 array elements.

Instructions: Input records are to be read, and the value found in the AMØUNT field is to be stored in sequential positions in the AMT-TABLE, as AMT elements. The number of elements read in should be calculated as N. Then, when all values have been stored, the AMT-TABLE array is to be scanned, and the smallest and largest values are to be found. These are to be stored as SMALL and LARGE, respectively. When all values have been scanned, SMALL and LARGE are to be displayed.

14. Data input and working storage areas for this problem appear as shown in Table 7-8.

Table 7-8

Item Description	Name	Field Type	Field Size	Field Places to Right of Decimal
Input file name	IN-FILE			
Input record name	IN-RCD			
Record contents:				
Amount field†	AMT	Num. Comp.	5	0
Independent working storage items:				
Subscript-1	N	Num. Comp.	1	0
Subscript-2	M	Num. Comp.	1	0
Indicator	I	Num. Comp.	1	0
Temporary storage location	TEMP	Num. Comp.	5	0

†This field appears five times in the input record and should be defined by an ØCCURS clause.

Instructions: The input file contains a single record, which in turn contains five values as entries in an array. This record is to be read. Then the five values are to be sorted into order, from the smallest to largest. After the values have been sorted, they should be displayed one at a time with their element numbers.

15. In cash flow analysis the present investment amount and amounts of future returns are sometimes known with acceptable certainty. In these instances the discount rate equating present investment with future yields must be determined through trial and error, using the formula

$$P = \frac{F}{(1 + r)^n}$$

where

P = Present value
F = Future value
r = Interest (discount) rate
n = Number of periods

To find the appropriate discount rate, a possible rate is arbitrarily chosen. All future yields are discounted by this rate, and their sum is compared with the actual investment cost. A sum larger than the true cost indicates a discount rate too small, and vice versa. Should a rate too low be chosen first, it will then be increased and the process of computation repeated. Gradually, the discounted sum of future yields will approach the investment cost. It is often impractical to search for the exact discount rate equating yields and cost; instead, the cost is straddled with computed present values above and below it.

Data input and working storage areas for the problem described below appear as shown in Table 7-9.

Table 7-9

Item Description	Name	Field: Type	Field: Size	Field: Places to Right of Decimal
Input file name	RETURN-FILE			
Input record name	RETURN-RCD			
Record contents:				
Number of expected yield periods	N	Num. Comp.	2	0
Cost of investment	CØST	Num. Comp.	7	0
Expected future yields†	YIELD	Num. Comp.	6	0
Independent working storage elements:				
Discount rate, current	R	Num. Comp.	2	2
Discount rate, previous iteration	R-Ø	Num. Rpt.	2	2
Present value of expected yields	PV	Num. Comp.	7	0
Present value of expected yields, previous iteration	PV-Ø	Num. Rpt.	7	0
Subscript	I	Num. Comp.	2	0

†As many as 10 yield amounts may exist. Therefore, this item should be described as occurring 10 times.

Instructions: Data pertaining to an investment's cash flow, including the investment amount, number of expected yield periods, and amount of expected yields, are to be read in from a single record. In this, N indicates the number of expected yields, which never exceeds 10, and this corresponds to the number of expected yields recorded as YIELD (I).

After reading the input record, the proper discount rate is to be sought by trial and error. A rate of 3 percent is to be used first. This should be advanced in increments of 1 percent until the discounted sum of future yields falls below the investment cost, indicating that the proper discount rate has been straddled.

With each unsuccessful test, the discount rate used and the resultant discounted value of future yields should be saved, as R-Ø and PV-Ø, respectively. Then, when a discount rate too high is finally found, the old rate and sum of yields should be displayed with an appropriate message. After displaying the old values, the newly computed values should be moved to the old areas (thus acquiring editing symbols); then, they in turn should be displayed with a proper label.

APPENDICES

APPENDIX A

COMPLETE LIST OF RESERVED WORDS

The words shown below are an inherent part of the COBOL System. Users should avoid using these words for data or procedure names.

ABOUT
ACCEPT
ACCESS
ACTUAL
ADD
ADDRESS
ADVANCING
AFTER
ALL
ALPHABETIC
ALPHANUMERIC
ALTER
ALTERNATE
AN
AND
APPLY
ARE
AREA
AREAS
ASCENDING
ASSIGN
AT
AUTHOR
BEFORE
BEGINNING
BITS
BLANK
BLOCK
BY
CF
CH
CHARACTERS
CHECK
CLASS
CLOCK-UNITS
CLOSE
COBOL
CODE
COLUMN
COMMA
COMPUTATIONAL
COMPUTE
CONSTANT
CONFIGURATION
CONTAINS
CONTROL
CONTROLS
CONVERSION
COPY
CORRESPONDING
CURRENCY
DATA
DATE-COMPILED
DATE-WRITTEN
DE
DECIMAL-POINT
DECLARATIVES
DEFINE
DEPENDING
DESCENDING
DETAIL
DIGITS
DISPLAY
DIVIDE
DIVIDED
DIVISION
DOLLAR
DOWN
ELSE
END
ENDING
ENTER
ENVIRONMENT
EQUAL
EQUALS
ERROR
EVERY
EXAMINE
EXCEEDS
EXIT
EXPONENTIATED
FD
FILE
FILE-CONTROL
FILE-LIMIT
FILE-LIMITS
FILLER
FINAL
FIRST
FLOAT
FOOTING
FOR
FORMAT
FROM
GENERATE
GIVING
GO
GREATER
GROUP
HASHED
HEADING
HIGH-VALUE
HIGH-VALUES
HOLD
I-O
I-O-CONTROL
IDENTIFICATION
IF
IN
INCLUDE
INDEX
INDEXED
INDICATE
INITIATE
INPUT
INPUT-OUTPUT
INSTALLATION
INTO
INVALID
IS
JUSTIFIED
KEY
KEYS
LABEL
LAST
LEADING
LEAVING
LEFT
LESS
LIBRARY
LIMIT
LIMITS
LINE
LINE-COUNTER
LINES
LOCATION
LOCK
LOW-VALUE
LOW-VALUES
LOWER-BOUND
LOWER-BOUNDS
MEMORY
MINUS
MODE
MODULES
MOVE
MULTIPLE
MULTIPLIED
MULTIPLY
NEGATIVE
NEXT
NO
NOT
NOTE
NUMBER
NUMERIC
OBJECT-COMPUTER
OBJECT-PROGRAM
OCCURS
OF
OFF
OH
OMITTED
ON
OPEN
OPTIONAL
OR

OTHERWISE
OUTPUT
OV
OVERFLOW
PAGE
PAGE-COUNTER
PERFORM
PF
PH
PICTURE
PLACES
PLUS
POINT
POSITION
POSITIVE
PREPARED
PRIORITY
PROCEDURE
PROCEED
PROCESS
PROCESSING
PROGRAM-ID
PROTECT
QUOTE
QUOTES
RANDOM
RANGE
RD
READ
RECORD
RECORDING
RECORDS
REDEFINES
REEL
RELEASE
REMARKS
RENAMES
RENAMING
REPLACING
REPORT
REPORTING
REPORTS
RERUN
RESET
RESERVE
RETURN
REVERSED
REWIND
RF
RH
RIGHT
ROUNDED
RUN
SA
SAME
SD
SEARCH
SECTION
SECURITY
SEEK
SEGMENT-LIMIT
SELECT
SELECTED
SENTENCE
SEQUENCED
SEQUENTIAL
SET
SIGN
SIGNED
SIZE
SORT
SOURCE
SOURCE-COMPUTER
SPACE
SPACES
SPECIAL-NAMES
STANDARD
STATUS
STOP
SUBTRACT
SUM
SUPERVISOR
SUPPRESS
SYMBOLIC
SYNCHRONIZED
TALLY
TALLYING
TAPE
TERMINATE
THAN
THEN
THROUGH } Equivalent
THRU }
TIMES
TO
TYPE
UNEQUAL
UP
UPPER-BOUND
UPPER-BOUNDS
UNIT
UNTIL
UPON
USAGE
USE
USING
VALUE
VALUES
VARYING
WHEN
WITH
WORDS
WORKING-STORAGE
WRITE
ZERO
ZEROES
ZEROS

APPENDIX B

The four programs in this Appendix contain characteristic COBOL commands. Through inspection of these, the reader may see the way particular instructions appear in the context of a more comprehensive situation than represented by the short illustrations in the previous chapters.

These programs are related to particular examples in the text. The flow chart for each problem and a detailed description of the situation being programmed may be found in some previous chapter. For convenience in reading each illustration, however, a brief review of the processing situation is furnished, as well as comments on the unique facets of the program.

ILLUSTRATION 1

This is a very simple, straightforward program. It is based on the extended illustration of Chapter 3, and accordingly stresses MØVE and simple computational commands. The flow chart for this problem may be found in Figure 3-10 (page 50).

In this problem, sales records are being read which contain certain identifying information, the number of units of inventory sold, and the sales price per unit. From this input must be computed the sales amount for each transaction and the amount of sales tax associated with the sale. These values are written out for each input record, and control totals of the number of records processed, the number of inventory units sold, and the amount of sales and sales taxes are being maintained.

The Chapter 3 flow chart is not followed exactly in the procedure division, because the illustration includes commands not yet introduced in the text. The first of these to be noticed is the AT END conditional, transferring control of the computer to a paragraph where control totals may be displayed and files closed. This conditional is discussed at length in Chapter 4.

Another difference between the flow chart in Chapter 3 and the illustrative program may be seen in the way certain data elements are calculated. Where a data item is computed and must be used both for output and in subsequent computations, the value is computed in a working storage field which does not contain any editing symbols. Its value may then be moved to the output field for writing and also used in further calculations. The characteristics of computational data fields are fully explored in Chapter 6.

223010A

COBOL PROGRAM SHEET

ILLUSTRATIØN 1

PAGE 1 3	PROGRAM: SALES ACCØUNTING	SYSTEM	SHEET 1 OF 3
0 0 1	PROGRAMMER: Mc CAMERØN	DATE	IDENT 73–80

```
SERIAL
4   6  CONT A   B
          8   12  16  20  24  28  32  36  40  44  48  52  56  60  64  68  72

01     IDENTIFICATIØN DIVISIØN.
02     PRØGRAM-ID. SALES-ACCØUNTING.
03     AUTHØR. F. A. MCCAMERØN.
04     REMARKS. EXAMPLE 1. THIS IS DRAWN FRØM THE EXTENDED
05         ILLUSTRATIØN ØF CHAPTER 3.
06     ENVIRØNMENT DIVISIØN.
07     CØNFIGURATIØN SECTIØN.
08     SØURCE-CØMPUTER. IBM-7040.
09     ØBJECT-CØMPUTER. IBM-7040.
10     INPUT-ØUTPUT SECTIØN.
11     FILE-CØNTRØL. SELECT SALES-FILE ASSIGN TØ IN.
12         SELECT ØUT-FILE ASSIGN TØ ØU.
13     DATA DIVISIØN.
14     FILE SECTIØN.
15     FD  SALES-FILE DATA RECØRD SALES-RECØRD LABEL RECØRD
16         ØMITTED RECØRD CØNTAINS 66 CHARACTERS.
17     01  SALES-RECØRD.
18         02  DATE                        PICTURE 9(6).
19         02  CUS-NAME                    PICTURE A(20).
20         02  C-NUM                       PICTURE X(5).
21         02  TC                          PICTURE XX.
22         02  INV-NØ                      PICTURE 9(7).
23         02  DIS-CLASS                   PICTURE 99.
24         02  UNIT-CØST                   PICTURE 999V99.
25         02  SLS-NØ                      PICTURE 9(7).
```

COBOL PROGRAM SHEET

223010A

PAGE 1 3 | PROGRAM: SALES ACCØUNTING | SYSTEM | SHEET 2 OF 3
PROGRAMMER: MC CAMERØN | DATE | IDENT. 73 80

```
SERIAL A   B
01          02  CØM-CLASS                 PICTURE 99.
02          02  NØ-UNITS                  PICTURE 9999.
03          02  UNIT-PRICE                PICTURE 99V99.
04          02  FILLER                    PICTURE XX.
05      FD  ØUT-FILE DATA RECØRD ØUTPUT-RECØRD LABEL RECØRD
06          ØMITTED RECØRD CØNTAINS 132 CHARACTERS.
07      01  ØUTPUT-RECØRD.
08          02  FILLER                    PICTURE X(5).
09          02  NAME                      PICTURE A(20).
10          02  FILLER                    PICTURE X(5).
11          02  T-DATE                    PICTURE 9(6).
12          02  FILLER                    PICTURE X(5).
13          02  UNITS-SØLD                PICTURE Z,Z99.
14          02  FILLER                    PICTURE X(5).
15          02  U-PRICE                   PICTURE $Z9.99.
16          02  FILLER                    PICTURE X(5).
17          02  SALES-PRICE               PICTURE $ZZZ,ZZ9.99.
18          02  FILLER                    PICTURE X(5).
19          02  SALES-TAX                 PICTURE $Z,ZZ9.99.
20          02  FILLER                    PICTURE X(5).
21          02  TØTAL-PRICE               PICTURE $ZZZ,ZZ9.99.
22          02  FILLER                    PICTURE X(29).
23      WØRKING-STØRAGE SECTIØN.
24      77  SP                            PICTURE 9(6)V99.
25      77  TAX                           PICTURE 9(4)V99.
```

COBOL PROGRAM SHEET

223010A

PAGE 1 3: 003	PROGRAM: SALES ACCØUNTING	SYSTEM	SHEET 3 OF 3
	PROGRAMMER: MC CAMERØN	DATE	IDENT. 73–80

```
SERIAL  A   B
01      77  RCD-CNT PICTURE 9(6) VALUE ZERØ.
02      77  TØT-UNITS PICTURE 9(7) VALUE ZERØ.
03      77  TØTAL-CHARGES PICTURE 9(8)V99 VALUE ZERØ.
04      77  DIS PICTURE $ZZ,ZZZ,ZZZ.99.
05      PRØCEDURE DIVISIØN.
06      PAR-1. ØPEN INPUT SALES-FILE, ØUTPUT ØUT-FILE.
07          MØVE SPACE TØ ØUTPUT-RECØRD.
08      PAR-2. READ SALES-FILE AT END GØ TØ END-RØUTINE.
09          MØVE CUS-NAME TØ NAME. MØVE DATE TØ T-DATE.
10          MØVE NØ-UNITS TØ UNITS-SØLD. MØVE UNIT-PRICE TØ U-PRICE.
11          MULTIPLY NØ-UNITS BY UNIT-PRICE GIVING SP. MØVE SP TØ
12          SALES-PRICE. CØMPUTE TAX RØUNDED = SP * .03. MØVE TAX
13          TØ SALES-TAX. ADD SP, TAX GIVING TØTAL-PRICE.
14          ADD 1 TØ RCD-CNT. ADD NØ-UNITS TØ TØT-UNITS.
15          ADD SP, TAX TØ TØTAL-CHARGES.
16          WRITE ØUTPUT-RECØRD. GØ TØ PAR-2.
17      END-RØUTINE. DISPLAY 'TØTAL RECØRDS PRØCESSED, ' RCD-CNT.
18          DISPLAY 'TØTAL UNITS SØLD, ' TØT-UNITS.
19          MØVE TØTAL-CHARGES TØ DIS.
20          DISPLAY 'TØTAL SALES AND FREIGHT CHARGES, ' DIS.
21          CLØSE SALES-FILE, ØUT-FILE.
22          STØP RUN.
```

ILLUSTRATION 2

This illustration is based on the extended example in Chapter 4, and its flow charts may be seen in Figures 4-15, 4-16, and 4-17 (pages 105, 106, and 107, respectively). It is concerned with the processing of inventory data, and involves reading old balance records and inventory receipts and issues information, and creating new balance records, cost accounting data, and reorder data.

Three input files are used:

MATERIALS-BALANCE, containing old inventory records

REC-FILE, containing inventory receipts records

ISS-FILE, containing inventory issues records

Three output files are prepared:

NEW-MAT-FILE, containing new inventory records

REØRDER, containing inventory reorder records

CØST-ACCØUNTING, containing cost accounting data based on inventory issues

The use of sequential account numbers as a control device should be noted in this illustration. Such a check may be seen in lines 12 and 13 of page 4 of the program.

Account numbers are also used to determine when all records associated with a particular inventory item have been processed. In the case of inventory receipts processing, a change in account numbers transfers the program to a new branch where average costs are computed and the processing of issues records is begun. This may be seen in the BLØCK-3 paragraph on page 4. BLØCK-4 on the same page controls the processing of issues records.

The PERFØRM command may be seen on page 4, lines 16, 21, and 25, to permit the removal of long processing routines to a separate paragraph. These are good examples of the value of the simple PERFØRM instruction.

This is the longest program in the Appendix. A careful study of it, and its source information and flow charts in Chapter 4, will give the reader a better understanding of the language.

223010A

COBOL PROGRAM SHEET   ILLUSTRATIØN 2

PAGE 1 3	PROGRAM: INVENTØRY ACCØUNTING	SYSTEM	SHEET 1 OF 5
0 0 1	PROGRAMMER: MC CAMERØN	DATE	IDENT. 73–80

```
SERIAL
4  6  A   B
      8   12  16  20  24  28  32  36  40  44  48  52  56  60  64  68  72
01    IDENTIFICATIØN DIVISIØN.
02    PRØGRAM-ID. INVENTØRY-ACCØUNTING.
03    AUTHØR. F. A. MCCAMERØN.
04    REMARKS. THIS PRØGRAM IS BASED ØN THE EXTENDED ILLUSTRATIØN
05            IN CHAPTER 4.
06    ENVIRØNMENT DIVISIØN.
07    CØNFIGURATIØN SECTIØN.
08    SØURCE-CØMPUTER. IBM-7040.
09    ØBJECT-CØMPUTER. IBM-7040.
10    INPUT-ØUTPUT SECTIØN.
11    FILE-CØNTRØL. SELECT MATERIALS-BALANCE ASSIGN TØ U04.
12            SELECT NEW-MAT-FILE ASSIGN TØ U05.
13            SELECT REC-FILE ASSIGN TØ UC6.
14            SELECT ISS-FILE ASSIGN TØ U07.
15            SELECT REØRDER ASSIGN TØ ØU.
16            SELECT CØST-ACCØUNTING ASSIGN TØ U08.
17    DATA DIVISIØN.
18    FILE SECTIØN.
19    FD  MATERIALS-BALANCE DATA RECØRD BAL-RCD LABEL RECØRD
20            ØMITTED RECØRD CØNTAINS 66 CHARACTERS.
21    01  BAL-RCD.
22        02  NØ-BAL                     PICTURE 999.
23        02  DESC                       PICTURE A(10).
24        02  ACTIVITY-CØUNTERS.
25            03  C-REC                  PICTURE 999.
```

223010A

COBOL PROGRAM SHEET

PAGE 002	PROGRAM: INVENTØRY ACCØUNTING	SYSTEM	SHEET 2 OF 5
	PROGRAMMER: MC CAMERØN	DATE	IDENT. 73–80

```
01         03  C-ISS                     PICTURE 999.
02     02  YTD-INFØ.
03         03  U-REC                     PICTURE 9(6).
04         03  U-ISS                     PICTURE 9(6).
05         03  CØST-R                    PICTURE 9(7).
06         03  CØST-IS                   PICTURE 9(7).
07     02  ØN-HAND-INFØ.
08         03  UNITS                     PICTURE 9(4).
09         03  T-CØST                    PICTURE 9(4)V99.
10         03  U-CØST                    PICTURE 9V99.
11     02  RØP                           PICTURE 999.
12     02  RQTY                          PICTURE 9999.
13     02  FILLER                        PICTURE X.
14 FD  NEW-MAT-FILE DATA RECØRD NEW-BAL-RCD LABEL RECØRD
15     ØMITTED RECØRD CØNTAINS 66 CHARACTERS.
16 01  NEW-BAL-RCD                       PICTURE X(66).
17 FD  REC-FILE DATA RECØRD REC-RCD LABEL RECØRD ØMITTED RECØRD 18.
18 01  REC-RCD.
19     02  NØ-REC                        PICTURE 999.
20     02  UNITS-REC                     PICTURE 9(4).
21     02  INV-CØST                      PICTURE 9(4)V99.
22     02  FGT                           PICTURE 999V99.
23 FD  ISS-FILE DATA RECØRD ISS-REC LABEL RECØRD ØMITTED RECØRD 18.
24 01  ISS-REC.
25     02  NØ-ISS                        PICTURE 999.
```

COBOL PROGRAM SHEET

223010A

PAGE 003 | PROGRAM: INVENTØRY ACCØUNTING | SYSTEM: | SHEET 3 OF 5
PROGRAMMER: MC CAMERØN | DATE: | IDENT.

```
SERIAL  A   B
01          02  UNITS-ISS                PICTURE 9(4).
02          02  JØB-NØ                   PICTURE 9(4).
03          02  FILLER                   PICTURE X(7).
04      FD  REØRDER DATA RECØRD REØRDER-REC LABEL RECØRD ØMITTED
05          RECØRD 132.
06      01  REØRDER-REC.
07          02  FILLER                   PICTURE X(5).
08          02  NØ-ØRD                   PICTURE 999.
09          02  FILLER                   PICTURE X(5).
10          02  DESC-ØRD                 PICTURE A(10).
11          02  FILLER                   PICTURE X(5).
12          02  QUANTITY                 PICTURE Z,Z99.
13          02  FILLER                   PICTURE X(99).
14      FD  CØST-ACCØUNTING DATA RECØRD MAT-USED LABEL RECØRD ØMITTED
15          RECØRD 18.
16      01  MAT-USED.
17          02  ITEM                     PICTURE 999.
18          02  JØB                      PICTURE 9(4).
19          02  NØ-UNITS                 PICTURE 999.
20          02  RM-CHG                   PICTURE 9(4)V99.
21          02  FILLER                   PICTURE X(2).
22      WØRKING-STØRAGE SECTIØN.
23      77  BAL-CTRL PICTURE 999.
24      77  TØT-ØLD-BAL PICTURE 9(8)V99 VALUE ZERØ.
25      77  TØT-REC PICTURE 9(7)V99 VALUE ZERØ.
```

223010A

COBOL PROGRAM SHEET

PAGE 1 3	PROGRAM INVENTØRY ACCØUNTING	SYSTEM	SHEET 4 OF 5
0,0,4	PROGRAMMER MC CAMERØN	DATE	IDENT. 73 80

```
SERIAL CONT. A   B
4    6       8   12
0,1,    77    TØT-ISS PICTURE 9(7)V99 VALUE ZERØ.
0,2,    77    TØT-NEW-BAL PICTURE 9(8)V99 VALUE ZERØ
0,3,    77    IS-CST PICTURE 9(4)V99.
0,4,    77    DIS PICTURE $ZZ,ZZZ,ZZ9.99.
0,5,
0,6,    PRØCEDURE DIVISIØN.
0,7,    BLØCK-1. ØPEN INPUT MATERIALS-BALANCE, REC-FILE, ISS-FILE,
0,8,          ØUTPUT NEW-MAT-FILE, REØRDER, CØST-ACCØUNTING.
0,9,          MØVE ZERØ TØ BAL-CTRL, NØ-REC, NØ-ISS.
1,0,          MØVE SPACE TØ REØRDER-REC.
1,1,    BLØCK-2. READ MATERIALS-BALANCE AT END GØ TØ FINISH.
1,2,          IF NØ-BAL NØT GREATER THAN BAL-CTRL STØP 'BALANCE RECØRD ØUT
1,3,  -       'ØF SEQUENCE' GØ TØ BLØCK-2 ELSE MØVE NØ-BAL TØ BAL-CTRL.
1,4,          ADD T-CØST TØ TØT-ØLD-BAL ØN SIZE ERRØR STØP 'CUMULATIVE TØTA
1,5,  -       'L ØVERFLØW' GØ TØ BLØCK-2.
1,6,    BLØCK-3. IF NØ-BAL = NØ-REC PERFØRM REC-PRØCESS, ADD INV-CØST,
1,7,          FGT TØ TØT-REC, GØ TØ BLØCK-3B ØTHERWISE IF NØ-REC LESS
1,8,          THAN NØ-BAL GØ TØ BLØCK-3B ELSE NEXT SENTENCE.
1,9,    BLØCK-3A. CØMPUTE U-CØST RØUNDED = T-CØST / UNITS. GØ TØ BLØCK-4.
2,0,    BLØCK-3B. READ REC-FILE AT END GØ TØ BLØCK-3A. GØ TØ BLØCK-3.
2,1,    BLØCK-4. IF NØ-BAL = NØ-ISS PERFØRM ISS-PRØCESS THRU CØST-ACTG,
2,2,          GØ TØ BLØCK-4A.
2,3,    BLØCK-5. IF NØ-ISS LESS THAN NØ-BAL GØ TØ BLØCK-4A.
2,4,    BLØCK-5A. WRITE NEW-BAL-RCD FRØM BAL-RCD. ADD T-CØST TØ TØT-NEW-B
2,5,  -       AL. IF UNITS LESS THAN RØP PERFØRM RE-ØRDER. GØ TØ BLØCK-2.
```

COBOL PROGRAM SHEET

223010A

PAGE 1 3: 0,0,5	PROGRAM: INVENTØRY ACCØUNTING	SYSTEM	SHEET 5 OF 5
	PROGRAMMER: MC CAMERØN	DATE	IDENT. 73 80

```
SERIAL CONT. A   B
4    6       8   12  16  20  24  28  32  36  40  44  48  52  56  60  64  68  72
0,1  BLØCK-4A. READ ISS-FILE AT END GØ TØ BLØCK-5A. GØ TØ BLØCK-4.
0,2
0,3  REC-PRØCESS. ADD 1 TØ C-REC. ADD UNITS-REC TØ U-REC.
0,4      ADD INV-CØST, FGT TØ CØST-R RØUNDED.
0,5      ADD UNITS-REC TØ UNITS. ADD INV-CØST, FGT TØ T-CØST.
0,6
0,7  ISS-PRØCESS. CØMPUTE IS-CST RØUNDED = UNITS-ISS * U-CØST.
0,8      ADD IS-CST TØ TØT-ISS. ADD 1 TØ C-ISS.
0,9      ADD UNITS-ISS TØ U-ISS. ADD IS-CST TØ CØST-IS RØUNDED.
1,0      SUBTRACT UNITS-ISS FRØM UNITS. SUBTRACT IS-CST FRØM T-CØST.
1,1  CØST-ACTG.
1,2      MØVE NØ-BAL TØ ITEM. MØVE JØB-NØ TØ JØB.
1,3      MØVE UNITS-ISS TØ NØ-UNITS. MØVE IS-CST TØ RM-CHG.
1,4      WRITE MAT-USED.
1,5  RE-ØRDER. MØVE NØ-BAL TØ NØ-ØRD. MØVE DESC TØ DESC-ØRD.
1,6      MØVE RQTY TØ QUANTITY. WRITE REØRDER-REC.
1,7  FINISH.
1,8      MØVE TØT-ØLD-BAL TØ DIS. DISPLAY 'SUM ØF ØLD BALANCES ' DIS.
1,9      MØVE TØT-REC TØ DIS. DISPLAY 'SUM ØF RECEIPTS     ' DIS.
2,0      MØVE TØT-ISS TØ DIS. DISPLAY 'SUM ØF ISSUES       ' DIS.
2,1      MØVE TØT-NEW-BAL TØ DIS. DISPLAY 'SUM ØF NEW BALANCES ', DIS.
2,2      CLØSE MATERIALS-BALANCE, REC-FILE, ISS-FILE, NEW-MAT-FILE,
2,3      REØRDER, CØST-ACCØUNTING.
2,4      STØP RUN.
2,5
```

ILLUSTRATION 3

This program is concerned with the preparation of depreciation schedules for assets using the declining-balance method of depreciation. It is based on an example in Chapter 7, and its flow chart may be found in Figure 7-9 (page 192). The program illustrates two major points.

The first is the creation and writing of report headings. The heading itself, under the group name HEAD-1, is set up in the constant section of the data division. It may be seen on lines 18-25 of page 2 and line 01 of page 3.

The fact that headings are to be written means that two different formats are to be written as output records. Therefore the output record may not be described as having any special format, but merely as containing the proper number of output spaces. Such a record, called DEP-Line, may be seen on line 24 of this illustration's first page.

The data group containing report contents is then described in working storage and may be seen on lines 07 through 16 of page 2. It is given the name LINE.

The report heading is written on line 07, page 3, by the command:

WRITE DEP-LINE FRØM HEAD-1.

Report contents are written on line 22, page 3, by the command:

WRITE DEP-LINE FRØM LINE.

Thus, by use of the "WRITE ... FRØM ..." option, two or more line formats may be written out through a single record.

The second significant feature of this program is found in the use of the "PERFØRM ... VARYING ... UNTIL ..." command. It is used to control the iterations in which depreciation amounts are computed and written out, and also to provide the value of one of the data items, YEAR. The PERFØRM command is to be found on lines 11 and 12, page 3, and its range may be seen on lines 15 through 22 of the same page.

COBOL PROGRAM SHEET ILLUSTRATIØN 3

223010A

PAGE 1 3	PROGRAM: DEPRECIATIØN SCHEDULE	SYSTEM	SHEET 1 OF 3
0,0,1	PROGRAMMER: MC CAMERØN	DATE	IDENT. 73–80

```
SERIAL CONT. A   B
4    6       8   12
01   IDENTIFICATIØN DIVISIØN.
02   PRØGRAM-ID. DEPRECIATIØN-SCHEDULE.
03   AUTHØR. MCCAMERØN.
04   REMARKS. THIS PRØGRAM ILLUSTRATES THE CREATIØN AND USE
05       ØF HEADINGS, AND THE NATURE ØF THE PERFØRM CØMMAND.
06       IT IS BASED ØN THE FLØW CHART IN FIGURE 7-9.
07   ENVIRØNMENT DIVISIØN.
08   CØNFIGURATIØN SECTIØN.
09   SØURCE-CØMPUTER. IBM-7040.
10   ØBJECT-CØMPUTER. IBM-7040.
11   INPUT-ØUTPUT SECTIØN.
12   FILE-CØNTRØL. SELECT ASSET-PCH, ASSIGN TØ IN.
13       SELECT DEP-SCH, ASSIGN TØ ØU.
14   DATA DIVISIØN.
15   FILE SECTIØN.
16   FD  ASSET-PCH DATA RECØRD ASSET-DATA LABEL RECØRD ØMITTED
17       RECØRD 24.
18   01  ASSET-DATA.
19       02  CØST                        PICTURE 9(7)V99.
20       02  SCRAP                       PICTURE 9(6)V99.
21       02  USE-LIFE                    PICTURE 99.
22       02  FILLER                      PICTURE X(5).
23   FD  DEP-SCH DATA RECØRD DEP-LINE LABEL RECØRD ØMITTED RECØRD 132.
24   01  DEP-LINE                        PICTURE X(132).
25
```

223010A

COBOL PROGRAM SHEET

PAGE 002 | PROGRAM: DEPRECIATIØN SCHEDULE | SYSTEM | SHEET 2 OF 3

PROGRAMMER: MC CAMERØN | DATE | IDENT. 73–80

```
01  WØRKING-STØRAGE SECTIØN.
02  77  NUM                            PICTURE 99V9(8).
03  77  DEN                            PICTURE 9(4)V9(8).
04  77  DEP                            PICTURE 9(7)V99.
05  77  ACCUM PICTURE 9(7)V99 VALUE ZERØ.
06  77  BAL                            PICTURE 9(7)V99.
07  01  LINE.
08          02  FILLER                 PICTURE X(5).
09          02  YEAR                   PICTURE 99.
10          02  FILLER                 PICTURE X(5).
11          02  CUR-DEP                PICTURE $Z,ZZZ,ZZZ.99.
12          02  FILLER                 PICTURE X(5).
13          02  ACC-DEP                PICTURE $Z,ZZZ,ZZZ.99.
14          02  FILLER                 PICTURE X(5).
15          02  BALANCE                PICTURE $Z,ZZZ,ZZZ.99.
16          02  FILLER                 PICTURE X(71).
17  CØNSTANT SECTIØN.
18  01  HEAD-1.
19          02 FILLER PICTURE X(4) VALUE SPACE.
20          02 YR PICTURE A(4) VALUE 'YEAR'.
21          02 FILLER PICTURE X(5) VALUE SPACE.
22          02 C-D PICTURE X(12) VALUE 'CUR. DEPREC.'.
23          02 FILLER PICTURE X(4) VALUE SPACE.
24          02 A-D PICTURE X(14) VALUE 'ACCUM. DEPREC.'.
25          02 U-D PICTURE X(19) VALUE '   UNDEPREC BALANCE'.
```

COBOL PROGRAM SHEET

223010A

PAGE	PROGRAM	SYSTEM	SHEET
1 3	DEPRECIATIØN SCHEDULE		3 OF 3
003	PROGRAMMER: MC CAMERØN	DATE	IDENT. 73 80

```
SERIAL CONT. A   B
01          02 FILLER PICTURE X(70) VALUE SPACE.
02     PRØCEDURE DIVISIØN.
03     ØPEN-FILES. ØPEN INPUT ASSET-PCH, ØUTPUT DEP-SCH.
04          MØVE SPACE TØ LINE.
05     READ-DATA. READ ASSET-PCH AT END CLØSE ASSET-PCH,
06          DEP-SCH, STØP RUN.
07     WRITE-HEADING. WRITE DEP-LINE FRØM HEAD-1.
08          MØVE SPACE TØ DEP-LINE. WRITE DEP-LINE.
09     CØNTRØL-PAR. CØMPUTE DEN = (USE-LIFE * (USE-LIFE + 1)) / 2.
10          MØVE USE-LIFE TØ NUM. MØVE CØST TØ BAL.
11          PERFØRM DEP-CØMP VARYING YEAR FRØM 1 BY 1
12          UNTIL YEAR GREATER USE-LIFE.
13          STØP 'PRØCESSING ØF THIS ASSET CØMPLETE'.
14          MØVE ZERØ TØ ACCUM. GØ TØ READ-DATA.
15     DEP-CØMP.
16          CØMPUTE DEP RØUNDED = NUM / DEN * (CØST - SCRAP).
17          MØVE DEP TØ CUR-DEP.
18          ADD DEP TØ ACCUM.
19          MØVE ACCUM TØ ACC-DEP.
20          SUBTRACT 1 FRØM NUM.
21          SUBTRACT ACCUM FRØM BAL GIVING BALANCE.
22          WRITE DEP-LINE FRØM LINE.
```

ILLUSTRATION 4

This illustration is designed to depict certain techniques used to process data arrays. It includes the reading, manipulation, and writing of one- and two-dimensional matrices.

The proper method of allocating memory space for storage of arrays is shown in the data division of this illustration. Two-dimensional arrays named ACCT-1, ACCT-2, and TØT are set up on the first page. The manner in which rows are named should be noted, and careful attention should be given to the fact that no PICTURE clause is assigned at the row level. The row name is further subdivided by a subordinate column name showing the number of elements per row, and here the PICTURE clause is given. This relates the PICTURE clause to each element in each row of the matrix.

The PERFØRM command is quite useful in processing arrayed data. On page 2 of this illustration may be seen PERFØRM commands controlling the reading, manipulation, and writing of arrayed data.

The problem on which this illustration is based may be found in Chapter 7, on pages 200-208. The flow diagram is shown in Figure 7-18 (page 207). This material should be reviewed as the following program segment is studied.

223010A

COBOL PROGRAM SHEET

ILLUSTRATIØN 4

PAGE 1 3	PROGRAM: ARRAY PRØCESSING	SYSTEM	SHEET 1 OF 3
001	PROGRAMMER: MC CAMERØN	DATE	IDENT. 73–80

```
SERIAL CONT. A   B
4    6       8   12

01       DATA DIVISIØN.
02       FILE SECTIØN.
03       FD  IN-FILE DATA RECØRD IN-RCD LABEL RECØRD ØMITTED RECØRD 18.
04       01  IN-RCD                         PICTURE 9(18).
05       FD  ØUT-FILE DATA RECØRD ØUT-RCD-ENTRY LABEL RECØRD ØMITTED
06           RECØRD CØNTAINS 132 CHARACTERS.
07       01  ØUT-RCD-ENTRY.
08           02  FILLER                     PICTURE X(10).
09           02  ØUT-RCD  PICTURE Z(10) ØCCURS 6 TIMES.
10           02  FILLER                     PICTURE X(62).
11       WØRKING-STØRAGE SECTIØN.
12       77  I                              PICTURE 9.
13       77  J                              PICTURE 9.
14       77  GRAND                          PICTURE 9(6) VALUE 0.
15       01  ACCT-1.
16           02  EXP-1 ØCCURS 5 TIMES.
17                   03  BAL-1 PICTURE 999 ØCCURS 6 TIMES.
18       01  ACCT-2.
19           02  EXP-2 ØCCURS 5 TIMES.
20                   03  BAL-2 PICTURE 999 ØCCURS 6 TIMES.
21       01  TØT.
22           02  T-EXP ØCCURS 5 TIMES.
23                   03  T-BAL PICTURE 9999 ØCCURS 6 TIMES.
24       01  ACCT-BAL.
25           02  ACT PICTURE 9(5) ØCCURS 5 TIMES.
```

223010A

COBOL PROGRAM SHEET

PAGE 002	PROGRAM: ARRAY PRØCESSING	SYSTEM	SHEET 2 OF 3
	PROGRAMMER: MC CAMERØN	DATE	IDENT. 73–80

```
       01  MØNTH.
           02  MØ PICTURE 9(5) ØCCURS 6 TIMES.

       PRØCEDURE DIVISIØN.
       CØNTRØL-PAR. ØPEN INPUT IN-FILE, ØUTPUT ØUT-FILE.
           MØVE SPACE TØ ØUT-RCD-ENTRY.
           PERFØRM READ-1 VARYING I FRØM 1 BY 1 UNTIL I GREATER 5.
           PERFØRM READ-2 VARYING I FRØM 1 BY 1 UNTIL I GREATER 5.
           PERFØRM ADD-MATRIX VARYING I FRØM 1 BY 1 UNTIL I GREATER 5
           AFTER J FRØM 1 BY 1 UNTIL J GREATER 6.
           PERFØRM MV-AR THRU WR-AR VARYING I FRØM 1 BY 1
           UNTIL I GREATER 5.
           PERFØRM ALL-CØMP VARYING I FRØM 1 BY 1 UNTIL I GREATER 5
           AFTER J FRØM 1 BY 1 UNTIL J GREATER 6.
           PERFØRM WRITE-MØ VARYING I FRØM 1 BY 1 UNTIL I GREATER 6.
           WRITE ØUT-RCD-ENTRY.
           MØVE SPACE TØ ØUT-RCD-ENTRY.
           PERFØRM WRITE-AC VARYING I FRØM 1 BY 1 UNTIL I GREATER 5.
           WRITE ØUT-RCD-ENTRY.
           DISPLAY GRAND.
           CLØSE IN-FILE, ØUT-FILE.
           STØP RUN.

       READ-1. READ IN-FILE, AT END NEXT SENTENCE.
           MØVE IN-RCD TØ EXP-1 (I).
```

223010A

COBOL PROGRAM SHEET

PAGE 1 3	PROGRAM: ARRAY PRØCESSING	SYSTEM	SHEET 3 OF 3
0 0 3	PROGRAMMER: MC CAMERØN	DATE	IDENT. 73 80

```
SERIAL CONT. A   B
4   6      8   12   16   20   24   28   32   36   40   44   48   52   56   60   64   68   72
01   READ-2.  READ IN-FILE, AT END NEXT SENTENCE.
02       MØVE IN-RCD TØ EXP-2 (I).
03   ADD-MATRIX.  CØMPUTE T-BAL (I, J) = BAL-1 (I, J) + BAL-2 (I, J).
04   MV-AR.  PERFØRM MØVE-RTN VARYING J FRØM 1 BY 1 UNTIL J GREATER 6.
05   WR-AR.  WRITE ØUT-RCD-ENTRY.
06   MØVE-RTN.  MØVE T-BAL (I, J) TØ ØUT-RCD (J).
07   ALL-CØMP.  ADD T-BAL (I, J) TØ ACT (I).
08       ADD T-BAL (I, J) TØ MØ (J).
09       ADD T-BAL (I, J) TØ GRAND.
10   WRITE-MØ.  MØVE MØ (I) TØ ØUT-RCD (I).
11   WRITE-AC.  MØVE ACT (I) TØ ØUT-RCD (I).
```

INDEX